DATA CENTRES
AS INFRASTRUCTURE

DATA CENTRES
AS INFRASTRUCTURE

Frontiers of Digital Governance
in Contemporary India

EDITED BY

Manish K Jha and Ritam Sengupta

Orient BlackSwan

DATA CENTRES AS INFRASTRUCTURE: FRONTIERS OF DIGITAL GOVERNANCE IN CONTEMPORARY INDIA

ORIENT BLACKSWAN PRIVATE LIMITED

Registered Office
3-6-752 Himayatnagar, Hyderabad 500 029, Telangana, India
e-mail: centraloffice@orientblackswan.com

Other Offices
Bengaluru, Chennai, Guwahati, Hyderabad, Kolkata,
Mumbai, New Delhi, Noida, Patna, Visakhapatnam

© Orient Blackswan Private Limited 2022
First published by Orient Blackswan Private Limited 2022

ISBN 978-93-5442-265-2

035731

Typeset in
Sabon LT Std 10/12
by Manmohan Kumar, Delhi

Printed in India at
Thomson Press, New Delhi 110 020

Published by
Orient Blackswan Private Limited
3-6-752, Himayatnagar, Hyderabad 500 029, Telangana, India
e-mail: info@orientblackswan.com

This book is dedicated to

❧ RANABIR SAMADDAR ☙

For his inspiration to push the boundaries of
research and intellectual engagement

Contents

LIST OF IMAGES

PREFACE

Data Centres as Infrastructure: Frontiers of Digital Governance in Contemporary India examines specialised infrastructures within cities that cater to collection, interpretation, storage, dispersal, and control of data and information flows. The flows are mediated through dedicated geographies and physiologies of 'Data Centres'. The volume describes Data Centres as a combination of materiality and immateriality, centralisation and decentralisation of data and information. The chapters illustrate Data Centres not only as technical infrastructures but also as political institutions that make and exercise new forms of power.

Like numerous books and edited volumes that have taken shape as the outcome of collaborative research projects led by the Calcutta Research Group (CRG), this volume is yet another attempt to explore an emerging field of research on data and society within the social science fraternity in India. The idea had its inception during an intellectual deliberation between Professors Brett Neilson and Ned Rossiter of Western Sydney University (WSU), and Professor Ranabir Samaddar, Distinguished Chair at CRG, and was taken forward by the authors of this volume. The authors are deeply indebted to Professor Samaddar for his intellectual guidance and sustained persuasion for a timely completion of the project. The research programme was supported by a modest grant from the WSU, which made it possible for us to pursue an interest in this field. The authors were fortunate in being supported and encouraged by Brett Neilson throughout the length of the project.

We are thankful to Professor Paula Banerjee and Dr Anita Sengupta, former Directors of CRG for anchoring and facilitating this research project. The CRG had also organised an authors' workshop for the presentation and discussion on the chapters of this volume. It was immensely valuable for gaining critical understanding of the theme. Similarly, we are beholden to Bibhas Chaudhuri and late Rajarshi Sengupta for providing us insights on data economy and the digital world as a whole. We are grateful to the entire team of the CRG. We are also deeply appreciative of the inputs provided by various informants and discussants who shared their views despite the highly secretive nature of the work environment at Data Centres.

Finally, the authors would like to thank Orient BlackSwan for showing interest in our attempt to engage with this theme of contemporary relevance, and publishing this volume. We want to acknowledge the inputs of Roopa Sharma, Nilanjana Majumdar, and particularly, Debangana Pal at Orient BlackSwan in shaping the final form of the volume. We are also immensely grateful for the rigorous feedback and critical comments of two anonymous reviewers that allowed us to significantly sharpen and deepen the arguments presented in the various chapters.

Publishers' Acknowledgements

The publishers would like to thank the Internet and Mobile Association of India (IAMAI) for their kind permission to reproduce certain parts of the report, 'Make in India: Conducive Policy & Regulatory Environment to Incentivize Data Center Infrastructure', May 2016, as an Appendix to the present volume.

ABBREVIATIONS

AC	Alternating Current
AI	Artificial Intelligence
AIPEF	All India Power Engineers' Federation
AMR	Advanced Meter Reading
APAC	Asia-Pacific Region
AT&C	Aggregate Technical and Commercial (losses)
AVGC	Animation, Visual effects, Gaming, and Comics
B2C	Business-to-Consumer
BEL	Bharat Electronics Limited
BFSI	Banking, Financial Services, Insurance
BMRPD	Bombay Metropolitan Regional Planning Board
CAGR	Compound Annual Growth Rate
CBD	Central Business District
CCC	Customer Care Centre
CCTV	Closed-circuit Television
CIDCO	City and Industrial Development Corporation of Maharashtra
CMC	Computer Management Corporation
CMD	Chairman and Managing Director
CMEL	Computer Mechanics and Electronics Laboratory
CRG	Calcutta Research Group
CSDS	Centre for the Study of Developing Societies
CSO	Central Statistics Office
DC	Data Centre
DCR	Development Control Regulation
DISNIC	District Information System of National Informatics Centre
DoE	Department of Electronics
DTR	Distribution Transformers
ECIL	Electronics Corporation of India Ltd.
ERP	Enterprise Resource Planning
EU	European Union
FLAG	Fibre-Optic Link Around the Globe
G2C	Government-to-Citizen
GDP	Gross Domestic Product
GDPR	General Data Protection Regulation
GIC	Global In-house Centre

GIS	Geographic Information System
GoI	Government of India
GST	Goods and Services Tax
HIDCO	Housing Infrastructure Development Corporation
HIPAA	Health Insurance Portability and Accountability Act
IaaS	Infrastructure as a Service
IAMAI	Internet and Mobile Association of India
IBM	International Business Machines
IBMC	International Business Machine Corporation
IGY	International Geophysical Year
IISc	Indian Institute of Science
IIT	Indian Institute of Technology
IITT	Integrated IT Townships
IMF	International Monetary Fund
IoT	Internet-of-Things
IP	Internet Protocol
IPDS	Integrated Power Development Scheme
IPP	Independent Power Producer
ISI	Indian Statistical Institute
ISO	International Organization for Standardization
iSPIRT	Indian Software Product Industry Roundtable
IT	Information Technology
ITBPM	Information Technology and Business Process Management
ITES	Information Technology Enabled Services
JNPT	Jawaharlal Nehru Port Trust
LBT	Local Body Tax
MARG	Modern Architects' Research Group
MCGB	Municipal Corporation of Greater Bombay
MCRG	Mahanirban Calcutta Research Group
MEA	Middle East and Africa
MEDC	Maharashtra Economic Development Council
MERC	Maharashtra Electricity Regulatory Commission
MDAS	Meter Data Acquisition System
MIDC	Maharashtra Industrial Development Corporation
MLA	Member of Legislative Assembly
MMR	Mumbai Metropolitan Region
MoSPI	Ministry of Statistics and Programme Implementation
MSBTE	Maharashtra State Board of Technical Education
MSEB	Maharashtra State Electricity Board

MUDC	Multi-user Data Centre
NASSCOM	National Association of Software and Services Companies
NDA-II	National Democratic Alliance-II (re-elected in 2019)
NeGP	National e-Governance Plan
NIC	National Income Committee
NICNET	National Informatics Centre Network
NM	Navi Mumbai
NMMC	Navi Mumbai Municipal Corporation
NoC	No Objection Certificate
NSS	National Sample Survey
PCAST	President's Council of Advisors on Science and Technology (US)
PCI	Payment Card Industry
PDP	Personal Data Protection (Bill)
PFC	Power Finance Corporation
PPP	Public-Private Partnership
PwC	PricewaterhouseCoopers
R&D	Research and Development
R-APDRP	Restructured Accelerated Power Development and Reforms Programme
RCA	Radio Corporation of America
REM	Revenue and Energy Management
SaaS	Software as a Service
SAP IS-U	SAP (Systems Applications and Products in Data Processing) company's 'Industry Specific Solution for Utilities Industry' software
SDC	State Data Centre
SEEPZ	Santacruz Electronics and Export Processing Zone
SEZ	Special Economic Zone
T&D	Transmission and Distribution
TCS	Tata Consultancy Services
TIA	Telecommunication Industry Association
TIFR	Tata Institute of Fundamental Research
TIFRAC	Tata Institute of Fundamental Research Automatic Calculator
TMC	Trinamool Congress
TTC	Trans Thane Creek
UIC	Uptime Institute Certification
UIDAI	Unique Identification Authority of India

UN	United Nations
UNCTAD	United Nations Conference on Trade and Development
UNIVAC	Universal Automatic Computers
UPI	Unified Payments Interface
US	United States
USSR	Union of Soviet Socialist Republics
VAT	Value Added Tax
WBSEB	West Bengal State Electricity Board
WBSEBEA	West Bengal State Electricity Board Engineers' Association
WBSEDC	West Bengal State Electricity Distribution Company
WBSEDCL	West Bengal State Electricity Distribution Company Limited
WBSETCL	West Bengal State Electricity Transmission Company Limited
WDC	World Data Centre
WSU	Western Sydney University
ZCC	Zonal Call Centres

Introduction

The State in/of Data Centres in India

RITAM SENGUPTA AND MANISH K JHA

LOADING...DATA CENTRES AS GOVERNANCE/THE GOVERNANCE OF DATA CENTRES

There is a peculiar but effective way in which our current suspension within the spate of digital media seems to defy the exercise of reflexivity. Such media aim to be ubiquitous by exuding the semblance of an almost atmospheric/immersive quality—a cloud, which can be engaged with only through its own interfaces that are (ideally) coordinated seamlessly. These interfaces in turn offer forms of command as logical or naturalised modes of interaction between nodes in a supposed network. The relevance of this virtuality gains weight as entire genres of communication, ranging from bureaucratic decisions and corporate calculations to intimate afterthoughts and philosophical musings, all vie for relevance in the (seeming)[1] metalanguage of data and code. This edited volume nonetheless seeks to take a step back and return reflexive attention to certain material conditions of possibility which structure this contemporary digital predicament of ours, of being immersed in certain 'virtualised' terms of existence and significance. It does so by following a call sounded in recent times to relate virtualised infrastructural forms like the Internet or the Cloud to their very actual locations and operations, not so much to negate the reality of the virtual, but rather to better comprehend the political, economic, resource-intensive, and rule-bound bases of the performances of virtualisation.[2] What immediately comes to light when we trace our 'clouds' back to their actual sites of operation are Data Centres, underwater cables, commercial and technical standards of functioning, including network protocols and programme parameters, and globally divided and specialised software, and maintenance workers in potentially diminishing numbers. Among these, we focus in this volume on Data Centres, which have recently evolved as the key infrastructure for the amassing and processing of the lifeblood of the globalised digital economy—data.

More precise definitions and categorisation of Data Centres are forthcoming in the following pages of this volume from multiple contributors. For this introductory act, it will suffice to mark out Data Centres as infrastructural entities that are both 'things' as well as 'relations between things'—as both an object as well as a principle of governance (Appel et al. 2018; Carse 2016; Johnson 2019; Larkin 2013: 329). The Data Centre principle is best described as a principle of aggregation through and onto which computing is rescaled, as beyond semi-autonomous and single-user/personal devices. This principle materialises as enclosures of user-generated data, a resource that can be reused by the remediation of these enclosures simply as storage retrieval, or in more cooked forms produced by the mediation of proprietary software or platforms catering to specialised needs.[3] As such an enclosure/infrastructure that is subscribed to directly or indirectly by entities across state-business-citizen-civil society divisions and through which much of the Internet seems to move its traffic, the Data Centre object is usually a well-protected and well-built structure, housing racks of servers and running variegated and continuous digital functions that consumes a remarkable measure of worldly resources in the form of water, energy, bandwidth, and land.[4] These objects thus, seem to require certain special allowances to reproduce their everyday conditions of existence. The contributors to this volume attempt to address both this object and the principle of governance that are Data Centres through individual cases that describe the historical and contemporary conditions of their being and becoming, within the developing orders of state and capital in a specific postcolonial location, that of India.

This directing of reflexive attention towards the material bases of the digitalised present is perhaps aided by our being situated within an interregnum, a certain intermediary phase of renegotiating the terms on which infrastructure like Data Centres can function within historically situated geographies like India. In this transitional phase, the process of making digital media ubiquitous and yet invisible is being executed through various state-enabled measures and actions, which in turn leave traces for identification in the public domain, like legal procedures, and so on. Using a metaphor from our virtualised existence, we can indicate this situation by the circling icon that appears on our digital interfaces to signal the status of 'Loading...' or 'Buffering...'—a phase that permits a distraction from the economy of infinite distractions, to look beyond the screen. And in this looking beyond, what comes into sharp relief is the very distinctive jostling for sovereignty over the control of data, its generation, its movement, and its valuations, that seem to have become extremely prominent in India in the last few years. Such controls, while heavily invested in the perpetuation of our virtual existence, remain also conventionally represented and encountered through legal arguments, nationalist economics, complications of citizenship and welfarist claims, and the formal and informal exercise of brute power, characteristic of the functioning of the state-capital nexus in the postcolonial nation. It is this fraught nature of the contemporary conjuncture that perhaps familiarises and helps us comprehend the development of digital data infrastructure in India as also a significant constituent of possible political and economic transformations ongoing in the region, before such infrastructures dissolve into the self-referential frameworks immanent to digital systems.

Certain battles waged to secure the stakes of power and profit, which could follow from the digital networking of Indian lives, livelihoods, and politics, have been fairly palpable. Among them has been the Aadhaar project which operationalised a universal and unique biometric ID, and demonetisation which revealed itself to be a process of compelling citizens into a system of digital payments. Over the course of the last two years, the continuing reign of COVID-19 has led to the intensification of the digitalisation of everyday life as virtualised technological coordination has forcefully competed to replace interpersonal connections. Meanwhile Indian citizens have been invariably subjected to furtive enrolment under a new digital index, that of the National Digital Health ID, through the virtually consolidated vaccination infrastructure (*The Print* 2021). These processes of creating new IDs and compelling the mediation of a variety of social processes and interactions through the architecture of digitised functioning have something in common. Along with being interventions in an emerging data economy, they also constitute attempts at certain fundamental and (arguably) violent reorientations in the political and economic constitution of India. What is also common to them is that the Indian state is a rather interested party in all of them. Yet another issue that can very seriously define the conundrum of control over matters of digital data is that of 'data localisation'. It urges the retention of data of particular geographical/ national origins and of particular kinds within the boundaries of the concerned geography/nation, thus heavily regulating cross-border data flows. It is then a kind of policy that reinstates national or regional states as gatekeepers of some sorts to moderate the otherwise time- and space-dissolving accelerationism[5] of the globalised data economy. The Indian state has of late sought to realise the full potential of this gatekeeping by quite controversially championing data localisation as necessary for national security as well as for being a boost to the Data Centre industry.

Taken together, these instances more than indicate an active role of the national state in mediating the production, transmission, processing, and consumption of data in contemporary India. However, as the chapters in this volume describe, there are also more subtle ways in which the state has come to be implicated in the question of data infrastructures in India, that are less palpable than the recent, very visible flourish of its regulatory and executive zeal. This 'Introduction' will sift through the chapters to show how the development and functioning of Data Centres in India continues to be critically reliant on the more subtle background activism of the state. Moreover, we will make the case that in tracing the manifestation of such activism, we can also understand how the postcolonial state-form is significantly mutating in the course of its implication within the new worlds of data capitalism. We will begin by setting up the comparative and trans-regional framework within which the studies for this volume were conceptualised, as part of a larger research project. We will then draw out the common thread about the mediating functions of the national state in matters of Data Centres in India from the respective chapters. Next, we will weigh these functions against the longer histories of the shaping of both postcolonial government as well as postcolonial capitalism, in order to try and distinguish the specific kind of political and economic transformation undergone by the state in India in the course of its involvement with contemporary data infrastructures. In the final section, we will nuance this story of transformation by returning to recent instances of the postcolonial state assuming its more conventional sovereign capacities of executive and regulatory action in order to induct Indian citizens within the orders of digital data infrastructure. This section will discuss matters like data localisation, which have not otherwise directly concerned the chapters in this volume but might have important consequences for the future functioning of data infrastructure in India.

THE BACKGROUND TO THE VOLUME: THE WSU PROJECT

This volume emerges from the research conducted as part of the project 'Data Centres in India', under the aegis of the Calcutta Research Group (CRG).[6] The project was itself a part of the larger research undertaking of the Western Sydney University (WSU) titled 'Data Centres and the Governance of Labour and Territory' that spanned a broader spatial ambit of Australia and the Asia-Pacific.[7] It is thus useful to explore how our respective conceptual and empirical forays into the study of Data Centres speak to the concerns of the larger transnational research endeavour proposed by the WSU. For this purpose, we will also be in dialogue with Brett Neilson (one of the principal investigators in the larger WSU research project), whose cogent engagement with the particulars of our research appears as the following (and first) chapter in this book. This dialogic enterprise we believe, will allow the formulation of more productive future lines of trans-regional and comparative enquiry about the gradually expanding scope of Data Centres as the most fundamental infrastructural ballast of the globalised and digitalised capitalist economy. It will also help in signalling questions of regional specificity within this latest phase in the globalisation of information technology capital.

Within the broader inter-regional, transnational scope of the WSU project, the object of enquiry was the large multi-user facilities that have assumed the moniker 'co-location Data Centres', located in the cities of Sydney, Hong Kong, and Singapore. These co-location facilities have largely been at the cutting edge in the global data industry. Their primary role is to provide storage, transmission, and processing facilities to multiple client organisations that often outsource their entire information processing operations to these facilities. The object of research and the location of research qualified each other. The project was interested in moving away from large single-user Data Centre facilities of a Google or a Facebook located in prime global North locations in order to study the relatively more dispersed dynamics in the globalisation of information technology capital that converged in the concerned cities, driving new forms of shared data concentration and its consequent logics of operations and governance (WSU 2016: 2). The locations of these cities are distinguished by their status as important nodes in the older trans-imperial oceanic networks. One important consequence of this historical legacy that the project identified as key to understanding the situation of Data Centres in these respective cities, was the landing of several submarine cables on their shores. With the clustering of co-location Data Centres near the international submarine cable stations in these cities, they could tap the demand for low-latency (high speed) communication in the entire Asia-Pacific region (and beyond) that is particularly suitable to high-frequency financial trading amongst other services (ibid.). Further, the project also sought to relate the clustering of Data Centres in these respective urban sites to the possibility of highly amenable regimes of taxation, labour and land, and dipping energy costs that were offered as part of their long-standing overtures as business-friendly locations (ibid.: 4). These helped maintain a competitive profile for these cities in comparison to alternatives in China, alternatives that were also susceptible to anxieties about data mobility being restricted by the stipulations of the Chinese state.

The clustering of several Data Centres in cities of the Asia-Pacific and Australia was not however, posed as simply a question of mobilising 'comparative advantages' specific to these locations. The WSU project in fact was interested in proposing a new kind of distribution of territorial power that was effectuated through the concerned Data Centres and their operations—a power neither imperial in the more familiar geopolitical terms nor an extension of the mandate of existing national states. Partly, this could follow from how business zones or industrial parks in the respective cities tended to detach from regulations of national territory to conform to translocal standards which apply to the architecture of Data Centres within their remit (WSU 2016: 2). The other significant possibility that the project has sought to highlight is how co-location Data Centres generate and command novel distributions of territoriality through technical protocols that operate to connect and disconnect individual client entities and their data pools within the same Data Centre (ibid.). This, as Neilson describes in his chapter in this volume, is referred to as 'peering' that could be the 'central business proposition of a multi-user centre'. Peering potentially allows connections to emerge between 'local/national enterprises' and 'global informatics and technical giants' without the intermediation of an external link. The WSU project problematises the forging of such connections as clues to diagramming newer non-spatial territorialities that work by creating novel modulations and rules of engagement for the movement of things, messages, and affects, and the governance of differentiated labour forces. The determinate quality of such modulations might also crystallise as newer algorithmic and artificial intelligence products in furthering the capitalisation of the data economy itself.

FINDING THE STATE IN DATA CENTRES OF INDIA

The case of Navi Mumbai, the 'satellite city' of Mumbai, as discussed by Manish Jha and Rishi Jha in the fourth and final chapter in this volume presents a set of issues similar to those proposed within the WSU project. The coasts of Mumbai have landing sites for several international submarine cable systems including Sea-Me-We-3, the Fibre-Optic Link Around the Globe (FLAG), and the i2i cable network linked through Singapore.[8] It is thus likely that this privileged geographical location along the western shores of India remains one important driver of a similar tendency (as in a Hong Kong or a Singapore) for co-location Data Centres to cluster in Mumbai and Navi Mumbai, with their count in the latter town now up to above thirty. However, in coming to terms with the specific case of Navi Mumbai, Jha and Jha develop a more categorical emphasis on the history of urbanisation within which this satellite town emerges as an attractive site for locating the 'tertiary sector' economy. They provide an account of how histories of urban development in postcolonial India came to intersect increasingly with the history of the development of IT (Information Technology) and ITES (Information Technology Enabled Services) industries, even as modernist commitments to citizen-centric urban housing and employment-intensive industrial development were side-tracked. They show that already by the 1990s, outsourced IT capital was wooed by the turning of Navi Mumbai into a 'neoliberal region state' where decisions towards making multiple relaxations in land, labour, and tax laws within emerging business districts and IT parks were made by CIDCO (City and Industrial Development Corporation of Maharashtra), as a para-state administration in partnership with corporate entities like Reliance. The state's function in the government of the urban was thus mutating from a stronger regulatory role in the decades of manufacturing sector dominance into 'an enabler "economic actor" of service sector phase', whereby its sovereignty came to be shared in some measure with key private business actors.

With the post-2000s rise of Data Centres in Navi Mumbai, this already divided sovereignty becomes more variegated. As Jha and Jha demonstrate, state-of-the-art co-location Data Centres like the CtrlS facility eventually function as entirely privatised islands within the already liberalised PPP-oriented (public-private partnership) urban form of the IT city. They then become zones within existing zones with respect to the large plots of land and built-up area they occupy, the high-skilled yet 'flexible' (see Chapter 4, this volume) labouring arrangements they deploy, and their encryption and transmission standards that eventually remain accountable on terms set entirely on transnational platforms. But what is worth noting from Jha and Jha's analysis is that even with this order of privatisation, the rather special demands made by such Data Centres on resources like water for cooling purposes, continuous power supply, expanded bandwidth, and impenetrable physical security imply that in this new phase of Data Centre-led urban development in Navi Mumbai, the state remains an important support system for such newly (re-)privatised zones of additional positive exceptions (which entails exemptions in terms of tax, land, and labour laws, arrangements for resources such as water, power, etc.). Using a term from Neilson's reading of Jha and Jha's chapter, this is one essential way in which the form of the state-of-the-art Data Centre gets 'Indianised', on count of how the state in India remains the most important mediating agency in the disbursal of certain natural and technological resources.

There is of course a second key modality, which emerges in the studies in this volume, of Data Centres becoming sites of sharing sovereignty. This is by way of a reverse process whereby state agencies become reliant on these privatised islands of digital operations for hosting and running their data storage and processing functions. This can be for instance inferred from how Jha and Jha describe the case of the banking industry in India, about 70 per cent of which is state-owned/nationalised. They point out that the banking industry's entry into the remit of Data Centres has to do significantly with its attempts at a kind of low-cost expansion towards the objective of financial growth and 'financial inclusion'. This entails an investment in alternative infrastructure like kiosks, micro-credit institutions, and mobile-banking in lieu of actual capital spending on physical bank branches. Such alternative infrastructure however, requires steady back-end support in terms of remote operations and software and hardware 'solutions', which are then provided by Data Centres. Jha and Jha argue that it is this resort to a Data Centre-d architecture that renders the state continuous with a form of 'extrastatecraft', a concept that they borrow from Keller Easterling to indicate how the territoriality of nation-state jurisdiction surrenders scope to the specific materiality of infrastructural forms (Easterling 2014). Nation-state regimes lose some control over movements of information and capital when certain kinds of infrastructure are in use. For instance, encryption standards that are used in banking services conducted through Data Centres do not allow easy decoding by state agencies. In recent smart phone-based banking apps, an unprecedented level of access to personal data often allows loaning companies a kind of individuated power over the creditor/consumer that cannot be overruled by the nation-state. Thus, though financial inclusion is a statist objective, its implications do not always suit the nation-state's rather finite regime of control.

The third chapter in this volume by Ritam Sengupta more directly broaches the issue of state agencies subscribing to a Data Centre-like architecture to run their operations. A significant push to the expansion of Data Centre services in India comes directly from the 31 'Mission Mode' initiatives (Ministry of Electronics and Information Technology [MeitY]. n.d.) commissioned by the National eGovernance Plan (2006) of the Indian government. The push also comes from the setting up of a unique State Data Centre (SDC) for each of India's twenty-nine states (IAMAI 2016). Additionally, multiple public sector but corporatised concerns—banks, utilities, or organisations like the UIDAI (Unique Identification Authority of India)—have also over the last decade, increasingly shifted to dedicated Data Centre-oriented operations. In drawing attention to the information processing revolution of sorts that the Indian state has been a participant in over the last decade or more, Sengupta

retains a focus, somewhat in contrast to the inclinations of the WSU
project, on 'captive' Data Centres that are single-user facilities. He
does this for two reasons. First, he claims that such dedicated facilities
are neither immediately making way for 'improved' co-location
varieties nor are they transitional in any simple sense since many
such single-user facilities have to be maintained as such for a long
time to come, by both state and businesses alike for operational and
legal-regulatory purposes. And second, he tries to move away from an
innovation-centric approach to viewing Data Centres, and questions
any strict binary division between 'captive' or 'co-location' varieties.
One implication of this could be gleaned from Sengupta's observation
that even a captive facility like the state-owned electricity discom
WBSEDCL's (West Bengal State Electricity Distribution Company
Limited) Data Centre, can yield to public-private sharing of data
by way of subscription to software and maintenance services of a
private concern (like TCS [Tata Consultancy Services] in this case).
Another implication that Sengupta pursues more definitively is how
WBSEDCL's Data Centre is itself an agency of assembling multiple
and divergent informational vectors that previously remained siloed
in separate divisional units of the organisation in a manner not unlike
the operations of multi-user co-location facilities and their 'peering'
arrangements.

The question of 'peering' and the new territorialities of governance
that it might spawn could not be probed directly in any of the
studies in this volume due to the extremely secretive and protected
character of Data Centre establishments. But in a related vein,
Sengupta's chapter adopts a client-end point of view to approach
the problem of how certain thresholds of organisational action came
to be recast within the Data Centre-d operations of the WBSEDCL.
He argues that one effect of this recasting is the establishment of a
graduated, but still greater degree of centralised control over the loss-
calculating and fault-monitoring system of the utility by its Kolkata-
based headquarters, against an older, apparently more dispersed
arrangement which privileged district offices within the organisation's
informational order. He also points out that the 'innovations'
introduced by medium of the re-centralised operations helmed by the
Data Centre, like for instance a new SAP IS-U[9] Enterprise Resource
Program (ERP), did not immediately become interoperable with
the legacy database of the organisation, specifically, its billing lists.
The consequences of this, Sengupta contends, remain quite ironic

as the objectives of the new software environment and WBSEDCL's organisational imperatives, seem to at times diverge significantly. Data Centre-d operations are then not simply triggers to speed and efficiency, they could also be implicated in perpetuating characteristic forms of interruptions, inefficiencies, and invisibilities that may further push us to go beyond an innovation-centric framework and locate Data Centres as one amongst other elements of significance in a dynamic information order.[10]

In terms of thinking along the specific provocation of the WSU project to understand Data Centres as being capable of carving out new objects and territories of governance, a couple more observations emerge from the studies of Jha and Jha, and Sengupta. The first of these pertain to the possible connections between national and transnational scales of governance that come to be apparently effectuated by the novel architecture of Data Centres. It is quite beyond doubt that by their very character, digital data infrastructures harbour the potential of provisioning 'minimum government with maximum governance', to use Jha and Jha's phrasing—a form of rule that constitutes an 'extrastatecraft' also by virtue of operating in a realm of abstraction, potentially autonomous from the messy terrain of the everyday operations of the postcolonial state. As Sengupta describes, this is a sovereignty that does not necessarily respond to questions of accountability that can be asked of a figurehead. It rather remains shaped by modulatory control that reacts to exceptions only when they come coded as 'feedback' via the parameters of particular software environments. Yet in many ways the unfolding of such forms of control remains critically geared towards the scale of the national population. India's much talked about 'demographic dividend', as Jha and Jha point out, remains thus the primary driver of bringing services like e-commerce and digital banking within the scope of data harvesting by Data Centre architectures, that continue to cater primarily to Indian clients. How 'solutions' standardised on a transnational scale negotiate this national scale of operations in India remains as of now an open question. And if these negotiations lead up to the proliferation of their own models of 'extrastatecraft', this need not immediately imply a kind of disembedding of governance of and by infrastructure from the realm of the nation-state. Instead, we need to pay more attention to how concerns of a national scale could actually be folded in/incorporated as a niche of sorts within the territorial logics of data infrastructure.

The second issue elicited from the studies by Jha and Jha and Sengupta that requires emphasis here is that the 'datafication' of specific arenas of governance as possibly effectuated by adopting Data Centre-d infrastructures, is not simply an overlaying of such infrastructure on an already operational mode of generating marketable objects and/or disciplined citizens, an available platform over which the data economy or data governance can henceforth unfold. Rather, datafication was to be a medium of making these arenas operable *at all*, in terms of securing the objectives of commodification, discipline, or financialisation. In Sengupta's study, this problem presents itself in the form of the instrumentalisation of data towards the objective of the curtailment of energy losses that result from technical dissipation and human theft of electricity. As he points out, the problem of 'loss' within the realm of electricity distribution in India has been historically reproduced as a question also of informatic lapses that the new digitised and Data Centre-d operations of the WBSEDCL aim to correct. This informatic correction has as its correlate, the objective of arresting the pilferage of power, and thus by implication, the re-commodification of energy against the populist slant towards 'free electricity'. Similarly, in Jha and Jha's study, the virtualisation of the banking industry via a Data Centre-oriented architecture is also described as means of securing a rapid and low-cost 'financial inclusion' of a massive number of people, hitherto outside the reach of formal banking services, that extended to only about 40 per cent of the Indian population till 2018.

It is not difficult to see that by its circular logic of functioning based on 'feedback' sequences, a possible process of governance by data infrastructures would have to seek sustenance from the very logics of commodification or financialisation that data re-programs and brings into being. A future credit scoring application for instance, will ride on newly financialised populations who move into the orbit of digital banking just as the modulatory control of a future smart meter will depend on the extent to which power consumption becomes amenable to a commodity logic against a precise digitised form of measurement. But as Sengupta's chapter shows, this eventuality of a transition to 'governance by data' could actually be complicated by the existing situation in which the creation of data infrastructure is not by itself entirely guaranteeing a passage to any new kind of commoditisation. This passage, in his case between uncertain measures of energy dissipation and 'free electricity' to a precise estimation of electricity consumption that by implication, is paid for, seems to indicate a necessity for the state to step in as an enforcer of principles that 'datafication' cannot quite direct on its own. And as he shows with the case of electricity distribution in West Bengal, the (populist) state's willingness to do so is not always a foregone conclusion. In any case, the instance of digitalised banking or of digitalised management of electricity distribution seem to present yet another scenario in which the potentially novel territories of governance opened up by Data Centre-d infrastructure might have to be supplemented by possible functions of the postcolonial state—in this case, those of working over and above market forces to link specific orders of people and things to chains of economic value-making. Before moving on, we would want to posit here that it is particularly on this count that the infrastructural rule of 'governance by data' seems to rest on the national state retaining some of its conventional capacities of sovereign action in the control of populations and commodities even as it pushes these entities into a virtualised (putatively) domain of 'extrastatecraft'. We will further clarify this proposition in the last section of this Introduction after revisiting in the following section, the historical lineages of state and capital within which the evolution of data and its infrastructures can be located in India.

Locating Data Infrastructures Historically

Within the WSU project, the rise of Data Centres is specifically framed in terms of the historical development of logistical capitalism. In his chapter, Neilson posits a series of historical analogies for Data Centres beginning with the fortified 'factories' of the early-modern European imperial powers around the world. These 'factories' bore the promise of free trade as they became sites of interaction for locals and foreign merchants. Yet they also allowed these imperial powers the scope to launch their territorial claims. With the more formalised colonised domains, the 'factories' became 'warehouses' that in turn were bestowed with logistical tasks of 'procurement, sale and negotiation' for the control of trade. As literature on capitalism has often discussed, buoyed by the post-War developments in military transportation and supply, logistics evolved as inseparable from and in many ways definitive of economic systems in the second half of the twentieth century (Cowen 2014). Henceforth the centrality of production in the value-addition and labour exploitation process was displaced, as value and labour could be sourced and manipulated along the entire chain of distribution and exchange. Production in global commodity exchanges was dispersed as production was itself becoming a function of highly synchronised demands of circulation that sought out export-processing zones of advantage across world regions (Tsing 2009). Consequently, a novel information order took shape that linked software and computing design with just-in-time production, containerisation, new modes of monitoring workers' performance, and the development of academic knowledge guiding the optimisation of supply chains (Neilson 2014: 85). To return to Neilson's chapter in this volume, the 'warehouse' of colonial trade was thus transformed in this logistical revolution into 'an increasingly automated environment'.

For Neilson, the Data Centre in many ways reclaims the logical place of the 'warehouse' within the colonial trading system (also, Jacobson and Hogan 2019). In Data Centres the informational order of logistics finds sites of concentration over which further advancements in computing capacities can be marshalled, towards both re-coordinating architectures of supply chains as well as commodifying the medium of such coordination, that is data. The clustering of Data Centres in Singapore might serve as a case in point. As Neilson and Tanya Notley discuss in a recent article, such clustering seem to reproduce the socio-economic geographical combinations of the nineteenth-century colonial economy that maintained Singapore as a 'logistical switch point' (Neilson and Notley 2019: 20). They contend that even though the postcolonial government's inclination was to develop Singapore as a separate industrial base that could allow the new nation to stand independent of regional trading networks (like those of rubber), the multiplication of Data Centres in Singapore more recently, has effectively re-confirmed its status as an intermediary site of coordination of regional commodity and labour exchanges. But even in their inheriting of older sites of logistical convergence, Data Centres could also generate their own distinctive modes, objects, and territories of governance within logistical distributions, through possible interactions forged by their means between regional and international geographies of digital data. As Ned Rossiter has argued, the emergence of large, co-location Data Centres in the Asia-Pacific region could mark 'a historic and paradigmatic shift from the extraction of surplus value from labour as a core structural dynamic of the capitalist mode of production to an arguably novel form of surplus data within an algorithmic capitalism' (Rossiter 2017: 7).

All the contributions to this volume confirm, to a certain extent, the status of Data Centres as key to logistical coordination in contemporary India, whether it be timely technological augmentation of power networks, or the synchronisation of manufacturing hubs around Mumbai, to take two examples. Yet in keeping with the reality of the massive exercise in database management launched by the Indian state in recent times, Ritajyoti Bandyopadhyay's (second) chapter in this volume also tries to think of an alternate genealogy for data infrastructures in India through the history of the Indian state's statistical programmes. If the Data Centre's function, as Neilson claims, is indeed to recast the archive as a storage site for diffuse and often disassociated data in order to transcend the conventional statistical imperatives of government, we ought to be able to account for exactly what is being transcended and how, in order to better comprehend the novelty of the modes of governance implicated in this rearrangement. In turn, it might also lead us to think of a different kind of capitalist lineage for data infrastructure in India, and thus a more precise understanding of the very political process of data being rendered 'surplus' in the current moment.

In narrating this history, Bandyopadhyay presents the Indian Statistical Institute (ISI) and the sample survey exercise that its erstwhile head P. C. Mahalanobis pioneered, as a unique occurrence situated at the intersections of certain global currents of mid-twentieth century. Primary amongst these were the environment of the Cold War 'big science' initiatives like that of the International Geophysical Year (1957–1958) that necessitated the accumulation and exchange of data on a gigantic scale, an associated investment specifically by First World nations in military research that pushed the boundaries of conventional computing and hardware and most significantly, the conception of the idea of a 'national economy' through a range of numerical indices devised since the 1930s (Aronova 2017; Bouk 2017). Taking the post-Independence scenario of the emergence of ISI, Bandyopadhyay shows how specific inflections of these developments came together to contribute to the development of sophisticated data gathering and processing initiatives in India. As a newly decolonised but also Non-Aligned nation, India did have certain technological benefits sourced from the international community. With respect to the case of computing, such sharing of technological devices and knowledge were also relatively uninhibited as ISI's status was primarily that of an educational institution and not a military facility. This resulted in the installation of advanced mainframe computing devices at the Institute, through which Mahalanobis ran his massive National Sample Surveys.[11] Bandyopadhyay points out that these surveys were quite different from discrete and periodic data collected by the Census in the way that they sought to achieve a certain largeness of scale both in terms of sample sizes as well as by way of being continuously conducted. He also ventures the suggestion that the statistical concepts and tools developed to process such sample surveys have had important contributions to make to current machine-learning algorithms and processing of Big Data. Eventually, these sample surveys sought to bring into existence 'a community of producers and consumers within an overarching national frame'.

In Bandyopadhyay's estimation, the key distinction between this moment of the ISI and National Sample Surveys, and that of today's Data Centres and Big Data is then perhaps marked not so much by a definite qualitative difference in terms of the epistemic and technical functions of data; both these moments are also somewhat continuous in terms of the prime objective of securing the development of the 'national economy'. The difference in the two respective phases is rather constituted by a 'more fundamental transformation' in the state-society relation in India, the main symptom of which is that the state is now intent on converting the constituent element of the 'national economy' idea that is data, into an object that can be commodified and traded along with being instrumentalised in more usual forms of government. According to Bandyopadhyay, in this recasting of statistical surveys as a 'corporate actor' dealing in Big Data, the 'national economy' is finally severed from a possible affective bond with the nation. The national economy thus becomes a dematerialised object that need not correlate with the actual well-being of populations. He further analyses that (digital) 'datum' is a somewhat unique commodity that while certainly involving labour in its production—the infinitesimally small act of clicking a link for instance—does not quite attain a status of being valueable in the chain of exchange due to its tendency towards infinite replicability, which reduces its reproduction time to almost nil. For him, the valorisation of data involved in its commodification is then possibly related to the algorithmic and technological processing that it undergoes to become interoperable with other sets of data. But this valorisation is also equally an effect of restricting the movement of data/ formation of data commons by building actual physical enclosures and through copyrights, patents, and other forms of property law. Bandyopadhyay finally suggests that Data Centres are such enclosures of the contemporary world.

There is however, a very obvious element of contingency that punctuates this transition narrative of the state becoming a counterpart of corporate actors from the world of logistical capitalism via its role in the commodification of data. As either directly stated or hinted at by several contributors in this volume, the present regime of digitised Big Data in India is also invariably haunted in many ways by a 'sparse data syndrome'.[12] In Bandyopadhyay's incursions into the archive of National Income accounting in India, he digs up several instances of genuinely robust diagnoses of such a syndrome. He thus shows how the National Income Committee of India (1951) remained quite interested in problems like the difficulties of measuring exchanges happening in India on non-cash terms, the lack of differentiation resulting in household enterprises performing functions otherwise taken up by industry, and the difficulty of estimating household incomes.[13] With the benefit of hindsight, we can perhaps read in these diagnoses early intimations of the problem of 'informality' that encompasses vast numbers of livelihoods and equally large parts of the production of goods and delivery of services in India till date. 'Informality' could in one sense denote the critical condition of an overwhelming majority of the Indian workforce (over 90 per cent) being employed under a definite lack of statutorily stipulated securities in terms of existing labour laws and regulations (Breman 2013). It could equally apply to the realm of small enterprises of manufacture and sales that work below the radar of formal registration in order to maintain slim but significant margins of profit (Sanyal 2007). It could also serve as a description for a wide variety of coping strategies for businesses and often, migrant labour populations, to skirt precarity by means of engaging in non-contractual forms of employment and credit relationships and illegal use of resources like water, electricity, and land (Chatterjee 2004). As Ranabir Samaddar (who guided the 'Data Centres in India' research project at CRG) has argued, the operations of this 'informality' do not really constitute an 'outside' to capitalism, but rather remain the strategic accretions through which postcolonial capitalism extracts surplus. They are in many ways then definitive of the character of postcolonial capitalism that remains parasitic on these heterogeneous and flexible modes of production and the associated modes of relatively costless social reproduction. These modes of production and reproduction can multiply without the medium of the formalised rule of law and can be dismantled as needed, to recuperate the processes of expanded accumulation (Samaddar 2018: 145–174).

Following from this, we can quite directly route the phenomenon of 'sparse data' in India to the conditions of the reproduction of 'informality' within a possible postcolonial capitalism. We can see that while a global and logistical rearrangement of capitalism was critically dependent on a new and sophisticated information order, its possible postcolonial constituents could actually have been founded in many ways on the bases of certain *strategically maintained* invisibilities and immeasurabilities.[14] The pioneering efforts of the likes of Mahalanobis to render these realms comprehensible through statistical innovations might have been representative of the newly decolonised state's interest in inaugurating a more liberal condition for the reproduction of capitalism in the region. Yet with a view to the contemporary, we could also infer that the order of postcolonial capitalism has actually (and expectedly) continued to sustain itself on the massive multiplication of 'informality', which in turn thrives by remaining penumbral to the vision of the state and other agencies of information in the region. The 'sparse data syndrome' then does not result from any possible shortcoming of the postcolonial orders of state and capital—it is rather founded in a relation of co-constitution with these orders.

Relocating the Sovereignty of the Nation-State in an Era of Data Centres

On the trail of this 'sparse data syndrome', we can now return to the issue raised in a previous section of this Introduction, of how the functioning of data infrastructures seems to rest on the supplementary drive of the national state towards realigning particular orders of people and things with trajectories of economic value-making. The proliferation of new kinds of digital data infrastructure, varieties of sensors, a considerable diffusion of high-speed Internet connections, and of course Data Centre-d architectures, has certainly made for an unprecedented opportunity for a re-induction of the various invisible components of 'informality' to the information and surveillance orders of state and capital in contemporary India. Not quite guaranteeing any imminent formalisation of rights and entitlements, such re-induction is however certainly geared towards the objective of rendering data 'surplus' and thus valuable. But as we have already pointed out with respect to the case of electricity and digitalised financial services, the presence of data infrastructure doesn't quite by itself guarantee this re-induction. In recent times in India, this re-induction has actually required the full exercise of the very conventional sovereign powers of the postcolonial state, deployed to legitimise various kinds of exceptional measures including the forced conscription of Indian citizens into mandates of digitalised governance. While the reader of this volume is more likely to encounter the state as being a transformed, corporatised actor that exists to enable IT capital and its own service-delivery onto the path of least possible friction, we choose to conclude this Introduction by offering certain nuances to this understanding of transformation. We do this by narrating particular instances of how the conventional sovereignty of the national state has of late, been summoned up again and again to prop up the development of digital data infrastructure and its implied function of governing by data. In making this conclusion, we also hope to then direct the reader towards future avenues of researching the development of such infrastructure that were not entirely explored in this volume.

The Aadhaar project perhaps best represents the recent state-aided quest for turning India's 'demographic dividend' into nodes of generating 'data dividends', and how this quest remains backed by a significant exercise of the state's executive power. Aadhaar, as is now well known, is a randomly generated number that associates with the biometrics of a person to constitute a form of identification. The number and the biometric information put together can henceforth make it possible to generate a unique identification for the concerned individual towards the objective of authenticating various kinds of functions.[15] To significantly abbreviate a more detailed history, the idea for such a biometric ID stemmed from post-Kargil War (1999) suggestions to enhance border security in areas like Kashmir to prevent infiltration (Mehmood 2008). Within a decade, this border security technology moved into the core of policy discussions about the delivery of welfare in India, which had started enrolling key private sector stakeholders including Nandan Nilekani, one of the chairmen of the IT company, Infosys. It was Nilekani's vision to think of Aadhaar as a technology of eliminating middling 'informal' agents and duplicates to deliver welfare (-as-service) directly to poorer beneficiaries (Chattapadhyay 2013; Nilekani 2009). It was also his vision scripted along with the IT industry think tank iSPIRT (Indian Software Product Industry Roundtable) to make Aadhaar the basis of authenticating a wide range of other transactions and service deliveries through creating a separate platform-based operation, India Stack, as a counter to what they call the 'data colonialisation' of large corporations like Google or Facebook (Dattani 2020; Nilekani 2017). In effect this sought to promote an indigenous data mining apparatus that was trained on Indian citizens with as little regard for their privacy and data security as the same large corporations against whom this apparatus was claiming its nationalism.

Several critics have pointed out that Aadhaar-based authentications that compel a person to maintain their bodily integrity through all stages of life and all circumstances remain unrealistic (Rao 2018; Sinha and Sethia 2017). They have also shown that the entire Internet-based infrastructure of authentication can malfunction enough number of times to deprive large numbers of people of their essential welfare endowments (Khera 2019a). The Supreme Court of India too initially forbade the government from making Aadhaar mandatory for welfare schemes (*India Today* 2015). Yet the Indian state, helmed by the Hindu nationalist Bharatiya Janata Party (BJP) since 2014, steadfastly pushed through its Aadhaar project, continuing to surreptitiously make it 'mandatory' for the access of such services (*The Wire* 2017a). This in turn, created a window also for several other services ranging from banking to mobile phone connections offered by private companies to demand Aadhaar-based validation of customers' accounts. In 2016, the NDA-II government at the Centre went on to enact the Aadhaar Act that legitimised the use of Aadhaar for authentication purposes by both public and private agencies. It 'passed' this as a 'Money Bill' that allowed it to skip the scrutiny of the Upper House (Rajya Sabha) of the Indian Parliament where it did not have majority (*Moneylife* 2018). Eventually it muscled the Supreme Court to ratify the constitutional validity of Aadhaar in September 2018. The Court finally made Aadhaar mandatory for welfare and subsidy-based functions while disallowing its use for private services (*The Economic Times* 2018b). By this time however, large numbers of Indians subscribing to all types of services ranging from e-commerce to telecommunications to banking had already linked their respective accounts to their Aadhaar ID. Moreover, Aadhaar had also already emerged as the dominant norm for identifying the subject of most financial transactions (*Quartz India* 2018). Legal-judicial concerns about the privacy of Indian citizens were thus already in the process of dilution. The Aadhaar project then in many ways could stand in as the most direct manifestation of the new Janus-faced form of the postcolonial state. On one hand, this state reinvents itself in the mould of a corporatised entity. And on the other hand, it continues to leverage its full executive strength towards overruling democratic and legal processes of safeguarding Indian citizens from potential violations of their rights and lives, and towards eliminating any possible alternative of making new digital technology speak to fair, free, and egalitarian concerns.[16] The founding and functioning of digital data infrastructures in contemporary India seemingly rests on both these stilts.

A more naked display of this executive strength came on 8 November 2016 when Prime Minister Narendra Modi banned the use of the higher denominations of Indian currency (Rs 500 and Rs 1000) without adequate notice. The declared objective of this infamous 'demonetisation' was the arresting of hoarded 'black money' (unaccounted and untaxed earnings) in the country, and citizens were egged on to sacrifice their basic conveniences for fulfilling their duty towards their motherland (*The Economic Times* 2016). But not long after, large advertisements splashed across Indian newspapers declared that this was a great opportunity for the citizens and a recently formed digital payments company (Paytm) to back each other up, with the former being coaxed to shift to cashless monetary transactions through the latter's mobile-based application. These ads were graced by images of the Prime Minister (*Business Standard* 2016). The platform India Stack had earlier that year already come up with a protocol for allowing interoperable payment transactions between different financial institutions and individuals in India called the Unified Payments Interface (UPI), at the back-end of which remained an Aadhaar-based system of identification.[17] The demonetisation experiment was a resounding failure in terms of arresting black money as several reports have now confirmed that almost the entire money calculated to be in circulation prior to the note ban was returned in banks for changing into new notes (*The Wire* 2017b). Eventually the government confirmed Paytm's narrative in a way by declaring that more than controlling 'black money', its objective for demonetisation was to kick-start the economy of digital payments in India (*The Wire* 2017c).

This coercion to go digital however had a severe human cost not unlike the mandatory use of Aadhaar for welfare services. Demonetisation saw scores of deaths being reported from across the country as going cashless quite literally meant going without food and other essentials for the less-privileged sections of the Indian population (*The Wire* 2018b). Moreover, large portions of production and services descended into a significant downturn as middle and small enterprises in India run entirely on cash (*Huffpost* 2019). In effect then, demonetisation was another experiment in the brutal exercise of executive power to drag the populace of India into the value-chain of digital data-making—a kind of 'primitive accumulation' that staked significant numbers of lives and livelihoods in the service of setting up the new surplus-making orders of data capitalism.[18] It is perhaps not a matter of much irony that this same kind of brutal power remains in display also to secure the very obverse of this process, that is to suspend the orders of data capitalism at will when it suits the imperialist designs of the current NDA-II government. Thus Internet services in the Kashmir region remained suspended for eighteen months following the abrogation of the constitutionally guaranteed Article 370 in August 2019, which had allotted the state certain specially sanctioned autonomies within the Indian union, even as this suspension made it extremely difficult for the normal functioning of commercial but also other essential services in the region (see *Outlook* 2020; *TechCrunch* 2021).

More recently, a slightly different order of sovereign action is being toyed with by the central government, which seeks to intervene in global conditions of data circulation more directly, admittedly in order to incentivise the setting up of Data Centres in India. This relates to the regulatory policy of data localisation, that is one element of the broader legal form of 'Data Protection'. As mentioned earlier, data localisation is specifically concerned with keeping data of particular geographical origins and of particular/'personal' kinds within the boundaries of the concerned region, thus significantly controlling cross-border data flow. Data Protection is a more general collection of legal concerns invoked in many nations within the globalised, networked data economy that potentially affect the scaling up of virtualised systems of data storage, management, and processing. These concerns are not synonymous with issues of individual privacy though they are often conceived as closely linked to such issues (Fuster 2014). Data Protection involves the regulation of what data is being collected, for what purposes, who it is being shared with, and how long it can be held by the agency collecting it, amongst other things (Lynskey 2015).

By August 2017, after the Supreme Court of India pronounced privacy to be a fundamental right of Indians (a right incidentally contested by the central government), concerns about legally specifying what this right entailed by enacting some version of Data Protection legislation became necessary for the government (*EFF* 2017). Meanwhile international developments like the adoption of the General Data Protection Regulation (GDPR) by the European Union (EU) also served as a prompt for India to develop a Data Protection regime. This was because GDPR created restrictions on the movement of the data of European citizens to domains that did not have sufficient standards of such protection, thus risking the business prospects of some IT industries in India (*Deccan Herald* 2018). Following this, the affirmation of Data Protection and by implication, data localisation, came embodied in several policies and laws conceived by the NDA-II government over its two terms in power at the Centre. This started with the Reserve Bank of India's (RBI) financial data regulations (2018) that stipulated that the storage and processing of all financial transactions-related data had to be within the borders of India (*The Wire* 2018a). Given the growing scope of the use of digital payments by the Indian population, this RBI directive compelled payments intermediaries like Mastercard, Visa, or Google Pay who wanted to stay relevant in the Indian market, to subscribe to or set up data infrastructures within the territorial confines of the country (*Medianama* 2019b). This move was followed by other orders issued by the government in terms of compelling data emerging out of other domains like e-commerce, healthcare, or insurance to be localised in India by means of acts like the (draft) Digital Information Security in

Healthcare Act (2018), or the (draft) National E-Commerce Policy (2019) (Basu and Nachiappan 2020).[19]

The most controversial of such legal measures has of course been the first version of the Personal Data Protection (PDP) Bill brought forward in 2018 by a committee set up under (retd.) Justice Srikrishna.[20] Almost all important global players, ranging from corporations like Google, Facebook, and Microsoft to international organisations like US–India Strategic Partnership Forum and the EU, expressed serious objections to its provisions (*Medianama* 2018). The main object of such objections was the Bill's data localisation clauses. The Bill strictly mandated 'data fiduciaries' to store 'at least one serving copy' of all personal data generated in India on a server or Data Centre located in India. The government was allowed to exempt certain categories of personal data from this requirement. It could however also declare certain categories of data 'critical' and require that they be stored only in India.[21] In other words, foreign internet intermediaries and services, such as Facebook, Uber, Google, Twitter, AirBnB, Telegram, WhatsApp, and Signal were all required to physically host user data in India. Along with concerns of security, such data localisation was deemed necessary to help Indian companies make productive use of data generated within India towards developing additional software, AI (Artificial Intelligence) products, and other data-driven services and tools (Sinha and Basu 2019). The objections to the data localisation ambitions of the Indian government have continuously multiplied across a range of international and trade forums including the 2019 G20 summit in Osaka (Basu and Nachiappan 2020). With the tabling of a second draft of the PDP Bill in the winter 2019 session of the Lok Sabha, the government heeded some of these objections and significantly reduced the localisation requirements of the 2018 draft bill. It first removed the mandatory requirement of mirroring all personal data in India. Localisation requirements were then restricted to two modified categories of data—a category of 'Sensitive Personal Data' that could be transferred outside India subject to conditions of consent and government permission, and a category of 'Critical Personal Data' that would still have to be stored and processed only in India (*SFLC.in.* 2019). However, in a new move, the government claimed unregulated access to any and every possible data generated by/off Indian citizens for national security agencies (*The Indian Express* 2020).

The 2019 PDP Bill has been modified again via consultation with a Joint Parliamentary Committee to lead up to a 2021 version now being presented at the Parliament. In the 2021 Draft PDP Bill, the requirement to mandatorily host both 'Sensitive Personal Data' and 'Critical Personal Data' on Indian soil has been re-introduced, with the cross-border transfer of 'Sensitive Personal Data' requiring more categorical permissions from the central government. Moreover, through the 2021 Draft PDP Bill, the government has sought control even over anonymised non-personal data (*Lexology* 2022). Once more such strict terms of data movement and data localisation have created controversy and the government is again mulling a complete re-draft of the Data Protection Bill (*The Economic Times* 2022).

The regulatory zeal with Data Protection, especially the question of data localisation, is perhaps still to evolve into hardened directives in India as the government continues to negotiate the (lately) complicated terrain of international trade agreements (Joshi 2020). When we began our research for the 'Data Centres in India' project in early 2017, the regulation of the data flows in and out of the country, but also between two entities in the same country, did not immediately seem to be an issue of major concern for the government (though this was to change shortly).[22] In fact, e-commerce giants like Flipkart reportedly benefitted immensely from cheaply hosting their consumers' data in the United States (US).[23] Perhaps our research for this volume, on count of being situated in such an incubatory phase of Data Protection regulations in India, has only managed to cast a tangential glance at these issues in terms of our taking stock of the landscape of Data Centres in India. But there has also been a genuine concern raised time and again by many observers of contemporary digital data infrastructures regarding how (in)effective (national) state regulation can actually be in the control of data. The point to be considered here is that even while the generation of data remains reliant on the architectural support of national states, its eventual trajectory in circuits of movement and processing could be quite unsuited to the custody of nation-states. Thus, in Easterling's propositions concerning 'extrastatecraft' that has remained an important guide to our understanding, such infrastructures constitute 'dynamic systems of space, information and power' that often 'generate de facto forms of polity faster than even quasi-official forms of governance can legislate them' (Easterling 2014: 10). Similarly, in Benjamin Bratton's design philosophy of *The Stack*, 'data do not really have a national career unless they are forced to produce one' and he understands current attempts at data localisation to be 'reactionary counter-policing that is of dubious value in the long run' (Bratton 2016: 36). The possibly transitional character of the attempt to control the trajectories of data by nation-states is also perhaps indicated in Neilson's point made in his chapter in this volume that 'storage of data in a facility located in a certain national territory... does not equate to ownership of this data'.

In concluding this Introduction, we would like to steer a somewhat different course from such observations in order to come to terms with the Indian state's newfound enthusiasm towards localising various kinds of data. India's data localisation measures are of course not unique. China and Russia are the obvious examples of such policies. But it is also remarkable that several large national economies between 2006 and 2016 had enacted at least eighty-four such measures (UNCTAD 2016). The most significant players in the global data economy, like the US for example, remain largely opposed to data localisation. Yet US President Trump's decision to quit the Trans-Pacific Partnership in January 2017 effectively interrupted the possibility of uninhibited data flow between the US and locations of the Asia-Pacific (*BBC News* 2017). Moreover, large corporations based on platform technologies like Facebook, Amazon, or Google actually run their own versions of data localisation whereby they create their own containers of data that do not really remain easily amenable to more open architectures (Mosco 2014; Srnicek 2017). Data localisation then must be understood as a key global trend in the governance of data that over the last decade seems to be returning some amount of control to nation-state governments within this latest phase of the globalisation of information technology capital (Chander and Lê 2015). To deny this reality would be to commit to an awkward conception of a global-by-design character of data infrastructures, which could be fast making way for a stricter regime of national controls that is hardly a transitional phase in relation to some ideal, eventual version of globalised data infrastructures.

The rise of the Data Centre industry in India was steep while it was riding the waves of India's 'GDP revolution' (Gross Domestic Product) (Samaddar 2018: 132). Over the last couple of years, it has however become quite obvious that the incessant growth of GDP has faced a definite roadblock in India, though the reasons for this are still being disputed (*The Hindu* 2020). Given this situation, it is not impossible that a renewed potential is being conceived for India's data industry via measures which compel various global corporations to create Data Centres in India. Which direction this will lead to in terms of the cross-border movement of digital data is as of now, difficult to determine. But it would be erroneous to consider the localisation of digital data within Data Centres in India as simply a mistaken modality of asserting ownership over this data. The Indian state is actually looking at more than the housing of data of Indians within the borders of the country. The draft PDP Bill of 2018 in fact had a little-noticed provision to set up something called a 'regulatory sandbox'.[24] This techno-legal form envisaged a bringing together of anonymised multiform data sets from several agencies and corporations for the future development of technological and algorithmic applications (Kharbanda 2019). A future credit-rating system for example, would require active combination of both social media data as well as financial information, and here a global corporation would have to participate in such a sandbox form or a platform if it were to have any contribution to the making of such applications. Related to this are other modalities by which the Indian government could possibly extend its claims on data produced within the country. Thus the *Economic Survey of India 2018–19* (GoI 2019), described how data, especially anonymised or non-personal data, was to be conceived as 'public good' (even if it was allowed to be moved outside the country) that could be processed by government-designed or even private platforms in order to make economic value within the country (Basu and Nachiappan 2020). The apparently sacrosanct categories of 'critical' or 'sensitive' personal data too would not necessarily be out of the scope of such economic value-making. These categories would perhaps describe a diversification of legal niches over which future algorithmic production can regenerate, if only by creating so-called 'privacy-enhancing technologies' (Koops and Leenes 2014; Lippert and Walby 2016). In enabling such production, Data Centres could indeed function, as Neilson observes (in this volume), as sites for the 'patching' of domestic and transnational spaces. But a future enquiry into Data Centres in India would certainly have to think of the national state as an important mediator of such patching together, if its regulatory zeal towards managing data flows and processing continues in the same way as it has till date.[25]

End Notes

1. The metalanguage gives off the appearance of being abstract enough to encompass all communication, but it need not actually be so.

2. Modalities of 'bringing the cloud back to earth' have been discussed in studies of developing economies of cloud computing (Mosco 2014; Hu 2015), 'platform' technologies (Srnicek 2017), the geopolitics of virtualised infrastructure (Amoore 2016; Burrington 2015a), the placement of the 'cloud' within commodity chains of rare-earth metals (Reading and Notley 2015), and data 'journeys' and geographies (Bates et al. 2016; Malecki and Wei 2009).

3. Data Centres still remain relatively under-researched. Andrew Blum's (2012) study of the Internet as a material form and Rob Kitchin's (2014) study of data infrastructures describe several aspects critical to a study of Data Centres. Ned Rossiter's (2016: 138–183) chapter in his book, *Software, Infrastructure, Labor,* remains a pioneering contribution that placed Data Centres within a larger theoretical framework of studying 'new media', or as he describes it 'logistical media'. The work of Mel Hogan (2015a) has remained focused on the study of Data Centres in prime locations of the global North. Recently two co-edited special issues (Johnson and Hogan 2017; Hogan and Vonderau 2019) have appeared on the topic of Data Centres that speak to the concerns of this volume. For studies attuned more specifically to the politics of digital data and the realms of control that they negotiate around the world, see the volume edited by Bigo, Isin, and Ruppert (2019).

4. Increasingly, scholars have been concerned with the water and energy infrastructure required for the form of cooling and powering systems deployed in large Data Centres (Burrington 2015b; Carruth 2014; Hogan 2015b, Jakobsson and Stiernstedt 2012).

5. Seen through the lens of an emancipatory vision, accelerationism describes an intensification of contemporary computational and other techno-scientific advances that allow for an escape from the gravitational pull of older social and economic orders. Such an intensification of quantitatively and technically enabled modes of rationalisation allows for a re-imagination of distributive politics and the commons that is both a possible route to the dissolution of modes of dominance and valorisation engendered by actually existing capitalism as well as a movement beyond nation-state-centric models of control (of trade, work, populations, etc.) (Williams and Srnicek 2014). Other more cautious observers state that in the case of 'the acceleration of capital flows through computational megaplatforms…We will have to wait and see what will and what will not "wither away" should planetary-scale computation approach peak platform optimization and ubiquity' (Bratton 2016: 58). The reassertion of nation-states in the management of data flows

presents a contingent situation that interrupts any immediately global-by-design or potentially emancipatory characteristic of data infrastructure and directs our attention to forms of reterritorialisation that are reshaping the nature of flows (of capital, information, and affect) and forms of subjectivation in the data economy, and a data-mediated society.

6. See http://www.mcrg.ac.in/Data_Centres/DataCentres_Home.asp (accessed March 2022).

7. See https://www.westernsydney.edu.au/ics/projects/data_centres_and_the_governance_of_labour_and_territory (accessed March 2022).

8. See https://www.datacentermap.com/india/ (accessed March 2022).

9. SAP IS-U refers to the SAP (Systems Applications and Products in Data Processing) company's 'Industry Specific Solution for Utilities Industry' software.

10. A comparable approach criticising innovation-centrism to understand the use of digital technology within Indian bureaucracy is laid out in Solanki (2019).

11. Another significant way of conceptualising the history of computers coming to India that focuses on the geopolitical aspects of technology transfer more closely is found in Menon (2018). The standard history of computers in India remains Subramanian (1992).

12. The term is originally from (Samaddar 2018: 132). This question of 'sparse data' is missed out in recent studies that otherwise effectively establish the continuities between colonial and postcolonial modes of data generation (Couldry and Mejias 2019), or those that describe a distinctive contemporary postcolonial character to global big data initiatives based on the adaptive character of such initiatives (as different from the colonial, ascriptive forms of statistical practices) (Ruppert and Isin 2019).

13. Other comparable studies of sample survey techniques and National Income accounting in India are Newbigin (2020) and Paidipaty (2020).

14. We are not suggesting that postcolonial lives and livelihoods are by their very character, within some sort of dimension of immeasurability. For a critique of that idea, see Dutta (2008).

15. See https://uidai.gov.in/what-is-aadhaar.html (accessed March 2022).

16. Several scholars have studied the Aadhaar project in greater detail on these terms. Two collections stand out here: the first being a volume edited by Reetika Khera (2019b), and the second, a special issue of the journal *South Asia* (Rao and Nair 2019). An earlier edited volume with a focus on Aadhaar and migrants is Ghosh (2013).

17. See https://www.npci.org.in/what-we-do/upi/product-overview#:~:text=Unified%20Payments%20Interface%20(UPI)%20is,merchant%20payments%20into%20one%20hood (accessed May 2022).

18. Economists like Arun Kumar (2017) and Jayati Ghosh, C. P. Chandrasekhar and Prabhat Patnaik (2017) have written deeply critical

accounts of demonetisation. A collection of critical pieces on demonetisation has appeared in the journal *Cultural Anthropology* (Dharia and Trisal 2017).

19. Both the draft act and the draft policy are yet to be passed into actual use through parliamentary or executive directive in India. Their concerns also overlap with the new Data Protection Bill (2021) and thus their execution awaits the finalisation of the more general data protection framework in India. Available at https://pib.gov.in/Pressreleaseshare.aspx?PRID=1578929 (accessed May 2022).

20. See https://meity.gov.in/writereaddata/files/Personal_Data_Protection_Bill,2018.pdf (accessed May 2022).

21. See https://www.prsindia.org/billtrack/draft-personal-data-protection-bill-2018 (accessed May 2022).

22. Questions of data protection was then as even now (in the absence of a formally passed data protection framework) governed by the provisions and amended (2008) sections of the Information Technology Act (2000) that do not really affect questions of cross-border data flow very strictly. For the Act and its amendments, see: https://meity.gov.in/content/information-technology-act-2000 (accessed March 2022).

23. Flipkart has now opened its second Data Centre in India (*Data Center Dynamics* 2019). Other global giants like Alibaba and Amazon (along with payments companies like Google Pay, Whatsapp Pay) have also readily agreed to host data or open Data Centres in India (*The Economic Times* 2018a). Indian companies like Paytm, PhonePe, and Reliance have cited concerns about 'data colonisation' and creating a level playing field to also actively support the government's data localisation policies (*Medianama* 2019a).

24. The provision for creating such a sandbox has also been continued in the Personal Data Protection Bill, 2021 (*iapp* 2022).

25. For another view on how the nation-state persists and remediates the question of Data Centres by participating in an exchange relation of sorts with large corporations, see Maguire and Winthereik (2021).

REFERENCES

Amoore, L. 2016. 'Cloud Geographies: Computing, Data, Sovereignty'. *Progress in Human Geography* 42(1): 4–24.

Appel, H., N. Anand, and A. Gupta. 2018. 'Introduction: Temporality, Politics, and the Promise of Infrastructure'. In *The Promise of Infrastructure*, H. Appel, N. Anand, and A. Gupta (eds), 1–38. Durham: Duke University Press.

Aronova, E. 2017. 'Geophysical Datascapes of the Cold War: Politics and Practices of the World Data Centers in the 1950s and 1960s'. *Osiris* 32(1): 307–327.

Basu, A. and K. Nachiappan. 2020. 'India and the Global Battle for Data Governance'. *Seminar* 731(July). Available at https://www.india-seminar.com/2020/731/731_arindrajit_and_karthik.htm (accessed March 2022).

Bates, J., Yu-Wei Lin, and P. Goodale. 2016. 'Data Journeys: Capturing the Socio-Material Constitution of Data Objects and Flows'. *Big Data & Society* 3(2): 1–12.

BBC News. 2017. 'Trump executive order pulls out of TPP trade deal', 24 January. Available at https://www.bbc.com/news/world-us-canada-38721056 (accessed May 2022).

Bigo, D., E. Isin, and E. Ruppert (eds). 2019. *Data Politics: Worlds, Subjects, Rights*. New York: Routledge.

Blum, A. 2012. *Tubes: A Journey to the Center of the Internet*. New York: Harper Collins.

Bouk, D. 2017. 'The History and Political Economy of Personal Data over the Last Two Centuries in Three Acts'. *Osiris* 32(1): 85–106.

Bratton, B. 2016. *The Stack: On Software and Sovereignty*. Cambridge, MA: MIT Press.

Breman, J. 2013. *At Work in the Informal Economy of India: A Perspective from the Bottom Up*. Oxford: Oxford University Press.

Burrington, I. 2015a. 'The Strange Geopolitics of the International Cloud'. *The Atlantic*, 17 Nov. Available at https://www.theatlantic.com/technology/archive/2015/11/the-strange-geopolitics-of-the-international-cloud/416370/ (accessed March 2022).

———. 2015b. 'A Visit to the NSA's Data Center in Utah'. *The Atlantic*, 19 Nov. Available at https://www.theatlantic.com/technology/archive/2015/11/a-visit-to-the-nsas-data-center-in-utah/416691/ (accessed March 2022).

Business Standard. 2016. 'Demonetisation: Paytm features Modi in its ad and has Kejriwal fuming', 10 November. Available at https://www.business-standard.com/article/current-affairs/demonetisation-paytm-features-modi-in-its-ad-and-has-kejriwal-fuming-116111000260_1.html (accessed May 2022).

Carruth, A. 2014. 'The Digital Cloud and the Micropolitics of Energy'. *Public Culture* 26(2): 339–364.

Carse, A. 2016. 'Keyword: Infrastructure'. In *Infrastructures and Social Complexity: A Companion*, P. Harvey, C. Bruun Jensen, and A. Morita (eds), 27–39. New York: Routledge.

Chander, A. and U. P. Lê. 2015. 'Data Nationalism'. *Emory Law Journal* 64(3): 677–739.

Chattapadhyay, S. 2013. 'Of identity, platform, and "new" information infrastructure of governance: Situating the Aadhaar project within the history of electronic governance in India'. Paper presented on 14–16 November at 'The Social and Cultural Life of Information' Conference, Sarai-CSDS (Centre for the Study of Developing Societies), New Delhi, India.

Chatterjee, P. 2004. *The Politics of the Governed: Reflections on Popular Politics in Most of the World*. New York: Columbia University Press.

Couldry, N. and U. A. Mejias. 2019. 'Data Colonialism: Rethinking Big Data's Relation to the Contemporary Subject'. *Television & New Media* 20(4): 336–349.

Cowen, D. 2014. *The Deadly Life of Logistics: Mapping Violence in Global Trade*. Minneapolis: University of Minnesota Press.

Data Center Dynamics. 2019. 'Flipkart opens data center in Hyderabad, India: Built in partnership with colo company CtrlS', 23 April. Available at https://www.datacenterdynamics.com/en/news/flipkart-opens-data-center-hyderabad-india/ (accessed May 2022).

Dattani, K. 2020. '"Governtrepreneurism" for Good Governance: The Case of Aadhaar and the India Stack'. *Area* 52(2): 411–419.

Deccan Herald. 2018. 'GDPR and its impact on Indian firms', 28 October. Available at https://www.deccanherald.com/business/economy-business/gdpr-and-its-impact-indian-700371.html (accessed May 2022).

Dharia, N. and N. Trisal (eds). 2017. 'Demonetization: Critical Responses to India's Cash(/less) Experiment'. Hot Spots series, *Fieldsights*, 27 September. Available at https://culanth.org/fieldsights/series/demonetization-critical-responses-to-indias-cash-less-experiment (accessed March 2022).

Dutta, A. 2008. 'Computing Alibis: Third World Teratologies'. *Perspecta* 40: 54–69.

Easterling, K. 2014. *Extrastatecraft: The Power of Infrastructure Space*. London and New York: Verso.

EFF. 2017. 'India's Supreme Court Upholds Right to Privacy as a Fundamental Right—and It's About Time', 28 August. Available at https://www.eff.org/deeplinks/2017/08/indias-supreme-court-upholds-right-privacy-fundamental-right-and-its-about-time (accessed May 2022).

Fuster, G. G. 2014. *The Emergence of Personal Data Protection as a Fundamental Right of the EU*, Law, Governance and Technology series, Vol. 16. London: Springer Science & Business.

Ghosh, A. 2013. *Branding the Migrant: Arguments of Rights, Welfare and Security*. Kolkata: Frontpage.

Ghosh, J., C. P. Chandrasekhar, and P. Patnaik. 2017. *Demonetisation Decoded: A Critique of India's Currency Experiment*. London and New York: Routledge.

Government of India (GoI). 2019. *Economic Survey 2018–19*, Vol. 1. New Delhi: Ministry of Finance, GoI. Available at https://www.thehinducentre.com/resources/article28283388.ece/binary/Economic%20Survey%20Volume%20I%20Complete%20PDF.pdf (accessed May 2022).

Hogan, M. 2015a. 'Facebook Data Storage Centers as the Archive's Underbelly'. *Television & New Media* 16: 3–18.

———. 2015b. 'Data Flows and Water Woes: The Utah Data Center'. *Big Data & Society* 2(2): 1–12.

Hogan, M. and A. Vonderau. 2019. 'The Nature of Data Centers'. *Culture Machine* 18: 1–12.

Hu, T-H. 2015. *A Prehistory of the Cloud*. Cambridge: MIT Press.

Huffpost. 2019. 'Indian Economy In Recession Thanks To Demonetisation, Says Economist Arun Kumar', 12 November. Available at https://www.huffpost.com/archive/in/entry/indian-economy-recession-demonetisation-black-money_in_5dc53e34e4b00927b231296c (accessed May 2022).

iapp. 2022. 'A look at proposed changes to India's (Personal) Data Protection Bill', 5 January. Available at https://iapp.org/news/a/a-look-at-proposed-changes-to-indias-personal-data-protection-bill/ (accessed March 2022).

India Today. 2015. 'Supreme Court nulls the mandatory status of Aadhaar Card scheme in India', 17 March. Available at https://www.indiatoday.in/education-today/gk-current-affairs/story/supreme-court-nulls-the-mandatory-status-of-aadhaar-card-scheme-in-india-244599-2015-03-17 (accessed May 2022).

Internet and Mobile Association of India (IAMAI). 2016. 'Make in India: Conducive Policy & Regulatory Environment to Incentivize Data Center Infrastructure', May. PLR Chambers. Available at https://www.medianama.com/wp-content/uploads/iamai-make-in-india-data-center-report-india.pdf (accessed March 2022).

Jacobson, K. and M. Hogan. 2019. 'Retrofitted Data Centres: A New World in the Shell of the Old'. *Work Organisation, Labour & Globalisation* 13(2): 78–94.

Jakobsson, P. and F. Stiernstedt. 2012. 'Time, Space and Clouds of Information: Data Center Discourse and the Meaning of Durability'. In *Cultural Technologies: The Shaping of Culture in Media and Society*, G. Bolin (ed.), 103–118. New York: Routledge.

Johnson, A. 2019. 'Data Centers as Infrastructural In-Betweens: Expanding Connections and Enduring Marginalities in Iceland'. *American Ethnologist* 46(1): 1–14.

Johnson, A. and M. Hogan. 2017. 'Introducing Location and Dislocation: Global Geographies of Digital Data'. *Imaginations: Journal of Cross-Cultural Image Studies* 8(2): 3–6.

Joshi, D. 2020. 'Interrogating India's Quest for Data Sovereignty'. *Seminar* 731(July). Available at https://www.india-seminar.com/2020/731/731_divij_joshi.htm (accessed March 2022).

Kharbanda, V. 2019. 'An Analysis of the RBI's Draft Framework on Regulatory Sandbox for Fintech'. *The Centre for Internet and Society Blog*, 8 May. Available at https://cis-india.org/internet-governance/files/analysis-of-the-rbi2019s-draft-framework-on-regulatory-sandbox-for-fintech (accessed March 2022).

Khera, R. 2019a. 'Aadhaar Failures: A Tragedy of Errors'. *Economic and Political Weekly* 54(14). Available at https://www.epw.in/engage/article/aadhaar-failures-food-services-welfare (accessed March 2022).

———— (ed.). 2019b. *Dissent on Aadhaar: Big Data meets Big Brother*. Hyderabad: Orient BlackSwan.

Kitchin, R. 2014. *The Data Revolution: Big Data, Open Data, Data Infrastructures and their Consequences*. London: Sage.

Koops, B. J. and R. Leenes. 2014. 'Privacy regulation cannot be hardcoded. A critical comment on the "privacy by design" provision in data-protection law'. *International Review of Law, Computers & Technology* 28(2): 159–171.

Kumar, A. 2017. *Demonetization and Black Economy*. New Delhi: Penguin Random House India.

Larkin, B. 2013. 'The Politics and Poetics of Infrastructure'. *Annual Review of Anthropology* 42: 327–343.

Lexology. 2022. 'What Does India's Data Protection Bill, 2021 Mean for Foreign Businesses?', 7 February. Available at https://www.lexology.com/library/detail.aspx?g=29cbffc9-1203-4792-95e4-fb2b43d98e66 (accessed May 2022).

Lippert, R. K. and K. Walby. 2016. 'Governing through Privacy: Authoritarian Liberalism, Law, and Privacy Knowledge'. *Law, Culture and the Humanities* 12(2): 329–352.

Lynskey, O. 2015. *The Foundations of EU Data Protection Law*. Oxford: Oxford University Press.

Maguire, J. and B. Ross Winthereik. 2021. 'Digitalizing the State: Data Centres and the Power of Exchange'. *Ethnos* 86(3): 530–551. Available at https://www.tandfonline.com/doi/full/10.1080/00141844.2019.1660391 (accessed March 2022).

Malecki, E. J. and H. Wei. 2009. 'A Wired World: The Evolving Geography of Submarine Cables and the Shift to Asia'. *Annals of the Association of American Geographers* 99(2): 360–382.

Medianama. 2018. 'List of Submissions on the Personal Data Protection Bill Made to MEITY', 23 October. Available at https://www.medianama.com/2018/10/223-personal-data-protection-bill-submissions/ (accessed May 2022).

Medianama. 2019a. 'Indian Data Should Be Owned By Indians, Not Corporations—Mukesh Ambani, RIL', 21 January. Available at https://www.medianama.com/2019/01/223-india-data-localisation-mukesh-ambani/ (accessed May 2022).

———. 2019b. 'Google Pay Will Comply With RBI's Data Localisation Norms "100%": Report', 13 November. Available at https://www.medianama.com/2019/11/223-google-pay-data-localisation/ (accessed May 2022).

Mehmood, T. 2008. 'Notes from a Contested History of National Identity Card in India: 1999–2007'. *South Asia Citizens Web*, 9 December. Available at http://www.sacw.net/article391.html (accessed March 2022).

Menon, N. 2018. '"Fancy Calculating Machine": Computers and Planning in Independent India'. *Modern Asian Studies* 52(2): 421–457.

Ministry of Electronics and Information Technology (MeitY). n.d. 'Mission Mode Projects'. GoI. Available at https://www.meity.gov.in/content/mission-mode-projects (accessed May 2022).

Moneylife. 2018 'Passing Aadhaar Act as Money Bill is Fraud: Justice Chandrachud', 26 September. Available at https://www.moneylife.in/article/passing-aadhaar-act-as-money-bill-is-fraud-justice-chandrachud/55403.html (accessed May 2022).

Mosco, V. 2014. *To The Cloud: Big Data in a Turbulent World.* New York: Routledge.

Neilson, B. 2014. 'Beyond Kulturkritik: Along the Supply Chain of Contemporary Capitalism'. *Culture Unbound: Journal of Current Cultural Research* 6(1): 77–93.

Neilson, B. and T. Notley. 2019. 'Data Centres as Logistical Facilities: Singapore and the Emergence of Production Topologies'. *Work Organisation, Labour & Globalisation* 13(1): 15–29.

Newbigin, E. 2020. 'Accounting for the Nation, Marginalizing the Empire: Taxable Capacity and Colonial Rule in the Early Twentieth Century'. *History of Political Economy* 52(3): 455–472.

Nilekani, N. 2009. *Imagining India: The Idea of a Renewed Nation.* New Delhi: Penguin.

———. 2017. 'Why India needs to be a data democracy'. *Livemint*, 27 July. Available at www.livemint.com/Opinion/gm1MNTytiT3zRqxt1dXbhK/Why-India-needs-to-be-a-data-democracy.html (accessed March 2022).

Outlook. 2020. '4G Internet Ban In J-K Extended "In The Interest Of Sovereignty Of India": Admin', 9 July. Available at https://www.outlookindia.com/website/story/india-news-4g-internet-ban-in-kashmir-extended-in-the-interest-of-sovereignty-of-india/356311 (accessed May 2022).

Paidipaty, P. 2020. 'Testing Measures: Decolonisation and Economic Power in 1960s India'. *History of Political Economy* 52(3): 473–497.

Quartz India. 2018. 'Aadhaar is voluntary—but millions of Indians are already trapped', 26 September. Available at https://qz.com/india/1351263/supreme-court-verdict-how-indias-aadhaar-id-became-mandatory/ (accessed May 2022).

Rao, U. 2018. 'Biometric bodies, or how to make electronic fingerprinting work in India'. *Body & Society* 24(3): 68–94.

Rao, U. and V. Nair. 2019. 'Aadhaar: Governing with Biometrics'. *South Asia: Journal of South Asian Studies* 42(3): 469–481.

Reading, A. and T. Notley. 2015. 'The Materiality of Globital Memory: Bringing the Cloud to Earth'. *Continuum* 29(4): 511–521.

Rossiter, N. 2016. *Software, Infrastructure, Labor: A Media Theory of Logistical Nightmares*. New York: Routledge.

———. 2017. 'Imperial Infrastructure and Asia beyond Asia: Data Centres, State Formation and Territoriality of Logistical Media'. *The Fibreculture Journal* 29: 1–20.

Ruppert, E. and E. Isin. 2019. 'Data's Empire: Postcolonial Data Politics'. In *Data Politics: Worlds, Subjects, Rights*, D. Bigo, E. Isin, and E. Ruppert (eds), 207–227. New York: Routledge.

Samaddar, R. 2018. *Karl Marx and the Postcolonial Age*. Cham: Palgrave Macmillan.

Sanyal, K. 2007. *Rethinking Capitalist Development: Primitive Accumulation, Governmentality and Post-Colonial Capitalism*. New Delhi: Routledge.

SFLC.in. 2019. 'Key Changes in the Personal Data Protection Bill, 2019 from the Srikrishna Committee Draft', 12 November. Available at https://sflc.in/key-changes-personal-data-protection-bill-2019-srikrishna-committee-draft (accessed May 2022).

Sinha, A. and A. Sethia. 2017. 'Aadhaar Case: Beyond Privacy, An Issue of Bodily Integrity'. *The Quint*, 1 May. Available at https://www.thequint.com/voices/opinion/aadhaar-case-privacy-and-bodily-integrity (accessed March 2022).

Sinha, A. and A. Basu. 2019. 'The Politics of India's Data Protection Ecosystem'. *Economic and Political Weekly* 54(49). Available at https://www.epw.in/engage/article/politics-indias-data-protection-ecosystem (accessed March 2022).

Solanki, A. 2019. 'Management of Performance and Performance of Management: Getting to Work on Time in the Indian Bureaucracy'. *South Asia: Journal of South Asian Studies* 42(3): 588–605.

Srnicek, N. 2017. *Platform Capitalism*. Cambridge: Polity Press.

Subramanian, C. R. 1992. *India and the Computer: A Study of Planned Development*. New Delhi: Oxford University Press.

TechCrunch. 2021. 'India is restoring 4G internet in Jammu and Kashmir after 18 months', 5 February. Available at https://techcrunch.com/2021/02/05/india-is-restoring-4g-internet-in-jammu-and-kashmir-after-18-months/ (accessed May 2022).

The Economic Times. 2016. 'In an attempt to curb black money, PM Narendra Modi declares Rs 500, 1000 notes to be invalid', 9 November. Available at https://economictimes.indiatimes.com/news/politics-and-nation/in-an-attempt-to-curb-black-money-pm-narendra-modi-declares-rs-500-1000-notes-to-be-void-from-midnight/articleshow/55315932.cms?from=mdr (accessed May 2022).

———. 2018a. 'Alibaba backs data localisation in India; looks to grow its cloud presence, 19 September. Available at https://economictimes.indiatimes.com/internet/alibaba-backs-data-localisation-in-india/articleshow/65869783.cms (accessed May 2022).

———. 2018b. 'Aadhaar verdict: Legal, but limit use to government benefits, says Supreme Court', 27 September. Available at https://economictimes.indiatimes.com/news/politics-and-nation/aadhaar-verdict-legal-but-limit-use-to-government-benefits-says-supreme-court/articleshow/65973337.cms?from=mdr (accessed May 2022).

———. 2022. 'Fresh legislation may replace Data Protection Bill', 17 February. Available at https://economictimes.indiatimes.com/tech/technology/fresh-legislation-may-replace-data-protection-bill/articleshow/89624369.cms (accessed May 2022).

The Hindu. 2020. 'Examining the slowdown', 28 January. Available at https://www.thehindu.com/opinion/op-ed/examining-the-slowdown/article30677218.ece (accessed May 2022).

The Indian Express. 2020. 'Justice Srikrishna calls new Data Protection Bill a blank cheque to the state', 29 February. Available at https://indianexpress.com/article/technology/tech-news-technology/justice-srikrishna-calls-new-data-protection-bill-a-blank-cheque-to-the-state-6292350/ (accessed May 2022).

The Print. 2021. 'Used Aadhaar for Covid vaccine? Modi govt created your digital health ID without asking you', 01 October. Available at https://theprint.in/health/used-aadhaar-for-covid-vaccine-modi-govt-created-your-digital-health-id-without-asking-you/742958/ (accessed May 2022).

The Wire. 2017a. 'Timeline: Twenty Two Mandatory Notifications for "Voluntary" Aadhaar Since January 2017', 9 March. Available at https://thewire.in/government/aadhaar-timeline-mandatory-notifications (accessed May 2022).

———. 2017b. 'Demonetisation: Nearly 99% of Scrapped Notes Came Back into System', 30 August. Available at https://thewire.in/banking/

demonetisation-99-of-scrapped-notes-came-back-into-system (accessed May 2022).

The Wire. 2017c. 'Instant Recall: How Modi Government Kept Changing Demonetisation's Goalposts', 31 August. Available at https://thewire.in/economy/modi-demonetisation-aims-golas (accessed May 2022).

———. 2018a. 'Unpacking RBI's Quest to Have All Payment Data Stored Within India's National Boundaries', 27 October. Available at https://thewire.in/business/rbi-payment-data-localisation-india (accessed May 2022).

———. 2018b. 'Two Years On, Modi Government Continues to Block Information on Demonetisation Deaths', 8 November. Available at https://thewire.in/government/demonetisation-deaths-modi-government (accessed May 2022).

Tsing, A. 2009. 'Supply Chains and the Human Condition'. *Rethinking Marxism* 21(2): 148–176.

United Nations Conference on Trade and Development (UNCTAD). 2016. *Data protection regulations and international data flows: Implications for trade and development.* New York and Geneva: United Nations. Available at https://unctad.org/en/PublicationsLibrary/dtlstict2016d1_en.pdf (accessed March 2022).

Western Sydney University (WSU). 2016. 'Data Centres and the Governance of Labour and Territory'. Unpublished project proposal. Sydney.

Williams, A. and N. Srnicek. 2014. '#Accelerate: Manifesto for an Accelerationist Politics'. In *#Accelerate#: The Accelerationist Reader,* R. Mackay and Armen Avanessian (eds), 347–362. Falmouth: Urbanomic Media.

Data Centres between North–South and East–West

Brett Neilson

As recently as 2014, *The Hindu Business Line* reported that India was unlikely to emerge as a global Data Centre hub. Citing factors such as outdated telecom policies and rolling power cuts, the newspaper noted that smaller rivals such as Singapore, Hong Kong, and Taiwan had outperformed India in this key sector of digital economy (Charlie 2014). Five years later, an industry report by consultancy firm Broad Group (2019) indicated that India is the world's second largest market for Data Centre infrastructure and the second fastest growing Data Centre market in Asia, after China. According to this report, 70 per cent of India's data is still stored beyond its shores, but new data localisation legislation means that growth will proceed rapidly, particularly in cities such as Mumbai, Chennai, Hyderabad, and Bengaluru. The significance of the Broad Group report lies less in its boosterism, which serves the Data Centre industry's search for new frontiers, than in its registration of the changing global geography of Data Centre location. One of the most important contributions of the chapters that make up this volume, which examines the past and present of Data Centres in India, is to take stock of this changing geography. Existing critical work on these facilities tends to focus on infrastructures located in the global North (see, for instance, Hogan and Vonderau 2019). By giving due attention to the conditions of emergence and operations of Data Centres in one of the world's most prominent rising markets for these infrastructures, the chapters in this book begin to ask how Data Centres contribute to the production of geographical and economic conditions that shift the axes of global power. In this way, the volume adapts the argument that 'postcolonial capitalism' is a global condition (Mitra et al. 2017) to the new modes of governance made possible by digital technologies.

Allow me to dwell briefly on my use of the term 'global North'. The contrast between the global North and the global South provides a means of identifying economic inequality between wealthy and impoverished world regions. The distinction has its origins in narratives of social modernisation and economic development that arose (and acquired an increasingly technocratic elaboration) in the wake of World War II (Brandt Commission 1980). Along with the East–West civilisational divide, which is a relic of Eurocentric spatial and cultural constructions, this split has structured many systematic approaches to world history and commerce. The title of this chapter seeks to draw attention to the ways in which the social, economic, and technical networks generated by Data Centres trouble these divisions, which have never corresponded to definitive geographical representations. A rigorous approach to the mutations of governance and power effected by Data Centre operations, I suggest, must account for material changes in the constitution of global space. Particularly when dealing with Data Centres in India, there is a need to interrogate how their tendency to establish weak social, as opposed to infrastructural, ties to their surrounding urban and national contexts intersects with their positioning within territorial and geopolitical arrangements predicated on international and regional competition.

This interruption of North–South economic divisions and East–West civilisational binaries by Data Centre operations is only part of the story I want to tell. The terms North–South and East–West also have a precise meaning in Data Centre technical jargon, where they describe different patterns of networking and traffic. North–South traffic is the movement of data between servers inside a Data Centre and external client machines that connect with them, usually by the mediation of a so-called access layer that controls which servers within a facility interact with any given client. East–West traffic, by contrast, is the passage of data between servers in the same facility, whether they are physical machines wired together by cables or virtual machines reassigned across different physical machines by Data Centre infrastructure management software. As the Data Centre business has expanded, and these infrastructures have come to house servers run by various commercial and governmental organisations, East–West traffic has become more intense than North–South traffic. This is because a query sent to a Data Centre by any single client machine triggers multiple interactions between servers to generate a response. Such arrangements are important for today's extractive data economies, enabling a situation where multiple parties benefit by accumulating data from client interactions. The question arises as to how these movements along the North–South and East–West axes of Data Centre traffic relate to the use of the terms North–South and East–West, as indicators of economic and civilisational difference. Without proposing a simple alignment between these different invocations of compass points, I suggest that the chapters that comprise this volume provide a privileged perspective from which to grapple with this question.

What is a Data Centre?

Before tackling the issue of how Data Centre traffic intersects the changing global arrangement of economy, politics, and territory, it is necessary to establish some basic knowledge for understanding the growing significance of Data Centres. In the twenty-first century, data is at the edge of strategies of economic expansion. The business model by which internet users contribute data to tech companies by using social media and other digital platforms is central to this expansion, although by no means the only method of extraction at work in the contemporary data economy. High frequency trading in financial markets, smart city initiatives, employee and workplace monitoring, health tracking, quantified self-applications, border control, government services, logistics industries, and political campaigning are just some of the areas in which the collection and analysis of data have become increasingly prominent in recent years. Indeed, data is becoming integral to everyday social relations, making the ways in which it changes the social order increasingly difficult to distinguish from other ongoing transformations.

Data Centres provide the critical infrastructural facilities for such changes, assembling servers under a single roof so that the organisations that place them there can capitalise on economies of scale and peering relations that offer competitive advantages. Although there are many different types of Data Centres, a minimal definition would recognise them as a *collocation* of servers for purposes of storage, transmission, and processing of data. Generating computational capacities that exceed those of servers housed at a distance from each other, Data Centres present a physical shell designed to host an ever-changing set of contents. In this sense, as Jesse LeCavalier (2016: 96) writes, a 'Data Centre is not a building full of computers but rather a computer with architectural qualities'.

As Ritayoti Bandyopadhyay writes in his contribution to this volume, the contemporary Data Centre is 'the key logistical installation that converts data into capital and governs the contemporary data economy'. In order to effect this conversion of data into capital, Data Centres must supply technologies that provide opportunities for the extraction and aggregation of data. Their capacity to generate value and further regimes of accumulation rests on two main capabilities. The first is the possibility to extract data at little or no cost, as in the case of social media platforms whose users agree to contribute data without payment in exchange for the provision of services. The second is the ability to aggregate data collected from various sources into so-called big data sets that offer opportunities for analysis with market relevance. Together, these techniques, which can involve multiple combinations of software, hardware, and human expertise, facilitate the expansion of one of contemporary capital's primary frontiers for the extraction and accumulation of value. Who the beneficiaries and victims of these processes are rests on contractual and technical relations among the organisations who have placed their servers in the Data Centre—relations that take on diverse forms depending on patterns of ownership, networking, and legal obligation.

A state-of-the-art Data Centre, such as the CtrlS facility investigated by Manish Jha and Rishi Jha in their study of Data Centres in Navi Mumbai, is a multi-user facility that allows different organisations to place or hire servers in a single installation. In such a situation, the wiring together of machines allows privileged forms of peering by which organisations connect directly with each other to exchange data rather than having to establish links through the slower public internet. However, many Data Centres are single-user or 'captive' facilities, such as the one run by the West Bengal State Electricity Distribution Company (WBSEDC) discussed in Ritam Sengupta's chapter. As Sengupta argues, even captive facilities, which generally house servers run by a single organisation, tend toward more 'open' architectures—a feature that has accompanied the shift of state-run data collection enterprises to a public-private partnership model. The large Data Centres run by companies such as Amazon and Google, for instance, are single-user facilities, but the machines they house host services and applications, including public cloud services, which many different users avail of (either on a paid basis, or free in exchange for allowing these organisations to extract data generated by their activities). To this single-/multi-user typology of Data Centres, it is possible to add other kinds of classification. The evolution of edge computing, for instance, brings a new type of Data Centre that operates in physical proximity to users or internet-of-things (IoT) devices to provide fast response times and/or filter data for processing back to a central facility.[1] The tiered system of Data Centre ratings is another relevant classification that categorises installations according to industry-set standards related to floor space, computing capacity, uptime, power usage, environmental efficiency, and so on.

Apart from the cables that link servers in Data Centres to client machines that operate at a distance from these facilities, the pattern of wiring that connects servers to each other in these installations is a crucial element of their design. These network topologies are variable and purpose-suited. With names like closed-tree, fat-tree, Clos, BCube, c-Through, Helios, and Hedera, they imply different trade-offs between network qualities such as speed, redundancy, path diversity, energy conservation, and scalability. A Data Centre that attracts business from high-frequency financial traders, for instance, is likely to have a Clos topology since this architecture reduces buffering and favours low-latency transmission that provides information from stock markets with minimal delay. By contrast, a sizeable commercial multi-user centre might prefer a fat-tree topology that modularises the servers used by different firms and connects them to each other via electronic switches that lead to a 'meet-me' (peering) room. When such a Centre supplies software, platforms, or infrastructure as a service, however, a more flexible architecture that utilises optical switches to reconfigure during runtime is an attractive option (Liu et al. 2013).

It is important to remember that Data Centres require certain preconditions of land and water that link them back to the basics of agrarian political economy. The energy usage of these facilities has been a preoccupation of environment-minded media scholars. They seek to debunk the myth of a clean digital economy (see, for instance, Carruth 2014 and Hogan 2015). Large multi-user installations keep diesel turbines idling over so they can kick into action if mains power fails. Like the 'dark satanic mills' that William Blake associated with the factories of the early industrial revolution, these facilities require fossil fuels. Yet, despite these continuities with previous forms of agrarian and industrial activity, the data economy presents a novel scale of operation that intensifies and multiplies the extractive capacities of digital technologies, allowing the extraction of not merely raw materials or alienated labour but patterns of social cooperation that generate data that can be stored, analysed, and sold. In temporal terms, this production of data as a commodity involves a massive reduction of turnover time with respect to earlier forms of commodity production and circulation, meaning that Data Centres enjoy a long lifespan as fixed capital to the number of turnovers they support. In spatial terms, the Data Centre has the capacity to centralise extractive operations in a single site and attract data transactions across wide (potentially planetary) geographical vistas. This technical capability of Data Centres makes their location particularly apposite as the economic advantage that parties accrue with servers in these facilities derives from human inputs to client machines that may be located at a vast distance. Data Centres thus acquire a geopolitical significance as they concentrate relations of capital and labour that unfold over wide expanses into a dense congregation of servers, switches, and wires. They are not only technical facilities but also political institutions that influence the wielding of power across diverse geographical scales. Considering how North–South and East–West traffic in Data Centres crosses the North–South and East–West axes of world power therefore, becomes a crucial task of political and economic analysis.

WHERE DO DATA CENTRES COME FROM?

As the contribution of Ritayoti Bandyopadhyay shows, Data Centres do not come out of anywhere but evolve in complex ways from former computing facilities as well as path-dependent patterns of cables and satellite technologies. Bandyopadhyay's rendering of the history of computing in India and the role of the Indian Statistical Institute (ISI) in amassing and managing large corpuses of data emphasises the deployment of these technologies for purposes of governance and population management. His account, in other words, raises the political significance of Data Centres as well as their economic role—a theme that, as we shall see, needs to encompass questions of sovereignty as well as governance. In any case, the emergence of the Data Centre from the mainframe computing room of the 1950s and 1960s is a process that crosses the personal computing revolution of the 1980s and the rise of the internet as a mass medium in the 1990s. Many industry commentators draw a parallel between the arrival of edge computing and the process of decentralisation that accompanied the diffusion of the personal computer in the 1980s. They note similarities between virtualisation in cloud computing and mainframe time-sharing technologies (Nemani 2011), and posit a cyclical movement between centralisation and decentralisation in the history of computing. Bandyopadhyay shows that the picture is more complicated than this and must take into account broader transformations such as the intersection of state governance with profit-making activities. The entanglement of Data Centres with historical forces becomes even more apparent if we attribute to them multiple genealogies, and consider also facilities such as cable stations and warehouses as their predecessor institutions.

The Data Centre, in many ways, has replaced the cable station as the crucial switch point for communication signals. Due to the point of presence technology, which allows the streaming of signal traffic into Data Centres, the cable station has become merely a site of power supply for the undersea cables that transmit digital information around the world. Nonetheless, the geography of the telegraph cables laid by imperial state powers in collaboration with private interests in the late nineteenth century has established patterns of path dependence that remain important for today's data economy. Therefore, not accidentally have cities such as Singapore and Hong Kong, which were early points of telegraph cable connection, emerged as Data Centre hubs in the early twenty-first century. We can argue about the changing forms of power and different kinds of space-time compression enabled by the telegraph as opposed to the internet and other contemporary networks of data transfer. Nicole Starosielski takes up these issues in her book, *The Undersea Network* (2015). However, the entanglement of these technologies with forms of imperial power, and the mutation of these forms of power in the postcolonial era remains a vital thread to follow in accounting for the political role of Data Centres. Such matters are particularly pressing when it comes to an understanding of the relevance of North–South Data Centre traffic, which has generally moved data from the global South to the global North, and also while examining the East–West traffic that is instrumental to the extractive capabilities of the contemporary Data Centre. Those aspects of Data Centre operations that derive from the cable station, such as the point of presence technology which connects servers in a Data Centre and the cables that transmit information to and from client machines, play a key role in setting the logistical position of a Data Centre as a site of control and extraction.

The entanglement of Data Centres with imperial power also becomes evident if we consider their affinities with the warehouse, another kind of facility important to their genealogy. At the level of architectural morphology, Data Centres bear a resemblance to the factories or *feitorias* established by European imperial powers around the globe during the early modern period. These fortified structures were *entrepôts* or fledgling free trade zones where local inhabitants interacted with foreign merchants. They acted simultaneously as marketplaces, storage houses, garrisons, and headquarters for the kinds of de facto government established by chartered companies. Importantly, they also functioned as footholds for making wider territorial claims, which played out in various ways with the twists and turns of colonial history. Factories thus played a role in the shift toward the formal kinds of imperial government that would emerge in the nineteenth century. With the establishment of formal colonial territories, they mutated into warehouses, which played a largely logistical role in the organisation of trade. The nineteenth-century warehouse was not only a site of an obvious division of labour but also a facility for procurement, sale, and negotiation. Across the course of the twentieth century, but particularly with the so-called logistics revolution that followed World War II, these functions moved elsewhere in the logistical chain, and the warehouse became an increasingly automated environment. Today Data Centres perform a warehousing function for a new kind of immaterial commodity, which requires material infrastructural support. That many Data Centres occupy old industrial warehouses is no accident. Likewise, the role of Data Centres in coordinating the labour of moving physical commodities in warehouses is a feature of today's logistical world (and part of the business model of organisations such as Amazon, Alibaba, and Flipkart). The warehouse is thus a double of the Data Centre, both its ghostly ancestor and commercial twin.

Doubtless, it is possible to locate other kinds of social institutions and infrastructures that provide genealogical background for the

Data Centre. The dream of the total archive continues to haunt these facilities, placing them in line with libraries, museums, and other collecting institutions. Despite the rapid turnover of storage media in computing (from punch cards to floppy disks and USB sticks), the fantasy of sucking up as much data as possible and making it accessible in readable form animates the contemporary Data Centre. As Jacques Derrida (1996) teaches, however, the archive is always partial. The contemporary Data Centre breaks with theory and practice based on organisational and governmental records to recast the archive as a storage site for diffuse and often dissociated data, including that posted to social media sites by users or that collected by sensors monitoring all kinds of physical movements and transformations. Data analysis promises to create value from this excess, which can theoretically be gathered from anywhere in the world. No longer linked to the statistical imperatives of national governance, Data Centres cast a territorial net beyond the borders of their containing states, connecting and linking client machines distributed across different global sites. Although so-called data sovereignty or localisation legislation attempts to restrict this distribution by requiring the storage of certain kinds of data on national territory, the role of Data Centres in creating new kinds of territory, much like the colonial factories of early modern times, needs to be taken seriously. Talk of 'data colonialism' (Couldry and Mejias 2019) needs to be supplemented with understanding of the role of North–South and East–West traffic in facilitating the extractive economy of Data Centres. That India is emerging as a Data Centre location and market signals that these patterns of data colonialism do not necessary follow those of modern imperialism or abide by the analytical markers of global North and global South. Tracking these patterns requires technical knowledge as well as an analytical handle on the changing operations of capital in a postcolonial world.

Manish Jha and Rishi Jha's study of how Data Centres evolve in the changing urban form and political economic environment of Navi Mumbai offers such an analysis. Importantly, their chapter links the presence of Data Centres to the emergence of a new labour territory and labour subjectivity in a situation where 'data is more important than any employee'. At stake is a workplace that is hierarchical, segmented, and surveilled. Characterised by various kinds of human-machine interface, and an imperative to avoid faults and downtime, which are inevitable in and an integral part of the system designed for resilience and redundancy, the labour regime at Data Centres combines a need for high tech knowledge with extreme precarity. The Data Centre, however, is a relatively labour-free zone, staffed mostly by male managers, technicians, and security personnel. It is at the client end of the North–South traffic relation that labour is most evident, regardless of how it is organised, located, or remunerated (or in the case of users of social media or other digital platforms not remunerated). The flashing lights and humming fans of the Data Centre, in other words, register the presence of distant labour forces, which are connected and organised into patterns of social cooperation by the network topologies that structure the flow of North–South and East–West traffic. If the way in which Data Centres convert data into capital seems magical or instantaneous, it is important to remember that the real engine of these developments is the living knowledge, intelligence, and subjectivity located at the client end of the North–South relation. To understand the significance of India's emergence as a Data Centre market, it is thus necessary to track the diverse and multiple locations in which labour forces and subjects generate the data that the country's facilities store, process, and transmit. Researching these relations and flows is a challenging task not only because of their multiplicity and extent but also due to matters of commercial confidence and technical black-boxing. Nonetheless, a diagram displaying these associations and interactions would be an important tool for understanding how digital techniques and technologies change India's geopolitical position in the world system.

What do Data Centres do?

Storage, processing, and transmission of data are the typical functions assigned to the Data Centre. In his chapter on the West Bengal State Electricity Distribution Company (WBSEDC) Data Centre, Ritam Sengupta shows how these functions combine into what he calls modulatory forms of governance and control. Focusing on how the feedback of data concerning 'loss' (primarily the unmetered use of power in the electricity grid but also financial and information loss) is constitutive for the operations of the Data Centre under question, Sengupta argues that the facility provides an important hinge between digitalised control and more traditional forms of bureaucratic organisation. The automated fault monitoring system that logs incidents of loss, for instance, requires manual acknowledgement by an operator before the system makes adjustments. Such a sequencing of action, however, is not bureaucratically neutral, because digital control mandates a reorganisation of administrative powers within WBSEDC. Sengupta shows how the cybernetic logic of Data Centre operations intersects other economic and political contingencies associated with the mutations of postcolonial capitalism and the workings of the Indian state. These transformations kick each other on, making the Data Centre a key institution through which to track the relation between digitally inflected forms of power and wider shifts in the political and economic constitution of the postcolonial world.

Although these relations, in Sengupta's account, are specific to the 'captive' or single-user Data Centre, they are by no means restricted to such installations. It is worth asking how the logics of postcolonial capitalism and the shifting valences of state governance influence the operations of a top-tier Data Centre such as the CtrlS facility discussed by Manish Jha and Rishi Jha. Is such a facility, with its multiple clients and complex systems of redundancy and resilience, simply a transplant of a state-of-the-art Data Centre, as found in the global North on to Indian territory? Jha and Jha answer this question in the negative by describing two parallel processes. First is the Indianisation of Data Centres or the location of these facilities on Indian soil in order to serve Indian clients. Second, they describe the practices of 'extrastatecraft' (Easterling 2014) that work in parallel, and include partnership and rivalry with the state to facilitate the insertion of these infrastructures into global networks of capital. On the one hand, Data Centres perpetuate modes of governance that draw on the experience of the postcolonial Indian state in dealing with populations, security, welfare, territorial management, and so forth. On the other hand, these installations have weak social ties with their surrounding environments and take root in a kind of urban form designed for purposes of logistics, finance, and extraction. A facility such as CtrlS is at once privately run and state-dependent. Data Centres become crucial switch points between the governmentalisation of the state, and the insertion of the state into wider networks of governance in which capital itself is the key political actor. They are sites of 'multiple, overlapping, or nested forms of sovereignty' in which domestic and transnational infrastructure spaces patch together.

The technical form of this patching is peering or the establishment of privileged connections between servers within Data Centres. At once facilitating exchange between local/national enterprises invested in a Data Centre, and their connection to global informatics and technical giants that maintain point of presence in an installation, peering is the central business proposition of a multi-user centre. The centrality of peering to Data Centre operations is the main reason that East–West traffic between servers in a facility has begun to outweigh North–South traffic between servers in a Data Centre and external client machines. I have already discussed how a single North–South query can generate multiple East–West interactions, and how this technical arrangement supports an extractive data economy by which multiple parties can accumulate data from a single source. However, it is also necessary to ask what purposes such data accumulation serves. Indeed, the selling of such data (or of information generated by its analysis) is a robust commercial motive. More importantly, machine learning and other artificial intelligence (AI) routines can train on such data to create new products and services. The evolution of machine learning and AI sits on the edge of contemporary economic development and geopolitical rivalries (witness the current 'tech war' between the US and China). Ownership of data thus becomes crucial to the digitalisation of the economy as it provides the commercial and technical basis for the development of artificial intelligence applications that are central to both current regimes of capital accumulation and projects of algorithmic governance.

The storage of data in a facility located in a specific national territory, however, does not equate to ownership of such data. This is one reason why data localisation laws requiring the storage of certain classes of data on national territory do not entirely address the issue of data extraction by global tech firms. If the presence of the Great Firewall around the Chinese internet and the inaccessibility of the Chinese internet market to foreign firms have occasioned extensive debate in relation to democracy and freedom, it also means that Chinese tech firms have been able to accumulate vast amounts of data from which they are now able to develop artificial intelligence applications. India sits in a different relation to such data holdings. Although the Aadhaar personal identification number and the parallel development of the India Stack provide opportunities for data accumulation, India's capacity to rival China as a developer of artificial intelligence applications is limited at present. However, given the vastness of its population, India can become data-rich quickly. Doubtless, then the development of Data Centres in India will not float freely from state issues of governance and population management, and the model of privately run facilities with state dependencies will continue for some time. All of which goes to show that patterns of North–South and East–West data traffic do not necessarily follow North–South and East–West divisions of global power.

END NOTES

1. Edge computing is a practice that brings data storage and processing technologies closer to sites of data extraction or production. The development of edge computing links to the growth of the internet-of-things (IoT), which is a system of interrelated computing devices or objects used to gather and transmit data across the internet or other networks.

REFERENCES

Brandt Commission. 1980. *North-South: A Programme for Survival, Report of the Independent Commission on International Development Issues.* Cambridge, MA: MIT Press.

Broad Group. 2019. *Data Centres India.* Available at https://www.broad-group.com/reports/data-centres-india (accessed May 2022).

Carruth, A. 2014. 'The Digital Cloud and the Micropolitics of Energy'. *Public Culture* 26(2): 339–364.

Charlie, A. 2014. 'India Losing out Data Centre Business to Small Nations'. *The Hindu Business Line*, 2 June. Available at https://www.thehindubusinessline.com/info-tech/india-losing-out-data-centre-business-to-small-nations/article23152064.ece (accessed March 2022).

Couldry, N. and U. A. Mejias. 2019. 'Data Colonialism: Rethinking Big Data's Relation to the Contemporary Subject'. *Television & New Media* 20(4): 336–349.

Derrida, J. 1996. *Archive Fever: A Freudian Impression.* Chicago: University of Chicago Press.

Easterling, K. 2014. *Extrastatecraft: The Power of Infrastructure Space.* New York: Verso.

Hogan, M. 2015. 'Facebook Data Storage Centers as the Archive's Underbelly'. *Television & New Media* 16(1): 3–18.

Hogan, M. and A. Vonderau. 2019. 'The Nature of Data Centers'. *Culture Machine* 18. Available at https://culturemachine.net/vol-18-the-nature-of-data-centers/ (accessed March 2022).

LeCavalier, J. 2016. *The Rule of Logistics: Walmart and the Architecture of Fulfilment*. Minneapolis: University of Minnesota Press.

Liu, Y., J. K. Muppala, M. Veeraraghavan, D. Lin, and M. Hamdi. 2013. *Data Center Networks: Topologies, Architectures and Fault-Tolerance Characteristics*. Cham: Springer.

Mitra, I. K., R. Samaddar, and S. Sen (eds). 2017. *Accumulation in Post-Colonial Capitalism*. Singapore: Springer.

Nemani, R. 2011. 'The Journey from Computer Time-Sharing to Cloud Computing: A Literature Review'. *International Journal of Computer Science & Engineering* 1(6): 267–273.

Starosielski. N. 2015. *The Undersea Network*. Durham: Duke University Press.

II

Infrastructuring Data Economy

Data Centres in Historical Context

RITAJYOTI BANDYOPADHYAY

INTRODUCTION

This chapter has a somewhat clumsy title but nonetheless, it serves its purpose. 'Infrastructuring' requires us to shift attention from the *structure* to a dynamic *process* through which infrastructures manifest in their own making and annulments. It is a process that 'owes as much to the agency as to conditioning' (Star and Bowker 2002; Thompson 1963). 'Data Economy' refers to the institutionalised form of manufacturing, processing, classifying, and storing of digitally encoded data through the mobilisation of Data Centres, server firms, individual smart devices, apps, network cables, and algorithms. The imperative of a data economy is to relentlessly manufacture and circulate data and build appropriate infrastructures for data to keep accumulating and circulating. Data Economy also refers to the datafication of production, consumption, and government. In other words, the arrival of the data economy signals the subjugation of the primary and secondary sectors of the economy by services and information. We are living in a conjuncture when the production of data is not anymore a byproduct of other activities (Sadowski 2019). Contemporary societies produce and manage data both as a means and an end in itself and govern futures through data. In a data economy, social transactions of our everyday life are data-mediated, and they are destined to produce and consume more data. Data economy offers a political reason to tame and inscribe the 'future' into the calculus of capital accumulation in the present (Mitchell 2014). The algorithmic capitalisation of the future is at the heart of the political economy in the twenty-first century. The act of infrastructuring draws us to the materialities of the data economy. In critical data studies, relatively less attention is paid to study what goes in the making and the domestication of 'Big Data', and also the implications of increasingly aggressive data-centric management of public life. A study of Data Centres prompts us to ask if these installations mark a new mode of governance (Samaddar 2018).

The arrival of data economy calls for both hardware and software developments, along with a fast evolution in the mode of storing data in Data Centres. To cite a recent example of the magnitude of these developments, it was reported in 2017 that to accelerate the transfer of data into its Data Centres, Amazon which has a fast-growing cloud computing facility, deploys 'trucks pulling shipping containers each packed with storage devices holding 100 petabytes' (*The Economist* 2017). To absorb such a volume of data, firms are seen to invest in the development of Data Centres. This is a ceaseless drive from basic units to the larger ones: 'from kilo to mega to giga to tera to peta to exa to zetta to yotta' (Doctorow 2008). Data are not anymore the stocks of digital databases of names and census accounts of 'personal data' consisting of age, marital status, sex, income, and expenditure records. The emergent economy has much more to do with the rapid algorithmic analysis of various 'real-time flows' of the huge cache of unstructured data, such as photos and videos circulating in social networks such as Facebook, reams of information from numerous CCTV (Closed-circuit Television) footages, the information generated by cell phones, GPS devices and by various app-based platforms. The research and development (R&D) units of giant IT companies struggle to cope with the requirements imposed by the 'data stream scenario' in applications with 'high real time demands' (Liu et al. 2014) for the seamless supply of information to thousands of users.

This chapter studies the socio-technical assemblages that emerge in the course of the infrastructuring of the data economy, with a focus on the emergence of Data Centres as a technological apparatus that makes the arrival, governance, and the valuation of digitally encoded data possible. Data Centres are often touted as the 'archives of digital capitalism', and the 'factories of the twenty-first century'. Further, the chapter presents certain anticipations of the data economy and its organisation in Data Centres in two inter-connected developments in the mid-twentieth century, that is, the birth of the idea of an integrated 'national economy' as a central 'object' of the postcolonial governmentality, and the triggering of the Cold War

'Big Science' initiatives that required data management at a cosmic scale. It identifies the Indian Statistical Institute (ISI) in Calcutta as a site where these two developments interfaced in the 1950s in the larger context of India's tryst with the Cold War-era developments in science and political economy. Taking the two decades since Independence as a key moment in the history of data in India, the chapter further shows how the ISI emerged as a significant player in the data-centric organisation of public life in the first couple of decades since decolonisation.

In what follows, the chapter presents a genealogy of the Data Centre–industrial complex in postcolonial economies (which has often been considered incalculable and hence ungovernable), outside the Euro-American and the Union of Soviet Socialist Republics (USSR) contexts. The chapter thus offers an exploratory agenda to study the contemporary data moment in the *longue durée*, with a view to make sense of our contemporary data-driven conjuncture. The chapter thus tries to work at the critical interface of two data moments, making use of one context to ask questions of another. It is always important to mark out the difference that the new data regime developed from the old governmental data. However, we believe, it is more challenging to track how the old data is reinvented, refashioned, and refunctioned at the time of 'Big Data', as statistical and census surveys are increasingly seen to embrace digital infrastructures such as electronic storage media and storage area networks for their upgradation. What are the anticipations of digital technology-driven life in the early postcolonial visions of development? What does this tell us about our futures, and how is it going to shape the realms of polity and policy?

It is only recently that scholars have started tracking the anticipations of Big Data in the analogue moment (Aronova et al. 2017). It is too commonplace to think of Big Data as just 'a cultural phenomenon' specific to the introduction of digital computers. As Aronova et al. (ibid.) mention, it is also important to critically trace the genealogy of certain 'features of modern data-driven science' which 'recognises underlying continuities' running through 'distinct eras of data' as well as 'genuine discontinuities' by 'comparing the historically contingent differences and relations' (ibid.: 8). In other words, what we need is a better understanding as to how the 'new' and the 'old' become contemporary to each other. The chapter attempts to accomplish this task. The scholarship has so far paid inadequate attention to the 'digital turn' in the global South where some of the key data experimentations are currently taking shape (consider for instance India's massive infrastructural project called the 'smart cities' project, or more importantly the Aadhaar project), and calling for a transformation in the realm of the state-citizen relationship as Indian cities are moving toward a domain of digital government from analogue technologies of government (Datta 2018).

In the last few years, social science literature on the internet and digital developments has focused critical attention to debunk the myth of the immateriality of the internet. Scholars, for instance, have analysed the physical infrastructures that comprise cloud computing, and they have shown the ways in which it is 'specifically and impactfully emplaced' (Johnson 2019: 2). In a fascinating monograph-length account, Jennifer Gabrys (2011) has tracked the afterlives of digital rubbish, while several others have drawn our attention to the ways in which the connections that Data Centres set up and thrive through, follow the pathways and trajectories of former imperial/colonial communication systems such as fibre optic cables, which were laid alongside the geo-medial framework of now decommissioned telegraph cables (Malecki and Wei 2009). In addition, the installation of the telegraphic network of the colonial empires established a public-private financial model of infrastructural work which informed contemporary public-private partnership under the neoliberal order of things. It is interesting to note that the Eastern Telegraph Company of London, which had by 1873 established monopoly over telegraphic traffic in most of the world, morphed into today's Eastern Communications which 'provides a range of services that include data facilities and data management for logistics industries' (Rossiter 2016: 152). The transformation in the profile of the said corporation is a 'legacy story of colonial infrastructure transformed and adapted over time' (ibid.: 152).

It is therefore, likely that imperial and colonial pathways of infrastructural development also conditioned the new geographies of connection and exclusion. As Zook (2006: 53; also, Malecki and Wei 2009: 362) reminds us, 'simple expectations of uniform geography or ubiquitous access are simply unreflective of the reality of the Internet', which follows and thrives on pre-existing social hierarchies and older trajectories of the nature of ownership and investment to infrastructure. Take for instance MacKenzie's (2014) perceptive analysis of the infrastructural networks of the Cermak

Data Centre in Chicago in which he shows how older private networks under the ownership of giant telecommunication firms end up enabling public internet in the successive era. So, to put it in simpler terms, infrastructural histories and path dependencies of prior developments continue to inform new developments. Several scholars have shown how old industrial buildings, warehouses, and other fixed capital associated with twentieth-century industrial establishments were 'retrofitted' to be converted into today's Data Centres. 'The resulting Data Centres', argue Jacobson and Hogan (2019: 80), 'function as a kind of infrastructural palimpsest that allows new technologies to inherit the socio-political arrangements' of the old and exhausted infrastructures.

Infrastructural regimes have a 'palimpsestic' attribute—one in which they 'constitute a mark on a layer, where the mark on one layer...produces an imprint on the layer below...and above' (Vigne 2020: 23). Usually, infrastructures develop 'incrementally' in a dynamic socio-spatial, temporal, ecological, and geological ecosystem amid 'partial knowledges and intransigent materialities' (ibid.). Hence, any infrastructural regime has to fall within the interstices of its prior and its future figurations, and its chronologies need not follow the terms and tenures of political regimes, 'although the two chronologies never stop interacting' and constituting each other. Infrastructures thus mediate and configure time while 'mediating exchange over distance, bringing different people, objects, and spaces into interaction' (Larkin 2013: 330). By tracing the analogue pathways of contemporary data infrastructures, the chapter contributes to this emerging literature in critical infrastructure studies.

The chapter is divided into four sections, each narrating a story of the emergence and transformations of the data economy. The first section identifies the contemporary Data Centre as the key logistical installation that converts data into capital and governs the contemporary data economy. The second section traces a history of Data Centres in the Cold War 'Big Science' era. This section presents the necessary context for the next section in which we study the emergence of the ISI as a key institution in the history of data in postcolonial India. It is in the ISI that the first experiment of converting data from analogue to the digital platform was carried out in India and perhaps for the first time in the world, outside the Iron Curtain. How did the local exigencies in India in the 1950s encounter the global developments? Who were the key players in this story? How did they create a data architecture for national development immediately after Independence? We wish to study some of the major developments in the field of data in the early postcolonial years that contributed to the birth of Data Centres in the postcolonial world. We will discuss both institutional and technological histories culminating in the current conjuncture of a data-driven government. In the Indian context, not much is known about the relationship between computerised Big Data and statecraft, except for the fact that here the defence establishment played a less significant role in the evolution of data infrastructure than in the well-documented western contexts (Chattapadhyay 2013; Menon 2018). How then are we to think of Indian history of Big Data—a history that developed in conjunction with the Cold War-era global order of things, yet one that displays significant ruptures from the Cold War and post-Cold War metanarratives of technological developments? In the fourth and final section, we track the advent of computers in India and further the discussion to the arrival of contemporary Data Centres in the country.

DATA CENTRES: WHAT DO THEY DO?

An article featured in *The Economist* (2017) draws a provocative and useful parallel between the oil refinery of the twentieth century and the Data Centre of the current century as follows:

> Both…fulfil the same role: producing crucial feedstocks for the world economy. Whether cars, plastics or many drugs—without the components of crude [oil], much of modern life would not exist. The distillations of data centres, for their part, power all kinds of online services and, increasingly, the real world as devices become more and more connected.

It is now argued that data are to the twenty-first century what oil was to the twentieth century and coal to the nineteenth century: the prime mover of change. What kind of commodity is a datum? In case of tangible physical things and services, reproduction requires the same amount of time and cost as that of the original commodity given all other conditions remain constant. Data represent a very different reality. While the initial creation of data commodity in the digital world may involve a huge amount of labour time, its reproduction (copying) engages negligible labour time and associated costs. As Rigi (2014: 912) points out, although a product of labour, the value of digital data 'approximates to zero', since as Marx (1894) says in *Capital*, vol. 3: 'the value of commodities is determined not by the labour time originally taken by their production, but rather by the labour time that their reproduction takes, and this steadily decreases as the social productivity of labour develops'. Digital data make a transition from a 'universal common' to commodities when access to them is restricted through enclosures, copyrights, patents, and other kinds of property laws. Thus, as Rigi and Prey (2015: 398) tell us, 'a price on data can best be understood as a form of monopoly rent (tribute)'. In the digital world, data are also produced when consumers use the internet and various social media to meet various needs of life. Such data do not have an exchange value, but their algorithmic processing by corporations such as Google and Facebook, and warehousing in Data Centres can potentially produce exchange value, which can be imposed on data by means of enclosure backed by the state (ibid.).

Let's now see what role Data Centres play in the commodification of data. As we have already mentioned in the previous section, the Data Centres are giant infrastructural installations to enable not just the massive collection and storage of data from thousands of sources, but also to connect data meaningfully to produce information for its exchange through accurate interfaces to data. Data Centres make it possible for multiple systems of applications to exchange information and to reciprocally manipulate the already exchanged information. In other words, Data Centres make data interoperable by ensuring connectivity and usability. As a physical warehouse of data, Data Centres thrive in a rental economy. Outsourced Data Centres perform two functions. The first of their operation is known as 'co-location service' which refers to renting out of space to host data archives of various organisations. It also includes power supply, cooling, physical security of data, and basic network connectivity. Customers pay monthly/yearly rentals to avail of these services while they offer their own servers at the Data Centre and provide their own IT resources to manage and maintain servers. The second service that an outsourced Data Centre offers to its clients is known as 'managed hosting services' in which the Data Centre provides its server to its clients and manages the server (monitoring and system reboot) with its own IT expertise.

Using Marx's terminologies it can be said that Data Centres represent a complex combination of 'constant capital' (plant and building, equipment, physical infrastructures of production, raw materials, auxiliary materials, energy, etc.), 'circulating capital' (the non-fixed parts of constant capital [e.g., energy] plus variable capital [labour power]), and 'fixed capital' (materials 'necessary for supporting production', such as plant and building, equipment, physical infrastructures of production). Marx says, fixed capital is that part of constant capital that is carried over from one turnover period to another (turnover period refers to production time plus circulation time). Marx tells us, constant capital along with variable capital (labour power) is implicated in the constitution of value (Marx 1867), while fixed capital and circulating capital explain the motion of capital that is, circulation of value (Marx 1885). In the making of data as a commodity, the turnover time is much less (which has a direct relation to profitability) than other tangible commodity production and circulation (that Marx for instance, considered), which means Data Centre as a network of fixed capital has a much longer lifespan, and it bridges a number of turnover times, and hence appears more fixed in relation to the fluidity of circulating capital. In this context, it is important to register that the distinction between fixed and circulating capital is more relative than absolute, in the sense that it is premised upon 'the comparative rotation speed' of various assets to be 'used up' (Jacobson and Hogan 2019: 82). It is in this comparative sense that Data Centres 'act as a landscape of immobile, fixed capital' (ibid.: 83).

In their material form, Data Centres are fixed installations that control data circulation at a planetary scale and create contexts and conditions for labour mobility. While securing data and ensuring their circulation, the Data Centres need to keep their software and hardware updated with new available versions, undertake maintenance, and administer platform operations, all of which require a massive deployment of labour regimes. Thus, while data have no exchange value as such, the processing of the same may accrue exchange value, and hence the workers performing tasks such as data warehousing and analytics do produce value and surplus value. Rigi and Prey (2015: 398–399) provocatively argue that 'these values are not transferred to the product' which get 'eternally embodied in the universal information commons...of general intellect'. In short, with data, use value tends to annihilate exchange value which strikes back through the imposition of the enclosure.

Multi-user Data Centres (MUDCs) of contemporary times emerged in the middle of the previous decade as emphasis gradually switched toward subscription and capacity-on-demand services in the IT industry (Zheli et al. 2013). The emergence of MUDCs was implicated in some of the key developments in the industry in the last couple of decades, that is, the enhancement of data transfer capacities, acceleration in data retrieval, and the ascendancy of technologies such as cloud, etc., and the spectacular increase in the operational capability of delineative processing of data. In aggregate then, by the mid-2000s Data Centres successfully superseded the networks of millions of semi-autonomous computing devices, which had dominated the earlier era. The mutation of these technologies in Data Centres has further reduced the turnover time, now to be understood as 'time taken for the advanced capital value to return to its initial form recovering its initial amount' (Park and Xu 2010), which is at the heart of the contemporary information and communication revolution in capital. Interoperability and seamless exchange of data between multiple users through Data Centres dissolve the 'transport paradigm that revolves primarily around the overcoming of *space* in favour of a paradigm in which the control and coordination of *timing* is at the forefront' (Klose 2009). In fact, this is the infrastructural history behind Walmart's reinvention of merchant capital as giant retail networks operating through the Toyotist principle (Hardt 1999) that hinges on a more efficient synchronisation between production and consumption. In high-frequency trading, more emphasis is paid in shortening the turnover time through low-latency within Data Centres, which makes the geography of Data Centres important as an increase in the distance between the DCs and their clients reduces speed. The synchronisation of intermodal transportation of goods through the quick exchange of data and information becomes the Data Centre's central mode of operation. Eventually, data becomes the driver of further decisions on the market, money transmissions, targeted policy regime, etc.

In India, Data Centres share a history with the so-called 'GDP revolution'. The annual growth of the Indian economy by 7 to 9 per cent for over a considerable number of years involved a significant growth in trade and finance that involved a proliferation in the volume of data associated with this economic expansion. During the eleventh Plan period (2007–2011), the boom was witnessed in three key sectors, namely real estate-construction-infrastructure-urbanisation complex, logistics-supply chain-data complex, and leisure-tourism-civil aviation complex. In other words, growth happened in the tertiary sector, and the developments in the tertiary sector took place within an ecosystem of interconnection. In the last decade, corporate investment in logistics increased significantly, even though 90 per cent of logistics is still unorganised and under the control of smaller players. The logistics sector has been growing at 10.5 per cent per annum and is slated to employ forty million by 2020. The sectoral investment in logistics is expected to reach US\$ 500 billion by 2025. The logistics sector in India has been a happy hunting ground for start-up ventures. In addition, the first two decades of the new century witnessed the growing integration of India's small-scale, home-based, and informal manufacturing activities with global supply chains of commodities. The logistics revolution and the supply chain revolution happened in close connection and in both, Data Centres played a crucial infrastructural role. They ensured credible IP (Internet Protocol) communications, storage, retrieval, and transmission (Samaddar 2018).

AN ANALOGUE HISTORY OF THE DIGITAL

The advent of Data Centres marked a specific moment in the larger history of computing—one that began with mainframes, personal computers, and the client-server model, and subsequently to 'distributed computing and software as a service' (Samaddar 2018: 131). Much of these developments, especially the networks of semi-autonomous computing devices, took place in the Cold War era that preceded the age of the Internet and digital capitalism. Therefore, it is important to follow the anticipations of the data economy in the Cold War era.

A distinct line of anticipation of Big Data can be attributed to what Timothy Mitchell (2014) describes as the emergence of 'new forms [of] political reason and calculative practice' in the 'mid-twentieth century' that constructed the 'economy as their object and introduced this feature into the government' (ibid.: 485). Attempts at aggregating 'price levels, wages, consumer spending, money supply, purchasing power and savings', created an effect of the economy which appeared governable and amenable to interpretative manipulations in the calculation of the growth rate (ibid.: 483). As Mitchell (ibid.) argues, in the post-War world, the economy emerged as a new 'interacting system' to 'bring the future into government', which also allowed division of a collective world into a series of governable units.

The emergence of the economy as new governmental rationality was backed by the proliferation of new organisations such as think-tank bodies, economics and statistical centres around the globe, including in the young nation-states such as India. Throbbing with quantitative positivism, these organisations would start deploying probabilistic statistical methods (already by the 1940s, numerically oriented statistical and operations research became popular worldwide to organise different aspects of life), and state-of-the-art computing machines (at the behest of organisations such as the IBM [International Business Machines]) to 'produce public economic knowledge outside the day-to-day contestations of political debate, contributing to the parallel effect of the economy as an object separate from the state that operated as a visible mechanism independent of the process of government' (Mitchell 2014: 490).

The economic expertise associated with such organisations was often preoccupied with the problem of growth: 'the increase in population, the expansion of trade, a surfeit or shortage of natural resources, or inflation in the supply of money' (Mitchell 2014: 491). What was new, in the mid-twentieth century was the growth of a 'less material' object: the economy which was a 'means of bringing the future into government—of governing populations through their futures' (ibid.). The rise of giant research wings in the United Nations (UN), the International Monetary Fund (IMF), and the World Bank along with a host of statistical research bureaus in the postcolonial countries gave the economy a robust shape with new kinds of data and figures (such as the GDP of nation-states) and their relationships appearing in and generating public discourses. The emergence and the consolidation of what Mitchell (ibid.) calls 'economentality' gave birth to new kinds of databases outside the reach of, but consistent with the old governmental databases, such as censuses. In the next section, we will see how the new data regime associated with economentality unfolded in the specific institutional context of the ISI and how this data regime transitioned from analogue to the digital mode between the 1950s and 1970s.

The second line of anticipation of Data Centres in the early Cold War context was closely associated with the emergence of what is known in history as the era of Big Science, led primarily by the US and the USSR, predominantly in the fields of nuclear physics, space, earth science, climatic science, and oceanography. The competitive deployment of satellites in space (starting with the Sputnik) began to produce data on the earth as well as the cosmos literally at a cosmic scale. Satellites, ever since their emergence during the Cold War, have been geopolitical instruments of communication (Malecki and Wei 2009; Warf 2007), which with their continuing 'political hegemony', 'proved to be ideal for broadcasting and coincided with the growth of television' (Malecki and Wei 2009: 363). Between 1965 and 1988, estimate Malecki and Wei, satellites also 'provided almost ten times the capacity of submarine telephone cables for almost one-tenth the price' (ibid.). Satellite continues 'to play a major role in radio, TV, broadcasting, broadcast data networks (weather, stock prices), video teleconferencing, credit-card verification, communications between field office and home office, and remote data collection and monitoring' (Hudson 1990: 275; see also Malecki and Wei 2009: 364), and until at least the late 1980s, satellites played the central role in the globalisation of financial services (Warf 1989). The competition between satellites and cables continued until recently.

During the last two decades, however, the picture of satellites' victory over cables in telecommunication would be reversed and 'cables had surpassed satellites as the preferred means of communication'. The new submarine cable emerging in the crucible of the old telegraph networks ultimately proved to be cost-effective. The Cold War-era fight between these two infrastructures of communication was also a political fight with satellites enjoying political hegemony over cable during the early decades of the Cold War. Data Centres began their journeys and operated for long through the interstices of this logistical conflict, and have been seen to have thrived through a combination of both undersea fibre access (primary connection) and satellite dishes (backup connection). It is further observed that new investments are underway to revamp satellite network at lower orbits for Data Centres which can again make it a cheaper and a viable alternative to fibre, especially when connectivities are made between far-flung areas. It is thus apparent that a history of Data Centre's making can be told through the developments in the fields of satellites and cables, which in turn share a long and fascinating history in the Cold War-era Big Science initiatives.

In fact, the International Geophysical Year or IGY (1957–1958) can safely be termed as a pre-electronic Big Data Centre (Aronova 2017). Huge cache of data on the physical environment was gathered and preserved in World Data Centres (WDCs) with an aim to serve scientific research and military precision (Korsmo 2010). As Alan Shapley, one of the chief architects of the IGY project wrote, it was literally 'a big data collecting being' (Aronova 2017: 308) which, as Aronova points out, anticipated a key feature of today's digital Big Data practices: 'the notion of centralised storage of open data, freely accessible to the users from around the world' (ibid.). It is in the context of the Cold War Big Science and world politics that the IGY and the WDCs indulged in an unprecedented circulation of data on physical environment and developed a 'regime of exchange and secrecy in which data became a form of currency' (Aronova et al. 2017: 12). The IGY mission involved scientists from as many as sixty-seven countries who were involved not just in the collection of data but also in transnational data interchange through the WDC system. Data were collected often for the sake of their accumulation without a clear understanding of their use in the immediate future. The microfilm technology was used to preserve data in WDCs, which substantially 'reduced the physical size of "data pieces" without having to convert the data to numeric values, which seemed especially appropriate for WDCs given the variety of data formats used in different IGY disciplines' (Aronova 2017: 317). The IGY continued to accumulate and circulate data via analogue microfilm technology even towards the end of 1960s when digital computers began to assume a central location in IGY disciplines. In the 1960s, microfilms became more user friendly, being amenable to 'search, organise and analyse analogue data' without converting them into a digital format. In fact, microfilm technology, in particular and analogue computing, in general, was still less expensive, 'reliable (if not terribly accurate), better developed, and far better supported by both industrial and academic institutions' (Edwards 1996: 44). For many in the 1950s and 1960s, microfilm-based systems such as MIRACODE appeared to be more efficient in data management than the emergent digital computers. Thus, an expert in the field of data management writes in 1967:

[MIRACODE] allows direct man-machine interaction with browsing capabilities that are impossible with computer systems operating in a batch-processing mode. Furthermore, its relatively low purchase price ... permits its consideration as a system for tasks, which could not justify the expense of renting and operating a suitable computer. Finally, it has some of the same powerful searching capabilities of a computer, employing Boolean logic on machine-readable optical codes (Janda 1967: 169–181; see also Aronova 2017: 323).

During all these years, however, the real development of digital computers was silently taking place in the US and the USSR under the aggressive patronage of defence establishments with a still vague objective to unify command, control, and communication within a 'single technological frame centred around electronic digital computers' (Edwards 1996: 44). According to one estimate, in the year 1950, the federal government/defence agencies in the US provided between 75 and 80 per cent of funding in computer research, while industry contributed 20 to 25 per cent of the total expenditure. In the early 1950s, the corporate share of R&D started growing. However, between 1949 and 1959 the major corporations developing computer equipment and technology, such as IBM, General Electric, Bell Telephone, Sperry Rand, Raytheon, and RCA (Radio Corporation of America), continued to receive substantial funding from military sources (ibid.). Edwards (ibid.: 63) cites the instance of the 'IBM's first production computer (the 701, also known as the "Defense Calculator"), first sold in 1953...developed at IBM's expense, but only with letters of intent in hand from eighteen Department of Defense customers'. Edwards further shows how in the 1960s, the private corporate sector slowly took up the centre-stage of R&D funding in organisations such as the IBM. Eventually, private investment in IBM's R&D gave it the technical superiority that played a key role in its dominance of the world computer market in the subsequent decades. IBM's success prompted other companies in the computer market to the path of internal R&D investment. Still, in the 1960s, the Pentagon's dominance in certain areas remained intact. In fact, as Edwards (ibid.: 66) calculates, 'almost half of the cost of semiconductor R&D between the late 1950s and the early 1970s was paid by military sources'.

Thus, a three-pronged development during the early Cold War years, that is, the birth of economentality in the field of government, the emergence of massive data banks in facilitating Big Science, and continued military presence in the research and development of computer technology drove us to a regime that began to produce spectacular amounts of data in new fields. However, the more important development in this era took place when a pervasive exercise, to produce what Bouk (2017: 86) calls 'data aggregates' through 'charts, tables, maps, or even algorithms' to 'fit individuals into the mass', came into prominence. Thus, the initial years of the Cold War era were marked by the zeal to measure everything from natural phenomena to the acts of individuals. If the nineteenth century witnessed an 'avalanche of printed numbers' (Hacking 1990), the inter-war period and the Cold War era witnessed the 'golden age of statistical graphics' (Friendly 2008). Needless to say, aggregations were the basic architecture to legitimise old abstractions like the nation. The idea of a unified national economy as an object constructed out of 'aggregate price levels, wages, consumer spending, money supply, purchasing power, and savings' (Mitchell 2014: 483) could now be measured due to the avalanche of new data in the forms of 'new business procedures, banking reports, household tax returns, and other forms of accounting' (ibid.). What then marks the early Cold War era is the emergence of a new data moment in the two domains, of economy and of Big Science, both of which interacted closely with the 'military-industrial complex'.

These developments coincided with the establishment of statistical bureaus in the recently decolonised nation-states seeking to accumulate data to deal with the issues of the economy (Ghosh 2016). In the postcolonial world, the birth of the economy produced a series of ambiguities in its attempts to quantify and account the vast array of unregistered and undocumented economic activities in the shadow of a fledgling fiscal and monetary regime. In such a condition, data appeared to be the only means to discipline an unruly economy, whose 'cooking' became one of the major operations of postcolonial governments. At the global level, on the other hand, the newly established governing organisations such as the UN and the World Bank began to set protocols and standards to make such disparate databases commensurable and comprehensible (Ward 2004).

The Making of an Economic Database in Early
Postcolonial India

Decades before the introduction of the census operations in India,
the colonial government insisted that the provincial governments
publish relevant statistical accounts in their Annual Reports. Between
1840 and 1865, such accounts were made uniform and published
in the form of the *Statistical Abstract for British India*. In 1862, the
British government in India constituted a Statistical Committee at the
behest of which the robust *Statistical Abstract for British India* came
out in 1868. Containing returns of provincial administrations, this
publication became a regular annual ritual of the British government
until 1923. Between the 1860s and 1880s, various branches of the
imperial government in India established statistical wings. Thus,
successive famines in the 1870s prompted the Agriculture Department
to come up with *Agricultural Statistics of British India* in 1886. In
1862, the Finance Department established a statistical branch, which
in 1895 morphed into a Statistical Bureau with the subsequent
addition of a commercial intelligence wing to it in 1905.

Until the inter-war period, however, official statistical enterprises in
India outside the census operation remained scattered, uncoordinated,
and largely decentralised. In 1925, the Indian Economic Enquiry
Committee was instituted which consisted of Sir M. Visvesvaraya
as Chairman, and Pt. Hari Kishan Kaul and Prof. Burnett-Hurst as
members. The objective of said Committee was to

> examine the material at present available for framing an
> estimate of the economic income of the various classes of
> the people of British India, to report on its adequacy, and to
> make recommendations as to the best manner [in] which it
> may be supplemented, and as to the lines on which a general
> economic survey should be carried out, with an estimate of the
> expenditure involved in giving effect to such recommendations
> (The Legislative Assembly Proceedings, 22 January 1925).

The Committee was also asked to review the 'question of the
adequacy of the statistical data available and the desirability and
possibility of supplementing it, and of undertaking an economic
enquiry' (National Statistical Commission n.d.). In addition, the

Legislative Assembly desired that the same Committee be asked to conduct the economic and the taxation enquiries. Eventually, the government appointed two separate Committees to undertake the task. The Committee's recommendation was that both central and provincial governments should come under one central authority, a central statistical bureau of the sort, with provincial branches to 'provide a common purpose and a central thinking office on the subject of statistics' (ibid.).

Nothing very significant happened before the end of World War II. In 1945, the Government of India appointed an inter-departmental committee which again recommended the establishment of: a) a central coordinating statistical office, b) statistical bureaus in provincial headquarters, and c) a statistical cadre. After Independence, P. C. Mahalanobis was appointed as the statistical advisor to the government in 1949 and in the same year, a micro-statistical unit was inaugurated in the cabinet secretariat which in 1951 emerged as the Central Statistics Office (CSO) being entrusted with the work of coordination with various organisations producing statistics. In 1949, a national income committee was set up with Mahalanobis as its Chairperson and V. K. R. V. Rao and D. R. Gadgil as members to estimate national income. The Committee was externally advised by a distinguished panel comprising J. R. N. Stone (Cambridge), Simon Kuznets (the University of Pennsylvania, who devised national income accounts in the US), and J. B. D. Derksen (the UN Statistical Office). It is at this point of trying to quantify national income with an aim to figure out the pattern of income distribution (which would form the basis of a general revision and rationalisation of the existing tax structure), and ultimately to predict the trend of economic growth in the country that the key functionaries of India's statecraft began to make an inventory of the existing economic database and infrastructures, and started taking into account the kind of statistical and infrastructural apparatus they required in order to think of an Indian economy. Thus, while setting up the Committee, the Government's resolution (No. 15(33)-P/49, dated 4 August 1949) mentioned the following:

> The Government of India have been giving consideration for some time to the inadequacy of the factual data available for the formulation of economic policies. One important gap is the absence of authoritative estimates of the national income and its

various components. The Government of India have accordingly decided to set up a committee to advise how best this gap could be filled up (GOI–NIC 1951, Planning Commission Papers, National Archives of India, p. 1).

The National Income Committee (NIC) encountered three major problems that appeared to the Committee members to be unique to the Indian condition when compared with the advanced industrialised countries, who had initiated the process of measuring their national economies a number of years ago. The first was what the Committee called the 'problem of measurability':

> ...when calculating the value of output, one normally proceeds on the assumption that the bulk of the commodities and services produced in the country are exchanged for money. In the case of India, however, a considerable portion of output does not come into the market at all, being either consumed by the producers themselves or bartered for other commodities and services. The problem of the imputation of value thus arises and takes on significantly large proportions in some sectors of the economy (GoI–NIC 1951, Planning Commission Papers, National Archives of India 1951, p. 12).

The second major problem that the Committee encountered emanated from India's 'comparative lack of differentiation in economic functioning':

> While it is true that we have a sector in our economy that is as differentiated and subject to modern income classification as in the west, it is also true that a major portion of our economy consists of household enterprises, simultaneously and without differentiation performing functions which would normally fall under different industrial categories. Thus, sizable groups among agricultural producers pursue other occupations in other industries, often in urban places or at any rate outside their domicile. Hence the customary classification of national income by industrial origin cannot be taken except as a rough approximation to a classification of distinct groups in the population, whose main income is derived from a single industry (ibid., p. 13).

Hence, the Committee felt the genuine need for a 'substantial revision of the industrial classification', but 'a much greater emphasis than is customary in the west upon social groupings connected with the character of the enterprise rather than with industry would not be more useful for India' (ibid., p. 13). Eventually that called for 'a great deal of analytical work' and a reworking of the existing classificatory schema 'developed in the west'. The third round of problems were concerned with 'the non-availability of statistical data for the estimation of income and related accounts in India' (ibid., p. 14), for which fresh surveys outside the scope of the measurement of national income appeared necessary. The lack of a robust database of household income tax encompassing a large cross-section of the country's population posited a significant challenge before the National Income Committee (Padipaty 2020). Overall, the task before the NIC was to create units of measurement and equivalence to enable the placement of the Indian case on a comparative scale in the competitive arena of nation-states. Ideologically, the economy invented thus, appeared to carry the very essence of the newly liberated nation—the amphitheatre of governmental action. Understandably, such a project needed to be backed by a credible process of survey that would bring into being a community of producers and consumers within an overarching national frame.

On 18 December 1949, Prime Minister Jawaharlal Nehru expressed his desire that a sample survey be organised 'covering the whole country to collect essential information'. Mahalanobis drafted a proposal for the National Sample Survey (NSS) and handed over the same to the Finance Minister C. D. Deshmukh on whose advice the National Income Committee finally recommended the use of the NSS data for national income estimation. Starting in 1950–1951, this multipurpose sample survey became the biggest and the most comprehensive sampling enquiry in the contemporary world. As a round-the-year and continuous data collecting and data processing machinery, the NSS was tasked to collect reliable data concerning production, consumption, and various other kinds of data to better comprehend the emerging trends in the national economy. The Annual Report of the ISI for the year 1950–1951 gives a comprehensive picture of the first round of NSS data collection:

The whole of rural India has been split up into 156 strata, the formation of each stratum depending on geographical contiguity and homogeneity in topographical characters. Wherever the necessary data have been available, each stratum has been further divided into four sub-strata according to the population of the village comprising them. A total of 1833 villages have been selected for the survey, and the quota of each stratum has been made proportional to its population. In each village, a random sub-sample of the households has been studied in respect of the principal occupation, and the households comprising the sub-sample have been divided into 'agricultural' and 'non-agricultural' groups, those engaged on a primarily agricultural enterprise being treated as agricultural and the rest as non-agricultural. Further sub-sample has been drawn in both of these groups for a detailed examination of general demographic and economic characteristics, production and cost data in the enterprises concerned and consumers' expenditure in the domestic field (ISIAR [ISI Annual Report, housed in ISI Kolkata] 1950–1951, p. 2).

Already in 1950, in a paper Mahalanobis stated that 'with an accepted level of precision the costs of (random) sample surveys are only about ten per cent of that of a complete enumeration' (see also Ghosh 2016: 6). His long-term interlocutor, Ronald A. Fisher mentioned in addition that in complex and vast countries such as China and India, sample surveys were a much more scientific and economically viable mode of statistical operation (ibid.).

Along with its routine work, the NSS also began to undertake occasional and special surveys on the pressing social and economic issues affecting the country. Thus, apart from expanding the scale of the sample survey, the NSS in ISI conducted a number of surveys on behalf of various ministries. Thus, in a couple of years of its operation, the NSS produced impressive ad hoc surveys on the displaced persons (due to Partition) in the states of West Bengal and Bombay (for Ministry of Rehabilitation), collected information on a countrywide basis for the Press Commission (for Ministry of Information and Broadcasting), surveyed the magnitude of unemployment in Calcutta and other metropolitan areas (for Planning Commission), came up with a study of the housing of the working class (for Ministry of Works, Housing and Supply), and so on. Soon, the NSS became one of the most credible databases for social and economic research, that is, the macro-economic and demographic policies of the government.

Within six years of its operation, the NSS became so robust that the American statistician and the pioneer of statistical quality management, Edwards Deming wrote:

> No country, developed, under-developed, or over-developed, has such a wealth of information about its people as India has in respect to expenditure, savings, time lost through sickness, employment, unemployment, agricultural production, industrial production. We in this country, though accustomed to working in large sample surveys were aghast at Mahalanobis' plan for the national sample surveys of India. Their complexity and scope seemed beyond the bounds of possibility, if not beyond anyone else's imagination, but they took hold and grew (Rudra 1996: 204).

Needless to say, such a permanent and accumulative work of data collection required the setting up of a permanent bureaucratic, scribal, field-level, and mechanical installation at multiple levels. A look at the Annual Reports of the ISI in the 1950s gives one a sense of how such an installation came into existence over a short period of a decade. Mahalanobis's induction to the core of the Nehruvian statecraft, on the other hand, brought into being a promising unification of official statistical initiatives with the research tradition in descriptive statistics of the ISI. The Institute began to receive liberal funding from the government that enabled it to quickly elevate its esteem within India. In addition, Mahalanobis's global intellectual collaborations made it a nodal point in thinking about the new sciences of the state and the new data regime for planning national development outside the well-known western set-up. On 9 December 1956, Chinese Premier Zhou Enlai visited ISI to specifically understand the modalities of the NSS operation in India. When he was visiting the NSS wing of the ISI, the following conversation took place between Enlai and Mahalanobis:

> Zhou Enlai: Which are the countries most advanced in statistics? Are you in touch with them?
> Mahalanobis: UK, USA and USSR. We are in touch with all three, and we accept from each what we find useful. We have found, however, that in applied work, it is not desirable to copy from any country. *In India, we are trying to adopt and develop the methods to suit our own needs.*

Zhou Enlai (nodding his head vigorously): Yes, yes. One group
of Chinese statisticians will soon come here. I want them to see
everything in detail. We want to learn from you...
(Mahalanobis to Pitambar Pant, 16 December 1956, File
No. 90, PCMMMA [Prasanta Chandra Mahalanobis Memorial
Museum and Archives], ISI Kolkata, pp. 11–12; emphasis ours).

Zhou's visit was followed by the visit of a Chinese delegation
to the ISI. After a careful survey of the NSS work of the ISI,
the delegation asked the Chinese government to a) introduce a
similar random survey in China, and b) establish an institute for
statistical learning along the lines of the ISI. Mahalanobis had
said, 'In India, we are trying to adopt and develop the methods
to suit our own needs'. A few years down the line, Mahalanobis
introduced a new method of analysing the NSS data called the
'Fractile Graphical Analysis', which C. R. Rao (1973: 480) describes
as 'a semi-parametric method for comparison of two samples' to
'find a disaggregated measure of changes in income inequalities or
disparities in consumption over time, a measure that reflected what
was happening to the levels of living of different income groups
over time' (Srinivasan 1996: 242–243). This mode of analysis was
seen as a decisive shift of theoretical perspective from aggregate
measures such as Gini Ratio to enable Mahalanobis to compare 'the
distribution of total consumption expenditure from NSS data for
the eighth round (July 1954–March 1955) when prices were low,
with the distribution for the sixteenth round (July 1960–June 1961)
when prices were high' (Srinivasan 1996: 244). His analysis revealed
that 'with an increase in prices, the distribution of expenditure on
consumption did become more equal' (Mahalanobis 1975: 1166;
Srinivasan 1996: 245).

Mahalanobis also devised a technique to address 'one of the long-
standing peculiarities' of the Indian labour question (when compared
with the advanced Western economies), that is, most of the workers
are involved in domestic home-based industries in which they did
not have tangible jobs to lose to be registered as unemployed, even
though they might not be having gainful work. To address this and to
standardise data in this field, the ninth round of the NSS collected data
on unemployment and underemployment 'on hours of work done per
week and number of days of gainful work during 30 days preceding
the day the interviews were conducted' (Srinivasan 1996: 246).

In a sense, the NSS brought into being a community of producers and consumers of an economy, articulated as the very essence of the liberated Indian nation. The task of nation-building revealed itself as the task of bringing producers and consumers into a single framework for governmental interventions in the form of national planning— one that would render the economy with anthropomorphic features (Deshpande 1993). Thus, the postcolonial economy became a site in which decolonisation (from enslavement to liberation) was to be performed in the complex exchange between the empty-homogenous time of the nation, and the dense-heterogenous time-space of governmentality. Interestingly enough, the Big Data phenomenon arrives at a moment in the postcolony (this was around the time of the so-called GDP revolution) when the conception of the economy is estranged from the collective conception of the nation.

The advent of the NSS overlapped with the emergence and continuation of the operations of a host of specialised public data collection institutions such as the Registrar General and Census Commissioner of India (under the Ministry of Home Affairs, mandated to organise decennial census operations, and linguistic surveys), Archaeological Survey of India, Botanical Survey of India, Forest Survey of India, Geological Survey of India, National Institute of Oceanography, Zoological Survey of India, and so forth. In addition, the Reserve Bank of India and various public-sector banks, the Securities and Exchange Board of India, the National Crime Records Bureau, etc., produced impressive corpora of sector-specific data (Samaddar 2018). In this context, the contribution of the NSS was to produce large-scale and continuous data (as opposed to the discrete and periodic data collected by the census operations) on the government and market initiatives to imagine the national population as a mass of consumers, hinged on the state-capital nexus (ibid.). A look at such initiatives may enable us to trace the history of state capability of the management of public data in India prior to the advent of the data economy.

Moreover, the early decades of the NSS contributed to the further development of statistics as a discipline, which became the backbone of machine learning algorithms in the subsequent decades. The following instance may be considered in this context. The Mahalanobis D square statistics (also known as Mahalanobis Distance) was widely deployed in the analyses of NSS data. The Mahalanobis distance 'is a measure between two data points in the space defined by relevant features'. A Mahalanobis distance metric is capable of adjusting the 'geometrical distribution of data so that the distance between similar data points is small'. This property of Mahalanobis Distance is widely deployed today to 'enhance the performance of clustering or classification algorithms, such as KNN classifier' (Xiang et al. 2008: 3601).

The Advent of Computers In India

A history of Data Centres cannot be written without studying the history of computing that commenced with 'mainframes, moving on to personal computers and the client-server model, and then to distributed computing and software as a service' (Samaddar 2018: 131). As we will see in this section, along with advanced experimentations in descriptive statistics, the NSS operation over the years also brought with it a hardware infrastructure that paved the way for the digital revolution in India. Thus, the General Report No. 1 on the NSS noted in 1951:

> To make suitable arrangements for the work of tabulation and analysis of the primary data, more than 100 additional computing clerks were appointed and given training in the Indian Statistical Institute. Since much of the work was to be done by tabulating machines, training was also given to a large number of punchers and verified in the Institute both in Calcutta and at its branch at Giridih in Bihar. Arrangements were made to hire the latest type of tabulating machines from the International Business Machine Corporation (IBM) of New York; and by the latter part of 1951, the Institute had two new models of IBM tabulators, a new multiplier and several sorters, reproducers, etc. in addition to some of the machines of the British Tabulating Machine Co. which the Institute had been using for some time. An electronic Statistical Machine (a high-powered combined sorter-tabulator) was also rented from IBM ('The National Sample Survey: General Report No. 1. First Round: October 1950–March 1951'. 1953, p. 59).

Already in 1947, Mahalanobis encountered an electronic computer in Harvard and understood its potential in executing data analysis for large-scale centralised planning in India (Menon 2018). Subsequently, in 1952, he urged the Union Cabinet to transform the 'project section of the ISI' into a 'National Statistical and Computation Laboratory for technical and large-scale applied work in the processing and analysis of statistical data and numerical computations' (Note submitted by P. C. Mahalanobis to the GoI, 20 February 1952, Planning Commission Papers, National Archives of India). Between 1950 and 1954, Mahalanobis conducted rounds of discussion in the US and in India to persuade the US authorities to help ISI procure the expensive UNIVAC (Universal Automatic Computers). However, his well-known sympathies with the Soviet bloc and his unalloyed commitment to socialistic planning appeared to be a stumbling block in this partnership. In fact, a secret report in 1953 from the US embassy in New Delhi to the State Department in the US mentioned Mahalanobis as 'a notorious fellow traveller and sympathizer of the Soviet Union' whose 'ideas are...a direct preparation for an authoritative solution to India's economic problems' (Menon 2018: 28).

In 1954, Mahalanobis mentioned that without computers 'we will never be able to cope with the tremendous volume of primary information which is accumulated through the NSS every month' (Mahalanobis to P. Pant, Pitambar Pant papers, NMML [Nehru Memorial Museum and Library], 23 June 1954). In 1955, two staff members of the ISI—S. K. Mitra and D. S. Kamat—were deputed on a special fellowship to the USSR to 'make a technical report on the electronic computers which the USSR Government had offered to institute' (ISIAR [Annual Report of the Indian Statistical Institute] 1955–1956, p. 15) at the ISI. In 1955, ISI started a computing centre to serve other scientific institutions of the country:

> Some service is already being rendered. A problem for preparing a table of values of an improper, convergent integral was received from Indian Institute of Technology, Kharagpur at the end of 1955, and was solved partly by an electronic calculator. Other problems have been received from the Indian Association for the Cultivation of Science, Calcutta and from the Indian Institute of Science, Bangalore, which are now being

run on the HEC-2M machine (ISIAR [housed in ISI Kolkata] 1955–1956, p. 16).

Already, since 1950, the ISI had been housing the Computer Mechanics and Electronics Laboratory (CMEL) to bolster learning and research in the fields of computation and computing machines (Banerjee 1983). In 1953, it assembled an analogue computer out of the 'war surplus materials' to solve simultaneous linear equations and to compute the NSS data (Banerjee 1983; Rajaraman 2012). The first digital computer in India was installed at ISI (an HEC-2M) in 1956. Subsequently, in 1959, the Institute, in collaboration with the USSR and the UN, got hold of a large computer known as the URAL. Thus, by 1950–1960, ISI emerged as a National Computer Laboratory, extending its infrastructural support to Ministry of Defence, the Atomic Energy Commission, the Meteorology Department, etc. The ISI staff members displayed considerable skill to handle and repair the newly installed complex machines. Thus, the ISIAR of 1956–1957 notes:

> The Institute staff not only maintained this complex and delicate machine but also spotted out the most frequent causes of breakdown and made a large-scale modification of the machine with a view to eliminating these causes. Some useful monitoring devices have already been added to this machine. Experiments have also been started to replace the mechanical switching device of HEC-2M machine by an all-electronic switch. Some experiments on magnetic gates have also been made (ISIAR [housed in ISI Kolkata] 1956–1957, p. 13).

Thus, between 1950 and 1956 a number of hardware experimentations took place in the ISI to ease out the computation of the increasingly accumulated raw NSS data. Engineers from the US and the USSR regularly visited the Institute and trained its technical staff. In later years, a number of technical staff members of the Institute who developed familiarity with digital computers were deputed to IISc (Indian Institute of Science) and TIFR (Tata Institute of Fundamental Research) to train their staff members when the first computers arrived in those campuses. At least a couple of skilled staff members from ISI joined the Bharat Electronics Limited (BEL) in Bangalore in the 1960s and contributed to the development of the computer programme in that organisation. Thus, by 1960, the ISI emerged as the only nodal centre to disseminate computer knowledge to the rest of the country. In 1964, the Institute rented an IBM 1401 system. To continue to pay IBM the rental money, the Institute had to contract more work from various government agencies and scientific establishments of the country (Rudra 1996). In 1968, the Government wished the Institute to install (on a loan basis) a state-of-the-art Honeywell 400 computer. The event drove the Institute's management to a workers' agitation. The workers claimed that the machine should not be used to displace the employees processing large-scale survey data such as the NSS. Finally, the machine got installed in 1970, which significantly enhanced the Institute's computational capabilities (ibid.).

Attempts at developing computers through indigenous expertise began in 1954 at TIFR. The new computer thus made was commissioned in 1956, which continued to serve the scientific community until 1964 under the name TIFRAC (Tata Institute of Fundamental Research Automatic Calculator) (Banerjee 1983). Again in 1961, Jadavpur University, in collaboration with the ISI started developing two solid-state, second-generation computers of advanced design, the first of which began working on 2 April 1966 (ibid.). In June 1964, the TIFR procured a US made computer called CDC-3600-160A. In IIT Bombay, the Minsk II computer was installed in 1967. Professor J. R. Isaac, along with five other faculty members, started the process of setting up the Computer Centre there.

Thus, in the period between the 1950s and the mid-1960s, research organisations and educational institutions were the biggest consumers of computer technology. An estimate suggests, in this period, thirteen out of sixteen computers in India were in operation in such institutions. This trend began to gradually change from the 1960s. Between 1962 and 1964, fourteen computers were installed, of which twelve computers found their way in R&D organisations. In 1965–1966, thirty more computers were installed, and the number rose to 200 by 1973–1974 (Banerjee 1983). Until this time, maximum procurement of computers happened through public funds. To provision and maintain computers in Indian establishments, IBM set up four Data Centres in Calcutta, Bangalore, Madras, and Bombay. The working capital of these Data Centres was meagre, but their profit margins were considerable (ibid.), as IBM was the only credible service provider in the Indian market.

India's defeat in the 1962 Indo-Chinese war has remained prominent in the history of computer policy in India. The defeat in the war made the Government aware of the need to refurbish technological capabilities both in civil and military fronts (Chattapadhyay 2013). In August 1963, Professor Bhabha, the doyen of atomic research in India, was asked to chair the Electronics Committee. The onus of publishing the Report of the Committee in 1966 was with Vikram Sarabhai, the doyen of space research in India. Among other things, the Bhabha Committee Report asked the Government to set up a Department of Electronics (DoE). The DoE came into existence in 1970, ending a period of ad hoc and autonomous developments in computer capabilities at the behest of a few educational and research institutions (Rajaraman 2012). Between 1971 and 1978, the DoE promoted 'self-reliant indigenous development of computers' (ibid.: 1), and as a result, a company named the Electronics Corporation of India Ltd. (ECIL) was founded and was 'financed to design, develop and market computers using primarily components made in India' (ibid.).

According to Rajaraman (2012), the second important moment of rupture arrived in 1978 with the fall of the Congress regime in 1977. The IBM was directed by the new government a) to reduce equity, b) to transfer 60 per cent of its ownership right, and c) to involve an Indian agency to produce IBM 360 series computers. Such actions eventually forced IBM to sell its Data Centres, equipment, and service operations to the CMC (Computer Management Corporation Private Ltd.). The exit of the IBM and the advent of a government-sponsored organisation in its place created the condition for the development of a *swadeshi* market in computer technology, which again had to face severe competition after liberalisation in the 1990s and eventually, the ownership of the CMC moved to an India-based transnational corporation.

In 1986, the Indian government started lifting controls on the industry and allowed among other things the import of totally assembled motherboards with processors. The reduction of import duties made computers affordable to a section of private users (Rajaraman 2012). In the same year, the Government permitted the software companies to import computers at much lesser import duty rates which made it possible for those companies to export software. Gradually, public perceptions about computers began to change as the computerised train reservation system made people's life easier (ibid.). The third breakpoint, according to Rajaraman (ibid.), came in 1991 when India had to open its economy and reduce controls over the local manufacturing companies. Soon, software and software services companies came together under the umbrella of the National Association of Software and Services Companies (NASSCOM), which remained remarkably successful in obtaining tax and various other concessions for its member companies. In the late 1990s, Indian software companies could manipulate the opportunity of the Y2K crisis and the confusions in the international market due to Euro conversion, and modified and improved a large number of 'legacy software systems' (ibid.). In addition, after the liberalisation of the economy, there had been a phenomenal increase in the volume of trade, finance, and insurance industries which led to an inundation of economic data, which in turn necessitated the installation of a robust data management infrastructure and a capacity to analyse data (Samaddar 2018).

Thus, by the start of the new millennium, India was ready for a Big Data avalanche that grew out of and was facilitated by a massive 'convergence' of information technology, broadcasting, and telecommunication. The early 2000s witnessed a major reorganisation of the existing diversity in e-governance through the introduction of twenty-seven Mission Mode Projects that touched upon an impressive number of 'service delivery verticals' (Chattapadhyay 2013), such as central excise, IT, e-Panchayat and various 'core and support infrastructures' (ibid.). The convergence of various e-governance initiatives presupposed an infrastructure to make data circulate among service providers, and between the service provider and the citizen. The Mission Mode philosophy enabled corporate firms to 'win' Mission Mode Projects and open captive Data Centres to ensure the accumulation and circulation of data. Thus, in 2017, Wipro Infotech won three Mission Mode Projects to open Data Centres in Maharashtra, West Bengal, and Gujarat (*India Infoline* 2010).

A couple of issues demand attention from the preceding discussion. First, it is quite evident that the act of governance has been transformed into profit-making market activity, dissolving the erstwhile social contract between the state and the market. The Data Centre-driven conjuncture is a moment when the state adopts the free market as its ' organising and regulating principle', and hence it becomes harder to identify the distinction between the state and the corporate sector, as both of them tend to embrace similar institutional practices as a state-corporate complex (Rossiter 2016). It is in this context that the economy gets 'evacuated' from its affective bond with the nation. Second, at least in India, the Mission Mode era has successfully contained, enveloped, and superseded the earlier regime of committees and commissions (Abraham 2017). The 'commission model' epitomised by the Atomic Energy Commission 'seeks the enhancement of the sovereign power', while the 'mission model' that became successful in telecommunication since the Rajiv Gandhi era was 'directed toward the furthering of biopolitical power' whose target is the 'national population' (ibid.: 675–676). The digital revolution between the 1980s and 2000s thus shares a bleeding boundary with a corresponding and a more fundamental transformation in state/society relation in India.

CONCLUSION

We have seen in this chapter that the Cold War geopolitics and the arrival of a mass society coincided with a growing trend to see the individual through a statistical lens. The individual needed to be emplaced properly in mass society. 'By making people into "statistical individuals,"' argues Bouk (2017: 96), 'it became possible to sort them according to the futures the statistics predicted they would have'. At the heart of the current Big Data moment lies the personalised aggregation of data in which all our actions become digitally coordinated, which makes real-time tracking of personal data possible. In India, personal data thus generated in real-time has of late, found a centralised home as nearly every resident of this country is made to register to the Aadhaar programme.

The Big Data phenomenon brings with it a rationality which appears to be estranged from personality and social contexts. This rationality often takes the form of unbending pronouncements calling for unique solutions to problems through the most efficient means, privileging all-embracing generalisations over contingencies of time and space. Big Data analysts hope that the pronouncements can be applied mechanically as 'computers reason better than humans'. The ascendancy of this rationality has witnessed the fall of the statistician in the terrain of high policy. In 2015, Larry Wasserman, for instance, noticed that the US President's Council of Advisors on Science and

Technology (PCAST) had no representation from the community of statisticians. He further reports that even the chief data scientist of the US Office of Science and Technology Policy was not a statistician. In India, the figure of the authoritative statistician eclipsed long ago as the bond between economy and the nation started losing its political relevance in the arena of competitive electoral democracy (in fact, the role was largely taken up by economists in the Indira Gandhi era, as Mahalanobis died a lonely Prometheus in Calcutta in 1972). In India, the Big Data moment witnessed the emergence of a new brand of technocrats as proponents of the said rationality, who have successfully surpassed the economist as well as the computer scientist in the new rule of experts. The birth of this algorithmic rationality at the behest of a new generation of technocrat-cum-entrepreneur demands much more careful attention.

To summarise, the chapter takes stock of the Big Data phenomenon and asks us to find traces of the phenomenon in the emergence of economentality, the mass society, Big Science and the military-industrial complex of the 1950s and the 1960s. In India, the era was marked by decolonisation, the emergence of a mass electorate, and the birth of the national economy as an imagined community of producers and consumers (Deshpande 1993). In these decades, the considerations of the 'national' and the 'developmental' would frame the architecture required to generate a database. In the Indian context, we have tried to show, the NSS did perform this precise task. It was already guided by the teleology of planned development of the Nehruvian era. From the 1980s, a role reversal began to take shape as data started determining what would be 'developmental' and what could be called the 'national'. Thus, today's digitally encoded data appears to be the axis of two imperatives—creating an abstracted economy of data itself, and that of national economy-making. The chapter then explores the kinds of relationships this history has with the phenomenon of Data Centres (which emerged in the 1950s in the context of the Cold War but became ubiquitous from the 1980s)—a key actor without which the contemporary arrival and valuation of Big Data remain unimaginable. Contemporary Data Centres create the infrastructure, both of storage as well as processing/ 'interoperability' that gives Big Data its 'bigness' and its currency. This interoperability also allows for a kind of marketisation of data—enabling the growing corporate control over data process, at the level of the Data Centre, wherein the Data Centre continues to serve as a market/exchange of data.

Today's Big Data phenomenon paradoxically co-exists with what Samaddar calls the 'sparse data syndrome'—one in which 'unavailability of granular and/or interoperable data…may lead to a lack of warning' (2018: 132). In this context, our current data conjuncture is marked by an interlocking presence of the old-world statistical data and the new world Big Data. In this semi-analogue-semi-digital moment, the census and NSS will certainly survive, but only by substantially accommodating Big Data elements within them and will continue to operate under an emergent regime of authentication.

References

Abraham, I. 2017. 'From the Commission to the Mission Model: Technology Czars and the Indian Middle Class'. *Journal of Asian Studies* 76(3): 675–696.

Aronova, E. 2017. 'Geophysical Datascapes of the Cold War: Politics and Practices of the World Data Centers in the 1950s and 1960s'. *Osiris* 32(1): 307–327.

Aronova, E., C. V. Oertzen, and D. Sepkoski. 2017. 'Introduction: Historicizing Big Data'. *Osiris* 32(1): 1–17.

Banerjee, P. S. 1983. 'Induction of Computers in India', Occasional paper no. 56. Calcutta: Centre for Studies in Social Sciences.

Bouk, D. 2017. 'The History and Political Economy of Personal Data over the Last Two Centuries in Three Acts'. *Osiris* 32(1): 85–106.

Chattapadhyay, S. 2013. 'Of identity, platform, and "new" information infrastructure of governance: Situating the Aadhaar project within the history of electronic governance in India', Paper presented on 14–16 November at 'The Social and Cultural Life of Information' Conference, Sarai-CSDS (Centre for the Study of Developing Societies), New Delhi, India.

Datta, A. 2018. 'The digital turn in postcolonial urbanism: Smart citizenship in the making of India's 100 Smart Cities'. *Transactions of the Institute of British Geographers* 43(3): 405–419.

Deshpande, S. 1993. 'Imagined Economies: Styles of Nation-building in Twentieth Century India'. *Journal of Arts and Ideas* (25–26): 5–35.

Doctorow, C. 2008. 'Welcome to the Petacentre'. *Nature* 455(4): 16–21.

Edwards, P. 1996. *The Closed World: Computers and the Politics of Discourse in Cold War America*. Cambridge, Mass.: MIT Press.

Friendly, M. 2008. 'The Golden Age of Statistical Graphics'. *Statistical Science* 23(4): 502–535.

Gabrys, J. 2011. *Digital Rubbish: A Natural History of Electronics*. Ann Arbor: University of Michigan Press.

Ghosh, A. 2016. 'Accepting Difference, Seeking Common Ground: Sino-Indian Statistical Exchanges 1951–1959'. *BJHS Themes* 1: 61–82.

Hacking, I. 1990. *The Taming of Chance*. Cambridge: Cambridge University Press.

Hardt, M. 1999. 'Affective Labour'. *Boundary 2* 26(2): 89–100.

Hudson, Heather E. 1990. *Communication Satellites: Their Development and Impact*. New York: Free Press.

India Infoline News Service. 2010. 'WIPRO Infotech Bags Three Mission Mode Projects for Data Centres', 13 May. Available at https://www.indiainfoline.com/article/news-sector-information-technology/wipro-infotech-bags-three-state-mission-mode-projects-for-data-centers-113101200225_1.html (accessed March 2022).

Jacobson, K. and M. Hogan. 2019. 'Retrofitted Data Centres: A New World in the Shell of the Old'. *Work Organisation, Labour & Globalisation* 13(2): 78–94.

Janda, Kenneth. 1967. 'Political Research with MIRACODE: A 16 mm Microfilm Information Retrieval System'. *Social Science Information* 6: 169–181.

Johnson, A. 2019. 'Emplacing Data within Imperial Histories: Imagining Iceland as Data Centres' "Natural" Home'. *Culture Machine* 18. Available at https://culturemachine.net/vol-18-the-nature-of-data-centers/emplacing-data/ (accessed March 2022).

Klose, A. 2009. *The Container Principle: How a Box Changes the Way We Think*. Cambridge, Massachusetts: MIT Press.

Korsmo, F. L. 2010. 'The Origins and Principles of the World Data Center System'. *Data Science Journal* 8: 55–65.

Larkin, Brian. 2013. 'The Politics and Poetics of Infrastructure'. *Annual Review of Anthropology* 42: 327–343.

Liu, X., N. Iftikar, and X. Xie. 2014. 'Survey of Real-Time Processing Systems for Big Data'. In *IDEAS '14: Proceedings of the 18th International Database Engineering & Applications Symposium*, Ana Maria Almeida, Jorge Bernardino, and Elsa Ferreira Gomes (eds), 356–361. Available at https://dl.acm.org/doi/10.1145/2628194.2628251 (accessed April 2022).

Liu, Z., Zhi Wang, Xiaochun Cheng, Chunfu Jia, and Ke Yuan. 2013. 'Multi-user Searchable Encryption with Coarser-Grained Access Control in Hybrid Cloud'. Fourth International Conference on Emerging Intelligent

Data and Web Technologies, IEEE. Available at https://ieeexplore.ieee.org/abstract/document/6631626 (accessed March 2022).

MacKenzie, Donald. 2014. 'At Cermak'. *London Review of Books* 36(23). Available at https://www.lrb.co.uk/the-paper/v36/n23/donald-mackenzie/at-cermak (accessed March 2022).

Mahalanobis, P. C. 1975. 'Consumption and Welfare'. In *The Gazetteer of India: Economic Structure and Activities, Vol. 3*, P. N. Chopra (ed.), 1160–1170. New Delhi: Ministry of Education and Social Welfare, Government of India.

Malecki, E. J. and H. Wei. 2009. 'A Wired World: The Evolving Geography of Submarine Cables and the Shift to Asia'. *Annals of the Association of American Geographers* 99(2): 360–382.

Marx, K. 1867. *Capital: A Critique of Political Economy*, Vol. 1. Charles H. Kerr and Company. Available at https://www.marxists.org/archive/marx/works/download/pdf/Capital-Volume-I.pdf (accessed March 2022).

———. 1885. *Capital: A Critique of Political Economy*, Vol. 2. Charles H. Kerr and Company. Available at https://www.marxists.org/archive/marx/works/download/pdf/Capital-Volume-II.pdf (accessed March 2022).

———. 1894. *Capital: A Critique of Political Economy*, Vol. 3. Charles H. Kerr and Company. Available at https://www.marxists.org/archive/marx/works/download/pdf/Capital-Volume-III.pdf (accessed March 2022).

———. 1993 [1939–1941]. *Grundrisse: Foundations of the Critique of Political Economy*. Penguin Classics. Also available at https://www.marxists.org/archive/marx/works/1857/grundrisse/ (accessed March 2022).

Menon, N. 2018. '"Fancy Calculating Machine": Computers and Planning in Independent India'. *Modern Asian Studies* 52(2): 421–457.

Mitchell, T. 2014. 'Economentality: How the Future Entered Government'. *Critical Inquiry* 40(4): 479–507.

National Statistical Commission. n.d. 'Indian Statistical System'. Available at https://mospi.gov.in/documents/213904/0/Ch+14+30.8.2001.pdf/d944ae06-bc59-ff09-9502-39d897b2ed0b?t=1599817175203 (accessed May 2022).

Padipaty, P. 2020. 'Testing Measures: Decolonisation and Economic Power in 1960s India'. *History of Political Economy* 52(3): 473–497.

Rajaraman, V. 2012. 'History of Computing in India, 1955–2010'. IISc Bangalore, Available at https://ethw.org/File:Rajaraman,_V._History_of_Computing_in_India,_1955-2010.pdf (accessed May 2022).

Rao, C. R. 1973: 'Prasanta Chandra Mahalanobis (1893–1972)'. *Biographical Memoirs of Fellows of the Royal Society* 19(December): 455–492.

Rigi, J. 2014. 'Foundations of a Marxist Theory of the Political Economy of Information: Trade Secrets and Intellectual Property, and the Production of Relative Surplus Value and the Extraction of Rent-Tribute'. *tripleC* 12(2): 909–936.

Rigi, J. and R. Prey. 2015. 'Value, Rent, and the Political Economy of Social Media'. *The Information Society* 31(5): 392–406.

Rossiter, N. 2016. *Software, Infrastructure, Labor: A Media Theory of Logistical Nightmares*. New York and London: Routledge.

Rudra, A. 1996. 'The Indian Statistical System'. In *Prasanta Chandra Mahalanobis: A Biography*, A. Rudra (ed.), 204–213. New Delhi: Oxford University Press.

Sadowski, J. 2019. 'When Data Is Capital: Datafication, Accumulation, and Extraction'. *Big Data & Society* January–June: 1–12.

Samaddar, R. 2018. *Karl Marx and the Postcolonial Age*. Switzerland: Palgrave Macmillan.

Srinivasan, T. N. 1996. 'Professor Mahalanobis and Economics'. In *Prasanta Chandra Mahalanobis: A Biography*, A. Rudra (ed.), 225–252. New Delhi: Oxford University Press.

Star, S. L. and G. C. Bowker. 2002. 'How to Infrastructure'. In *The Handbook of New Media*, L. A. Lievrow and S. Livingstone (eds), 151–162. London: SAGE.

The Economist. 2017. 'Data is Giving Rise to a New Economy', 6 May. Available at https://www.economist.com/briefing/2017/05/06/data-is-giving-rise-to-a-new-economy (accessed March 2022).

Thompson, E. P. 1963. *The Making of the English Working Class*. London: Pantheon Press.

Vigne, B. 2020. 'Omeya: Water, Work and Infrastructure in Ovamboland from 1915 to 1968'. Master's Thesis, Department of Historical Studies, University of Cape Town.

Ward, M. 2004. *Quantifying the World: UN Ideas and Statistics*. Bloomington: Indiana University Press.

Warf, B. 1989. 'Telecommunications and the Globalization of Financial Services'. *The Professional Geographer* 41(3): 257–271.

———. 2007. 'Geopolitics of the satellite industry'. *Tijdschrift voor Economische en Sociale Geografie* 98(3): 385–397.

Xiang, S., F. Nie, and C. Zhang. 2008. 'Learning a Mahalanobis Distance Metric for Data Clustering and Classification'. *Pattern Recognition* 41(12): 3600–3612.

Zook, Matthew. 2006. 'The Geographies of the Internet'. *Annual Review of Information Science and Technology* 40(1): 53–78.

III

Between Control and 'Feedback'

Narrating the Digitised Operations of a 'Captive'
Electricity Data Centre in West Bengal, India

RITAM SENGUPTA

INTRODUCTION: BETWEEN CONTROL AND 'FEEDBACK'

The pre-eminently logistical placement of Data Centres in networks of government, production, and trade aims to install an operation of control that is premised upon modulation and exceptionality (Deleuze 1992; Rossiter 2016; Zehle and Rossiter 2016). As a form of control within digitalised, software-oriented environments modulation executes a self-sufficient form of sovereignty that does not await sanction from any singular foundational principle or figurehead; rather, modulation performs sovereign exceptions as logical response to contingent events or phenomena, which are already translated on their own terms/parameters as feedback (Bratton 2016: 19–40). If, as Ned Rossiter (2016: 138) has argued, this modulatory activism of Data Centres involves dealing with 'low level demands prompted by minimal parametric variation', can there be an unpacking of this activism, of the inter-relay of feedback mechanisms emerging through the material being and becoming of actually existing Data Centres? This is the question that aptly introduces the analytical concerns of this chapter. In pursuing such concerns, this chapter will delve into the conditions and contingencies that make scope for the emergence of digitalised governance through Data Centre-driven operations. The objective will also be to gauge an array of effects over organisational configurations, distributed across specific evolutionary trajectories of digitalisation, effects that follow from the present of modulatory control to perhaps breed the future of feedback. On another count, such an enquiry would be a way of retracing virtualised digital infrastructures to their very material existences (Mattern 2016). And through this retracing, we will also attempt to understand how digitalised governance comes to be layered in relation to the non-digital.

This particular modality of problematising digitalised governance also follows from the functionalities that have evolved over a decade-long period around a specific Data Centre and the data processing and management scheme that it heads. This is the West Bengal State Electricity Distribution Company Limited (WBSEDCL) Data Centre and at issue, therefore, are the ways in which the management of an electrical network and its attendant bureaucracy has evolved in relation to the digitalised controls that the WBSEDCL has introduced. The WBSEDCL is a 'discom' (electricity distribution company) owned by the state of West Bengal in India, though it is run on corporate principles by the decree of federal law (The Electricity Act, 2003). It was created by the 'unbundling' of the erstwhile West Bengal State Electricity Board (WBSEB) in 2007.[1] Within the current distinctions of vocabulary that are proposed within the global Data Centre industry, the WBSEDCL's Data Centre would qualify as a 'captive' facility. The term 'captive', as will be elaborated, contains within its ambit a varying distribution of potentialities that do not immediately lend themselves to attributions of a singular, closed system. But a 'captive' digitalised operation like that conducted by WBSEDCL's Data Centre over the last decade or so, does however demand a certain descriptive-analytical preference for its core and dedicated pursuits.

The WBSEDCL's Data Centre is primarily geared towards handling digitised data streams emerging from an automated and remotely operable metering scheme for measuring the consumption and distribution of power established over the last few years. It also hosts a range of Information Technology (IT) 'solutions' that mediate the shaping of such data streams into technological, financial, and managerial inputs to run the activities of the organisation. This metering and digitised data infrastructure was initiated through the adoption of a central government funding programme— R-APDRP (Restructured Accelerated Power Development and Reforms Programme) in the state of West Bengal since 2008–2009.[2] The express mandate of the R-APDRP was to aid state-owned discoms to create an automated set-up for recording and transmitting data concerning matters of electrical distribution, in order to reduce

Transmission and Distribution (T&D) losses incurred by these companies.[3] T&D loss refers to the difference between the amount of energy entering the network after generation, and that which is expended or billed at the consumer's end. These losses are also referred to as 'Aggregate Technical and Commercial (AT&C) Losses' in more contemporary terminology.[4] Within alternating current (AC) distribution, such 'losses' are as such impossible to eradicate completely, though they can be minimised to negligible levels. There are, however, very specific conditions under which T&D/ AT&C losses have multiplied in post-Independence India. After the 'Green Revolution' of the 1960s and 1970s, unmetered agricultural connections on flat tariffs had become something of an electoral norm for catering to big famers' lobbies that was grafted onto the system of electricity distribution.[5] It is generally understood that this resulted in abundant unaccounted-for usage, under-billing, and pilferage, and consequently, aggravated T&D losses. Pilferage in turn impacted the technological functioning of the network by creating higher demands over sub-par wired infrastructure suitable to handling more modest loads. This is said to have also worsened 'losses' on a technical count.

Unlike several other states, electrical losses in West Bengal cannot be directly attributed to agricultural/irrigational use, which until recently amounted to just about 10 per cent of the total power consumption in the state. But 'losses' nonetheless were also rampant in West Bengal just like many other Indian states. In 2000–2001 under pressure to tidy up their finances from central and international bodies like the Planning Commission and the World Bank, state utilities had to redo their accounting of 'loss' figures. The erstwhile WBSEB produced revised estimates which showed that up to 40 per cent of the power it generated/bought was being lost in the course of transmission and distribution (2002 figures). This was a significant update from lower 'loss' figures from not much earlier (Chatterjee 2018: 133). As this relative uncertainty in calculation might indicate, the reproduction of 'losses' had also come to be based on a characteristically *informatic* conundrum, a problem shared by West Bengal with the rest of India. This conundrum consisted of the fact that since the 1970s, it was becoming extremely difficult to gauge exactly where the electrical network was becoming leaky in major parts of the country due to shortcomings of metering infrastructure. Alongside, the State Electricity Boards found incentive in under-reporting seemingly difficult-to-calculate T&D losses in order to draw subsidies (Tongia 2003). Meanwhile, the continuous reproduction of losses, both technical and revenue-related, was translating into the acute financial unviability of electricity distribution, leading to several monetary 'bailouts' of the state's electrical agencies after the 1990s. Eventually, it was this financial exigency that prompted the emergence of a scheme like R-APDRP that was to aid state-owned discoms like the WBSEDCL to establish an appropriate digitised infrastructure of metered data, distributed over various segments of the electrical network, in order to furnish standards for acting upon them.

In what follows, the chapter will elaborate on how the control of 'loss' has given impetus to Data Centre-led digitised modulatory control within the WBSEDCL's operations. 'Loss' or its management in this sense, is cast as part of the landscape of feedback, a landscape encompassing the timely governance of bureaucratic performance, technical amendments to electrical networks, and the possible arresting of the pilferage of power. This chapter will begin by setting up the WBSEDCL Data Centre as a distinct object of enquiry in two specific ways. It will at first distinguish the Data Centre from a world of globalised logistical governance and its infrastructural order. It will then elaborate on the very specific scale of operations that unfold through the Data Centre's existence as a 'captive' facility. In making this elaboration, the analytical utility of category distinctions proposed by the IT industry between 'captive' and 'co-location' Data Centres will be interrogated.

Further, the chapter will explore how a 'captive' Data Centre like the WBSEDCL facility eventually performed its own aggregation of previously dispersed vectors of information towards centralising organisational command over power distribution within the discom. This account of centralisation will allow us to approach the question of the relationship between digitalised control and feedback that unfolds through the operations of the WBSEDCL. In tracing the specifics of the digitised data management scheme in question, the chapter will eventually broach the possibility that this scheme functions often as a self-serving mandate that articulates the consistency of its parametric operation only by certain ways of self-circumscribing. To anticipate a later discussion in this chapter, the irony of this circumscribed operation is that even while producing certain positive effects on the electrical and bureaucratic network in question with the control of 'loss', the originary drive of this operation, does not sustain as an objective that this data management scheme eventually remains consistent with. The chapter will end with expanding upon this ironic implication of digitalised operations that function through 'minimal parametric variation'. It will show that such modulation stands out after all, as fairly *minimal* in its anticipation of the mediations of other 'non-digital' interventions, since it only responds to a rather limited assortment of contingencies on its own self-referential terms as 'feedback'. Other indications like that of power theft and its estimates (as will be shown) are noted and thus 'included', but they do not count and therefore, are merely folded over—perhaps in expectation of a non-digitalised, explicitly political intervention to emerge and 'resolve' the issues at hand.

SITUATING THE WBSEDCL DATA CENTRE AS A SITE OF
STUDYING DIGITALISED GOVERNANCE

The WBSEDCL's Data Centre began operations around 2009–2010. The Data Centre is located in Action Area 1A of New Town, Rajarhat in West Bengal where it sits right next to the towering heights of the 'IT Park' created by the builder group DLF (see Images 3.1, 3.2, and 3.3). Rajarhat is a north eastern suburb of Kolkata which is now constructed and managed by an autonomous body formed by the Government of West Bengal—the Housing Infrastructure Development Corporation (HIDCO). Major parts of this 'New Town' have been 'developed' as an IT 'hub' of sorts after a hugely controversial spate of land acquisition, and the deft manoeuvring (and flouting) of the state's environmental and other legal requirements by the HIDCO with the enabling assistance of local political power (Dey et al. 2016). Rajarhat's 'Action Areas' are now of course, something of a paradigm for the incentivisation of IT 'enclaves', with earlier commitments to 'low income housing' being subtly changed to accommodate land use by massive corporate settlements. For example, the DLF IT park (Image 3.5) has already been purchased by IBM, who have supposedly embarked on raising two more towers of 1.3 million sq. ft. each next to the existing one with the entire project amounting to about US\$ 79 million (Sengupta 2013).

As Dey, Samaddar, and Sen (2016: 242) have argued, the 'New Town' model as represented by Rajarhat (and not unlike the case of Navi Mumbai, as discussed by Manish Jha and Rishi Jha in the next

Image 3.1: Entry to the main building of the WBSEDCL Data Centre
Photograph: Ritam Sengupta

Image 3.2: Side view of the WBSEDCL Data Centre with cooling units in view
Photograph: Ritam Sengupta

Image 3.3: Side view of the WBSEDCL Data Centre with the DLF
IT Park as neighbour

Photograph: Ritam Sengupta

Image 3.4: The WBSEDCL Data Centre, the 33KV electrical
substation, and the DLF IT Park

Photograph: Ritam Sengupta

Image 3.5: The DLF IT Park, front view
Photograph: Ritam Sengupta

chapter in this volume) feeds into the emergence of a 'logistical city', that is also 'a city of peripheries'. The peripheral description here is not so much indicative of the margins of global capital. It rather signals the making of a globalised urban condition, whereby many physical peripheries of older metropolises are now joined together to repurpose them into preferential nodes of connectivity in the worldwide grid of transport terminals, warehouses, IT and financial infrastructure. In this global 'bypass'-ing of extant models of urban growth centered upon promises of housing and employment, infrastructural mediations continuously disembed locations from localities, even as these localities remain bound to certain limiting factors like that of securing the cheapest possible inputs in the form of labour and resources like land, water, electricity, and bandwidth (Easterling 2014). Data Centres have been understood by some scholars as infrastructural forms that while inheriting this geography of logistical coordination, also reconstruct the dimensions of virtualised control by occasioning newer connections across the data trails of disparate organisations and entities (Johnson and Hogan 2017; Neilson and Notley 2019). As infrastructural formations, Data Centres are governed by international regulations and ratings that pose particular standards concerning matters of data security, memory backup, encryption, and the availability of water and energy amongst other things (Hogan 2015; Maguire and Winthereik 2021). And in turn they purport to further disembed logistical functions from the register of national state jurisdiction by introducing modes of digitised governance with their own protocols and parameters of situating, relating, and moving things, people, and messages (Rossiter 2017).

How do we understand the WBSEDCL Data Centre in relation to the schematics of a possible 'logistical city'? While occupying a prime position at the core of New Town amidst its towering neighbours, the Data Centre cuts a strangely diminutive appearance in a standalone facility housed in an utterly unassuming building of two floors. The justification of its characteristically incongruous existence in a prized real estate settlement is however immediately brought into view, as it comes to be noticed that the Data Centre shares with the IT Park the power supply of a 33KV electrical substation, situated right between the two buildings (Image 3.4). If the 'peculiar ontology' of infrastructures is that 'they are things and also the relation between things' (Larkin 2013: 329), the WBSEDCL's Data Centre secures such relational prominence, amidst the behemoths of the global IT players, as the control unit that quite literally helps 'power' the very activities of such players. Yet even as it distils the key functions of logistics to govern the distribution of power, it is not immediately possible to attribute to it a global-by-design character. The Data Centre does qualify itself as a Tier 2 rated facility by engineering standards that operate internationally. This translates into a claim of 99.741 per cent availability with approximately twenty-two hours of downtime per year. This runtime is also warranted by a singular alternative source of redundancy with respect to power and cooling options. The Data Centre has a duplicate in a Disaster Recovery Unit at Berhampore, the central town of the Murshidabad district of West Bengal. But a Tier 2 facility still hardly qualifies as a cutting-edge technological set-up that remains defined by demands of an international data hosting and processing industry, an industry that is currently moving up from Tier 4 category Data Centres to an imagination of a Tier 5 rated arrangement (*Customer 1st Communications* 2017). Moreover, while the WBSEDCL does operate by standard IT 'solutions' packaged specifically for power utilities around the world, it is difficult to think about its operations as exceeding the conventional scope of government by agencies of the national state, or as being shaped by any immediately extra-national interconnections of data flows.

It is however certainly possible to pose the processes ensuing from the WBSEDCL's adoption of a Data Centre-d architecture of information management as a form of *encounter* between the existing problems and possibilities of localised government (by the state), and new kinds of digitalised governance that offer their own distinctive forms of control attuned to particular IT 'solutions'. Conversely, such encounters might also describe the interaction between the objectives of digitalised governance and possible limits against which such governance develops its operations—in other words, between the domain of 'soft' modulatory control, and the multiform terrain of feedback against which it hones its capacities. An understanding of such encounters might be obscured by the way in which the lens of 'innovation' (in modalities of digitalised control) is only trained on data infrastructures that are conceptualised as being overlaid on the scale of global logistical networking. Studying relatively localised infrastructure like the WBSEDCL Data Centre invites a move away from this specific kind of innovation-centrism, and directs attention to more dynamic scales-in-making where 'innovations' in digitalised governance are made or even unmade beyond the newness of such innovation claims, which are usually bloated to drive up their stakes, as they come to mediate the datafication of the world.[6] Such localised data infrastructure invoke the possibility that much remains to be unearthed from the in-betweens of apparently automated processes that turn 'all that is solid' into data and then all data into a mobile resource. As the next section will explain in greater detail, localisable infrastructural forms like the WBSEDCL Data Centre are also not immediately making way for any globally stacked up scheme of data sharing and management. In fact, national, provincial, or local governments could (and do very much) simultaneously maintain certain delimited silos of information management with their own specific forms and politics of interconnection, even as they otherwise open up to a broader, globally networked vision of data movement and processing. As one example of such delimited silos, the WBSEDCL's Data Centre both occupies the order of a 'logistical city' as well as points to how the uneven texture of logistical operations

retain the objectives of an identifiably local scale, even as this scale
is remade by the same operations.

If we cannot then very easily diagram the WBSEDCL Data Centre
into a planetary infrastructural collaboration as yet, how else do
we otherwise follow and understand its promised performance of
digitised governance? On returning to the concerned building in
Rajarhat, we find that its insides are not visible from the outside
and that it has a single entrance. An attempt to enter the building
reveals it as a fortified compound manned at the gate by security
staff. Once past the security check, the reception desk of the Data
Centre is the final frontier of public enquiries beyond which it is not
possible to proceed without the permission of the highest officials
of the WBSEDCL, permission which could not be obtained during
the period of this research. From the reception desk onwards, the
Data Centre thus begins to express an organisational protocol of
security and secrecy, pursued through authenticated checkpoints
that can only be cleared by authorised personnel. On this count, the
WBSEDCL Data Centre starts resembling all other Data Centres.
Yet here, the relatively localisable scale of operations of the Data
Centre both allows us as well as pushes us to launch a possible
ethnographic pursuit beyond its locked doors. Once we take the
environment of restricted access as a kind of confirmation of
the key status of the WBSEDCL's operations in a most ordinary-
looking building, tucked away behind the towers of the DLF IT
Park, the operations of the Data Centre can be traced beyond its
actual location. Such operations can be and need to be studied in
their distributed character, described in their actualised realm of
functioning within a perimeter that is marginally more accessible
to the researcher. In our case, this actualised site happened to be the
WBSEDCL's administrative headquarters at Salt Lake, Kolkata, not
too far away from the Data Centre.

These offices were a significant contrast to the situation of the
WBSEDCL Data Centre. They offered more or less easy mobility
between various levels and rooms, where apparently more relaxed
official interlocutors offered their carefully considered and argued
opinions with considerable frankness at times, without the immediate
restrictions of a security protocol. A primary empirical entry point for
the discussions in this chapter thus became a set of observations and
interviews conducted at the headquarters of WBSEDCL in Kolkata

and amongst senior engineer bureaucrats, mainly in four units—the Chairman and Managing Director (CMD) cell, the Information Technology cell, the Corporate Planning cell, and the Revenue and Energy Management (REM) cell. The interviews often ranged over critical reflections offered in response to the problems of a gradually corporatising company. These discussions, in a way shorn of the anxieties of data security, narrated a kind of quotidian life of digitised data production, processing, and management that transitions from the domain of proprietary hardware, software, and data ownership to the graphical interfaces and constrained actualities of problem-solving. One way of understanding such actualities could be to figure the Cloud, following Louise Amoore's suggestion, as exceeding the location of Data Centres to become 'instead a novel political space of calculative reasoning' and a bundle of techniques acting upon 'the threshold(s) of perceptibility' (Amoore 2016: 9). In following this conceptualisation, the study of digitised governance in this chapter will offer an analysis of how particular IT 'solutions' run via a Data Centre-d architecture of centralised information management, enact such alterations in the thresholds of organisational perception, and mediate possibly newer forms of calculative reasoning oriented towards loss control and system maintenance.

In this chapter, another empirical entry point to querying such recently standardised forms of digitised management within the WBSEDCL is provided through a set of contrarian positions found in the publications of the West Bengal State Electricity Board Engineers' Association (WBSEBEA)—positions that are those of 'users' intimately associated with the implementation of the WBSEDCL's digitalised operations. These positions perhaps describe a set of contingencies which otherwise remain presupposed as wrinkles in the folds of digitalised governance, the folds being stitched together by security protocol. Along with the claims of the upper management of the WBSEDCL, it is then also the domain of such contingencies that this chapter discusses in exploring the landscape of feedback, over and against which the modulatory control of digitised governance might be developing itself. But before opening up to scrutiny this landscape of feedback and its relationship with modulatory control, it is still useful to continue to develop the framework within which we can place the WBSEDCL's Data Centre as a form of data infrastructure, and subsequently, examine the kind of organisational transformations that the onset of a Data Centre-d architecture introduced within the bureaucratic order of the organisation.

A 'Captive' Data Centre?

In industry parlance, the WBSEDCL Data Centre would qualify as a 'captive' variety that deals with the data of a singular organisation and is dedicated to its requirements. However, what might sometimes get lost in the 'captive' description, is that it only gains greater distinction in reference to the more recent evolution of 'co-location' Data Centres that handle the data of multiple different organisations within the same facility. This is well illustrated in a recent Whitepaper on the Australian Data Centre market by Frost and Sullivan (F&S 2017) titled 'Not all Data Centres Are Equal'. The paper points out that 73 per cent of Australian Data Centre facilities (75,000 in number) are actually 'captive' facilities. Yet it strongly argues for a shift to 'co-location' or shared varieties of hosting on the grounds that these offer a greater scope of scalar expansion necessary for the multiplying data storage and processing needs of particular organisations. The paper urges such organisations to subscribe to third party entities since that would make it easier to handle other issues that accompany the demand for server-space, like 'power use efficiency' and cooling requirements, outsourcing of basic IT maintenance tasks, and also adopting more 'skilled' processing services and tools (ibid.: 11–14). It then goes on to describe a scale of Data Centre 'maturity' in terms of the adoption of 'best practices', with co-location varieties obviously occupying the apex of this scale. The evolutionary scales provided by the F&S paper thus mark out a prescriptive territory of the future with respect to which 'captives' might appear as something of a residual category. And yet in describing the various stages of outsourcing IT functions, the broader tenor of the report also, if only inadvertently, acknowledges that the evolution from 'captive' to 'co-location' might be a matter of phased adoption with multiple hybrid solutions existing in its trajectory.

The stark numbers of 'captives' also perhaps necessitate a different order of emphasis than that allowed for by the prescriptions of market research. In India too, 'captive' Data Centres are a fairly big segment of the ITBPM (Information Technology and Business

Process Management) industry—around 1,100 such Data Centres generate a share of US$ 23 billion of a total market of US$ 154 billion (Bain & Company 2017). 'Captives' have commanded this distinction within India's IT business especially on count of different forms of outsourcing, not only of 'backend', but also analytics tasks to affordable sites of storage, processing, and availability of skilled labour that have been typical of the globalisation of information technology capital over the last few decades. But the 'captive' market has also had its growth as units of data aggregation and processing have become uniquely urgent requirements within the institutions of the Indian state. A 2016 report by the IAMAI (Internet and Mobile Association of India) (for the IAMAI report, see Appendix, this volume) on the domestic economy of Data Centres cited as a prime field of development a range of Government-to-Citizen (G2C) and Business-to-Consumer (B2C) applications, which were to be hosted through multiple Data Centres, as commissioned by the National eGovernance Plan (NeGP) (IAMAI 2016). The NeGP of the Government of India (GoI), approved around 2006, drives the uptake of dedicated/'captive' Data Centre hosting for the 31 'Mission Mode' initiatives proposed as its constituents (Ministry of Electronics and Information Technology [MeitY] n.d.-a.). It also directly commissioned, by central policy and financial support, a State Data Centre (SDC) for each of India's twenty-nine states for managing the delivery of eGovernment services (MeitY. n.d.-b). In the same series could be placed the multiple public sector corporate concerns, namely banks like SBI (State Bank of India) or utilities like WBSEDCL, or the Data Centre of UIDAI (Unique Identification Authority of India), that have over the last decade maintained their own dedicated Data Centres. They have stuck to such dedicated server facilities both on count of following organisational policy of avoiding sharing data with other entities as well as by way of legal requirements of sensitive data security. The continued adoption of 'captive' Data Centres in India by both private as well as state organisations thus co-exists with the recent surge in the number (presently 140) of 'co-location' Data Centres, which are third-party organisations offering shared facilities and solutions. This in a way complicates the possibility of any imminent dissolution of institutional and organisational distinctions to make way for possible economies of scale arising out of interoperable and standardised offerings of storage, hardware, and software solutions by Data Centres of a strictly 'co-location' variety.

However, while the evidence of numbers qualifies 'captives' as a distinct area of enquiry, it is nonetheless imperative to avoid a hypostatisation of the category. 'Captives' are undergoing a kind of immanent transformation. A recent industrial repackaging of 'captives' as GICs (Global In-house Centres) in a NASSCOM report, presents the greater incorporation of 'big data'-based analytics and cloud solutions (Bain & Company 2017), as aspiration for 'GICs of the future'. This report resonates otherwise with a chorus echoed by other corporate players (Everest Group 2012), that the 'captive' denomination does injustice to the potential of scaling up by for instance, cloud adoption, that can be availed of also by dedicated digitised operations and management. The IAMAI report on the Indian Data Centre market made note of the fact that the Government of India's GI Cloud, or MeghRaj (that aims to support NeGP initiatives) 'will not be a standalone private cloud but will consist of several categories such as government-owned-and-operated cloud as well as government-shared cloud, owned and operated by the private sector' (IAMAI 2016: 9). The report concluded that 'the GI Cloud categories evince the critical role of private sector participation in data management, data flows and data centres in India' (ibid.).

Whether by ways of turning legacy data management architectures into 'GICs of the future', or by public organisations adopting private sector infrastructure, the category of 'captive' Data Centres in India has perhaps begun demonstrating a tendency of pushing dedicated operations over some form of shared or more 'open' architecture. This stems in a way, as recently argued by Ranabir Samaddar (2018: 131–137), from the genetics of the 'postcolonial experience', where the massive data gathering initiatives historically conducted and now inherited by the Indian state (see Chapter 2, this volume), requires in the present the mediation of a mixed governance regime of PPP type (public-private partnership), in order to both scale up as well as capitalise on data as resource, in a climate marked by business cycles of ever-enlarging production as well as commodification of data. To what extent 'captives' thus start resembling or yielding scope to 'co-location' varieties is a question for the future. But what is being pointed out here is that the scale-making capacities and by implication the concentration of capital, soft power, and information enabled by Data Centres is best understood via tracing the peculiar tendencies of topological transformation (that is, the specific ways in which constituent parts are linked and arranged to make a whole data management system/network) in the storage, processing, and management of data rather than by positing any uniform developmental trajectory of innovation (Neilson and Rossiter 2021).

Within the WBSEDCL's Data Centre-driven digitised operations, a tendency to shift to more open architecture has recently manifested as a requirement of capacity addition to manage and process a greater inflow of digitised data. In late 2017, the WBSEDCL thus floated a tender for contracting with a separate Tier 3 Data Centre and IT provider for the purposes of handling remotely available digitised data flowing in from new meters to be installed with consumer connections of electrical load between 15 and 50 KVA.[7] However, even earlier and within the dedicated server arrangement with which it commenced its Data Centre operations, the WBSEDCL had employed a third-party IT consultant—Tata Consultancy Services (TCS). TCS was employed initially in 2009 to aid in developing the metered data processing (MDAS [Meter Data Acquisition System]) application of the organisation. By 2012, TCS also became involved in the redesigning of the Enterprise Resource Planning (ERP) programme of the WBSEDCL through the replacement of an older Oracle-based system by a new SAP IS-U (Systems Applications and Products in Data Processing [SAP] company's 'Industry Specific Solution for Utilities Industry' software) module (both these software 'solutions' will be discussed later in this chapter). The overseeing of WBSEDCL's software architecture by TCS famously provoked a significant strain of opposition from the constituencies of the WBSEBEA. The engineers' association repeatedly pointed out in their official publication that the availability of personnel qualified to handle requisite software 'solutions' within the WBSEDCL obviated any need for a third-party contractor like TCS. Moreover, the relatively unregulated possession of key segments of digitised data by TCS was argued to have amounted to an unfair competitive advantage to the consultants in retaining their contractor status for long periods.[8] The 'captive' description might thus at times draw away focus from emerging forms of outsourcing adopted by dedicated operations like that of the WBSEDCL's Data Centre and the negotiations around it, even as such forms do not necessarily make 'co-location' varieties out of existing 'captives' in any straightforward sense.

The 'captive' description, however also perhaps falls short of indicating any sense of the reorganisation of power that is occasioned by the creation of such Data Centres. The 'captive' description, in other words, does not quite give a sense of how apparently dedicated digitised data management systems are themselves forms of re-aggregation of separate silos of information, a re-aggregation that also might have implied a reorganisation of the capacity and direction of organisational command. It is thus also in this sense, that a reading of the category of 'captive' as merely residual might lead to an obscuration, this time of the forms of evolution that 'captives' have already brought about in the respective informatic landscapes in which they have been set up. Analysis of recent GOI interventions like NeGP, 'Digital India', and Aadhaar (the unique biometric identification system/'platform' for India) has made the case that within the longer history of the Indian state's deployment of digitised networked information systems, these initiatives straddle the line between tendencies of operating by agency-, state-, and task-specific information systems, and exhibit proclivities towards linking these separate systems into centralised nodes of control and visibility that also afford a scaling up across wider governmental and commercial territorialities of database-d management (Chattapadhyay 2013). Thus the earliest forms of national scale database-d systems like the National Informatics Centre Network (NICNET) proffered two kinds of schemes—first, those of particular verticals retaining their delimited administrative scope, and second, something like the District Information System of National Informatics Centre (DISNIC) programme which for the first time, enabled states and the central government to have direct access to district-level demographic and socio-economic data. By 1985, the state governments were resisting the possible 'panopticon-like capabilities' of the central government arising out of access protocols of systems like DISNIC. The NeGP in a way continues to retain the extant system of separate silos of information management dedicated to particular service delivery 'verticals' like Income Tax, rural government, state-specific applications, etc. It is however through the Aadhaar 'platform' and the operation of shared clouds, that the GoI is seeking to coordinate and thus rein in these separate silos into an aggregate and constitutive systematics of obtaining, vetting, and processing governmental but also commercial information and services (Chattapadhyay 2013: 22; Ramanathan 2011). The UIDAI that manages Aadhaar prefers a 'captive' Data Centre to host its data. Yet by no means does that indicate a diminution of state power as exerted through database-d governance; in fact, if anything, it indicates an acute concentration of such power.

The WBSEDCL's 'captive' Data Centre and the software 'solutions' it deploys, translates similarly into an exposure to a centralised level of control since a significant portion of the digitised data collected and processed by the organisation becomes linked by funding conditionalities, also to the databases of central monitoring authorities. But if this centralised re-establishment of control over what is essentially a shared 'Concurrent' subject (electricity distribution) in the Indian Constitution, is a logical outcome of Data Centre-based information management; this is a logic that has also evolved within the disaggregated organisational formation of the WBSEDCL to secure a kind of unprecedented control over Divisional units by the Kolkata headquarters. The coming of the 'captive' architecture of a Data Centre-led digitised control thus, was also literally a capture of disaggregated vectors of command that preceded the era of total networking and digitisation. What was produced through such capture was, in the words of senior bureaucrat at the CMD cell of the WBSEDCL, a 'centralised operation with decentralised functioning'.

Organisational Restructuring in the Wbsedcl

To understand the nature of this 'centralised operation with decentralised functioning' we can begin by describing the specifics of the digitised reorganisation of the WBSEDCL's activities. Over the last decade or so, the assistance of the R-APDRP programme enabled the WBSEDCL to install machine-readable meters for all consumers as well as for a majority of Feeders and Distribution Transformers (DTRs), operated by the company as intermediary nodes on its power distribution network. The meters measuring the conduct of electricity through Feeders and DTRs and its consumption by 'bulk' consumers (consuming 50 KVA and above; cold storages, factories, etc.) are remotely accessible, and they are also equipped to log a multiform set of time-coded variables like load surveys, that are described as the 'health parameters' of the network. These meters also record 'exceptional events' like possible tampering or outages. Since late 2017, this form of metering is being extended also to other categories of consumers of smaller load requirements. Taken together, these constitute the AMR (Advanced Meter Reading) infrastructure of the WBSEDCL that is touted as something of an example in data generation initiatives amongst Indian utilities. It was also described by several higher officials at the WBSEDCL as constituting (potentially) a 'no-human-touch' system. The AMR infrastructure is complemented in turn by the GIS (Geographic Information System) mapping of each intermediary unit of power distribution operated by the WBSEDCL likes poles, consumer meters, and again Feeders and DTRs. This scheme was described as particularly effective in tracing every consumer connection as well as for the accounting of billing and AT&C losses down to the immediately relevant DTR. This was the most granular level till which such calculations were ever made by the WBSEDCL.

Since 2011, the GIS-specified and time-coded data generated by the AMR infrastructure is routed directly to the central server of the WBSEDCL Data Centre over a dedicated 'internet backbone' at speeds of 8 mbps. By 2012, the availability, coordination, and processing of the remote flow of metered data on energy, health parameters, and interruptions from all Feeders/DTRs and from 'bulk' consumers came to be coordinated by a common Meter Data Acquisition System (MDAS), a software 'solution' hosted over the Data Centre. The MDAS parses this data in primarily two ways. It makes available an automatically generated stream of AMR data over a common interface operable in all administrative/technical offices of the WBSEDCL. This includes an apparently 'real time' log of percentage figures of (AT&C) 'loss' and billing (in)efficiencies incurred for particular segments of distribution like Feeders, DTRs, and 'bulk' consumers. The second key affordance of the MDAS interface is a 'real-time' fault monitoring/complaint logging system. This system makes note of the 'exception reports' clocked by the metering system for particular intermediary units on the network and automatically issues instructions (referred to as dockets) for maintenance tasks at the level of the concerned office. Meanwhile, a parallel communication reaches a mobile technician's van closest to the GIS location of the unit in question. If a docket is not tended to, there is a systemic 'escalation' of the exception in the form of the system sending emails to higher levels of management. The escalation continues till the fault is rectified and a work completion report is submitted.

Having made note of this digitalised informatic rearrangement of the WBSEDCL's scheme of operations, we can now begin to approach the question of 'centralised operation with decentralised functioning' more directly in terms of the forms of administrative 'restructuring' that the organisation has undergone in the recent past. Eventually this will enable an understanding of how informatic rearrangement and administrative 'restructuring' were complementary processes that led up to a certain kind of centralisation of the WBSEDCL's operations through its Data Centre-d architecture of functioning. From 2005 onwards, two processes of administrative restructuring were initiated for state-owned utilities of West Bengal as part of a broader process of introducing 'reforms' in the electricity sector in India.[9] The first of these was an 'unbundling' of the long-existent West Bengal State Electricity Board (WBSEB) in 2007 to create two separate transmission companies WBSETCL (West Bengal State Electricity Transmission Company Limited) and the WBSEDCL. The allied second process was a 'Technocratic Model of Power Reform' that sought to corporatise the functioning of the new, relatively autonomous organisations like the WBSEDCL, towards the necessary objective of profitability. In line with these 'reforms' was the appointment of consultants such as PricewaterhouseCoopers (PwC) to 'rationalise' and 'restructure' manpower deployment, right after the inception of WBSEDCL and around the same time as it started implementing R-APDRP measures.

What followed was the introduction of independent directors recruited from top-tier executives with expertise in both technical as well as financial matters, who were employed from both within and outside the organisation. Alongside, there was slimming down of the 'bottom-heavy workforce' and the appointment of technical staff with some of the highest wages in the public sector. The 'restructuring' was also effected by way of a 'flattening' of the multi-layered administrative hierarchy by more reliance on outsourcing for tasks such as bill-collection—a form of 'discreet frontline privatization' (Chatterjee 2017: 13). This 'flattening' amounted to the termination of 40 per cent of staff recruited for billing functions,[10] and also the abolition by 2011 of the entire architecture of sub-Divisional offices, as some of the tasks executed by these offices were outsourced to private agencies.[11] While accounts of this 'restructuring' usually describe the process as having taken into suitable confidence the unions and associations of WBSEDCL's employees,[12] it is striking that till very recently, publications and public communications of organisations like the WBSEBEA have pointedly contested the PwC's suggested interventions. A November 2011 letter from the All India Power Engineers' Federation (AIPEF) to the Chief Minister of West Bengal thus criticised as 'unique' and 'destabilizing' the WBSEDCL's/PwC's proposals for the abolition of sub-Divisional offices and the usurpation of the responsibilities of 'revenue and maintenance activities' from the district level administration.[13] In August 2012, the WBSEBEA actually went ahead to submit its own alternative plan for 'restructuring' that interestingly made its suggestions on the bulwark of the claim that 'no additional manpower has been proposed in our proposal'.[14] The proposition went on to emphasise that what was needed was a 'synchronisation' of 'technology'—having 'a significant role to play in bringing forth the cherished result'—and 'a dedicated and committed workforce'. The key element of this 'synchronisation' was proposed as the re-institution of the responsibilities of sub-Divisional offices to oversee the work of maintenance and billing, now carried out by contractual agencies over which the resident Divisional engineers of the WBSEDCL had 'no delegated power' in the new schema.

Here it is somewhat difficult to comprehend how the WBSEBEA's push towards re-empowering Divisional units would sit together with its acknowledged inevitability of automation rendering the deployment of 'additional manpower' superfluous. Yet this juxtaposition does help us understand the extent to which corporatised administrative 'restructuring', initiated since 2005, had been enabled by the post 2008–2009 coming of Data Centre-d architectures of digitised control within the operations of the WBSEDCL. Unsurprisingly, this was also crucially mediated by the coming to prominence of the necessary task of controlling 'loss'—technical, financial, and informatic—as something of a *raison d'être* of post-liberalisation electricity distribution utilities in India. Divisional units, as some of the interlocutors of this study (themselves architects of 'corporate restructuring') described, had long had a more effective mandate over computerised billing as well as over measures of controlling AT&C losses, and conducting system improvement in comparison to the Kolkata headquarters. One key reason for this, as narrated by an REM cell official, was that when the erstwhile WBSEB had already by 1997–1998 embarked on a computerisation of consumer databases, it was the newly created Divisional computer centres that conducted the digitisation via manual inputting from registers of consumer billing. The management at the Kolkata headquarters seemed to have started taking T&D loss management 'seriously' sometime in 2001–2002—a transformation, described by a CMD Cell official, 'from a social service to a commercial operation'. After 2004, five Zonal Call Centres (ZCCs) were created (Zones—agglomerations of Divisions) which aggregated the Division-level metrics of energy usage and revenue. Divisions however sustained for a longer time as the basic units of loss detection. This preferential locus in a calculative chain ensured that initiatives of 'loss' or fault reduction and system improvement remained the prerogative of these units and the sub-Divisional offices under them. As hinted by another official, it might have also prompted more informal arrangements between Divisional units and the local electricity-consuming populations under their purview, of overlooking unpaid bills and issues of theft and under-reporting of consumption and billing amounts.

It is this preference of the Divisional units in an informatics order that was interrupted by the AMR and MDAS arrangement. This metering infrastructure is based on a direct linkage between the Data Centre at Rajarhat and remotely readable metering units installed at more granular levels of distribution (Feeders and DTRs) than the substations over which the Divisional units had knowledgeable jurisdiction. With a networked and GIS-specified access to 'loss'-making geographies, the cartography of 'loss'-control could henceforth be directly redesigned by the Kolkata headquarters, and contracted to external agencies on an acting-on-need basis, thus overriding Divisional competences and sovereignties.[15] It is this *logistical* redesigning of the data infrastructure of the WBSEDCL that can be argued to have been the sufficient condition for both the 'flattening' of administrative hierarchies as well as forms of 'discreet frontline privatisation'. Administrative power of such 'a centralised operation with decentralised functioning' could thus be read as an effect of literally rendering 'captive' the previously segregated informatics and (by implication) command vectors within a combined digitised operation, helmed now by the WBSEDCL's Data Centre.

THE VARIEGATED TERRAIN OF 'FEEDBACK'

The account of the alignment of the vectors of information with the vectors of bureaucratic command within the WBSEDCL's 'restructured' scheme of things that we have presented till now is still somewhat incomplete if we do not pursue its quotidian implications. In making a fuller appreciation of how such alignment comes to be performed within the everyday operations of the organisation, we can now also finally approach the introductory problem that this chapter opened with, that is, how the realm of digitalised control comes to encounter the possible terrains of 'feedback' within the administrative functions and objectives of the WBSEDCL. We can now situate 'feedback' as located somewhere in between parables of digital 'innovation' and 'potential', and the points over which the mandates of the Data Centre and its digitised IT 'solutions' encounter administrative contingencies. To be certain, not every element in this domain of administrative contingencies is moulded as 'feedback' within WBSEDCL's digitised operations. Often, contingencies lead up to more conventional chains of bureaucratic reasoning and command. Erring and non-performing officials still have to be pulled up by senior officials at 'performance review' meetings; and the movement from the logging of 'loss' and electrical 'health parameters' to the domain of planned executive action continues to involve significant issues of bureaucratic authority and decision-making, requiring often the full exercise of organisational sovereignties.

Yet what is particularly significant for pursuing an analytical focus on the relationship between digitalised control and 'feedback' as existing within the WBSEDCL's operations, is to mark out the peculiar insistence in narratives of 'innovation', on demonstrating how organisational decision-making within WBSEDCL can be made to assume continuity with the logics and processes of digitised datafication. This insistence is noticeable in a TCS account[16] about how innovative and digitised data management had benefitted the WBSEDCL. The account describes a newly performed 'correction' of the practice of not being sufficiently proactive in dealing with complaint calls made to certain Customer Care Centres of the organisation. The issue in the rectification of this 'problem' was not simply if the complaint was attended to or not. The problem having come to its notice, the WBSEDCL issued a directive that for all complaints called in by customers, a 'docket' had to be mandatorily created within the MDAS system by officials in charge at the CCC, much like the automatic generation of the same in case of interruptions logged in from remotely readable meters. The 'problem' thus 'rectified' then seems to have been much more than about disciplining lower officials—it was actually posed by TCS as an issue of 'business intelligence'. What transpired was evidently a material recasting of the intelligibility of an extant complaint and correction mechanism, overseen by human resources, as *feedback* in a logistical and digitised chain of command. It is here that Amoore's previously quoted suggestion of figuring the cloud as a set of techniques of acting upon the 'threshold(s) of perceptibility' becomes increasingly appropriate.

This kind of translating of organisational contingencies and exceptions into 'feedback' could also be highlighted as the key modality by which WBSEDCL's 'centralised operation with decentralised functioning' attempts to pay back its debt to the logistical infrastructure that supports its functioning. Such interventions into thresholds of organisational/logistical perceptibility however, might themselves be layered in particular ways in accordance with the structuring of WBSEDCL's digitalised operations. Contingencies do not always find uniform significance as 'feedback' within the ambit of digitised operations. One way in which the uniformity of becoming 'feedback' is modulated is by time lags. As described by the interlocutors of this study, within the current set-up of the AMR system of the WBSEDCL, processed 'loss' figures for non-urban Feeders and DTRs become available on the MDAS only belatedly, after a month of compilation, whereas for urban Feeders and DTRs these figures can be 'pulled' on an on-demand basis. Time lag could also effect the otherwise fully automated 'fault monitoring' system. The MDAS interface does not actually generate automatic notification of 'exception reports' within the scope of its interface, and the system thus awaits the manual acknowledgement of these reports by the operator attending to the screen in order for the automated docket and escalation system to be initiated. Such time lags describe a *phased* character of parametric responses that modulate their control by enacting a temporalised hierarchy of feedback mechanisms, which in turn seem to provide a distinctive shape to WBSEDCL's administrative priorities.

In his book-length analysis of 'logistical media' (*Software, Infrastructure, Labor*), Rossiter (2016: 29) perceptively invokes the term 'parameter' in two key and related ways. The first of these refers to a more general 'border concept' that 'delimits the range of activity and action'; and the second invocation made in relation to conceptions of computer science, describes a 'function or command' that establishes the reference for an 'actual argument', which then executes the concerned function. As described here, 'feedback' within the WBSEDCL's scheme of digitised operations—as for instance, in the case of the organisational instruction for compulsory docketing of complaint calls made by customers—could be understood as undergoing processing in a parametric environment in the second sense, as an argument that is already constituted in reference to the parametric affordances of the digitised complaint/fault monitoring system. On the other hand, it requires emphasis that the range of hierarchical, phased responsiveness described in relation to the possible time lags in fetching non-urban Feeder data, or in the monitoring of 'exception reports', also follow from the command of parametric affordance rather than from any presumed shortcoming of digitisation. The relationship between control and feedback here is dictated as delimited interventions which self-ordain a phased capacity for action, not necessarily seamless in its temporal coordination, but mediated instead by modes of punctuation programmed into the system.

However, could there be a somewhat different category of contingencies, whose consonance with parametric arrangements is neither immediate nor even subject to phased responsiveness, but might rather require the bringing about of *variations* in parametric conditions, to admit (or not admit) such contingency as feedback? Rossiter in a way treats this possibility with some amount of cynicism. Thus while admitting that 'minimal' variations could be affected in parametric constitutions (thus altering operations of a programme, model, or simulation), he concludes that logistical operations often do not conform to the general principles of second order cybernetics that propose a certain systemic malleability in response to 'feedback' or 'anomalies'.[17] His prime example in qualifying such 'closed' logistical operations is that of Enterprise Resource Planning software that 'refuses...feedback or noise...' (Rossiter 2016: 42). He explains that within the implementation of ERP software, 'the determination of relevance is an automated process choreographed by the algorithmic parameters of particular modules and their capacity to communicate with other modules' (ibid.: 120). There is thus little that is inherently compelling about specific kinds of 'feedback', which might compel such an algorithmic environment to adapt to its demands.

The Parametric Eschewal of 'Feedback'—
Erp at the Wbsedcl

Rossiter's suggestions might receive something of an apt but ironic exposition within a description of the encounters between 'feedback' and the parametric system of control emerging in the domain of the WBSEDCL's implementation of Enterprise Resource Planning (ERP). Such encounters became noticeably prominent especially since 2012, when an SAP IS-U software module made specifically for electrical utilities was adopted by the organisation by replacing its Oracle-based module of management. By 2016, the WBSEDCL had integrated key areas of billing, financial accounting, human and material management and maintenance under the SAP IS-U platform, which thus, also came to share in the databases of the MDAS. Effectively, this amounted to, in the words of an official, 'a multi-dimensional form of regulatory control' to synchronise work flow, capital investment, and revenue activities of the organisation, and thus was also a key modality of systematising its 'centralised operation with decentralised functioning'. In 2014, the WBSEDCL also received the German multi-national software corporation SAP's ACE Award for successful implementation of ERP at all its units following the implementation of R-APDRP.

However, ever since its implementation, the working of the SAP IS-U software seemed to have been a constant source of consternation for the engineering community represented by the WBSEBEA. Part of the charge against SAP IS-U seemed to have emerged out of an existing suspicion that the association harboured towards private contractors like PwC or TCS, the latter organisation being newly commissioned to manage the transition from the earlier legacy Oracle software system to the new SAP IS-U module. But even as the WBSEDCL started training its own personnel to take over the new software environment from TCS, and thus run it entirely over its dedicated Data Centre-d architecture, more 'technical' objections about the parameters of the software kept piling up on top of earlier apprehensions. Many of these objections were summed up in a late 2013 article by a WBSEDCL engineer in a publication of WBSEBEA. The article's central contention was that the execution of the SAP IS-U application was resulting in 'thousands of unbilled consumers' every month (Dutta 2013: 3–7). This was because within the prior

Oracle-based management, billing systems were 'modularized under each Division' under a server dedicated solely to that unit, but web-linked in turn with other administrative nodes on the network. For every Divisional unit, consumer meter reading happened according to a variety of meter reading dates, and a billing system dedicated to a Divisional denomination was able to 'uniquely' group consumers, according to the variety in their meter reading dates. The SAP IS-U application, however attempted to redesign the system by 'batch processing' the billing cycle of all consumers 'coded' onto the same DTR. But since the meter reading dates of these consumers taken from the earlier database continued to vary, the system seemed to have been continuously failing to account for the diversity in meter reading cycles under a single DTR. With the earlier system there also seemed to have been the scope for subjective 'validation' of meter-reading cycles over particular Divisional territories by the meter reading staff of the WBSEDCL; but within the new environment, in which reading is carried out remotely or by 'outside agencies' in a machine-readable form, such 'validation' was difficult to expect as the data only carried meaning as an input within the newly designed software environment.

The observation about the SAP IS-U environment as leading to confusion in billing cycles, and consequently, leaving several consumers unbilled has actually been repeated by WBSEDCL engineers and bureaucrats (members of the WBSEBEA) over the years.[18] When set against the background of the various modes in which contingencies are encountered within the development of modulatory control ensuing from a Data Centre-based architecture of WBSEDCL's digitised functioning, this continuing 'problem' would perhaps describe something of a limit case in the terrain of feedback mechanisms. This terrain, as it might be already evident, is fairly variegated. It ranges between the proactive casting of organisational issues as 'feedback' to a time-phased absorption of various 'feedbacks' by the parametric logics of the operating system. With the instance of the persistent inconsistencies in the implementation of a billing system within the SAP IS-U ERP environment, such parametric logics seem quite evidently to strain at their assumed minimalism while responding to 'feedback'. This minimalism serves the operations of the database-d management but does not seem to quite execute the goal towards which it is designed. In disallowing (the 'interoperability' of) extant metadata oriented-practices (billing according to monthly billing cycles and Divisional office codes), the ERP software remains true to its design of maintaining an accounting system down to the granularity of DTRs, a mandate that it shares with the MDAS. But this very systemic consistency of the software environment appears to have led up to the reproduction of anomalous outcomes, outcomes that do not quite make it as 'feedback', outcomes that ironically actually run against other organisational motives, for example, timely revenue generation and thus, the control of AT&C losses.

It would again not be entirely accurate to describe this as a limit of modulatory control. Neither is such control developing here, as Rossiter describes, as a characteristic refusal by ERP software of 'subjective' or 'affective noise' ensuing from the domain of organisational work, by casting them as irrelevant to organisational imperatives. Regular billing of customers is in fact *extremely* relevant to the WBSEDCL's organisational motives and hardly qualifies as 'affective noise'. Herein lies the irony involved in the development of modulatory control through the implementation of SAP IS-U within the WBSEDCL's operations. The recurring of essential organisational objectives as anomalies of sorts is in fact, an *effect* of modulatory control based on 'minimal parametric variation', variation that need not admit of certain classes of contingencies as 'feedback'. Such is the form of self-circumscription enabled by the self-serving logics of ERP software, a form which strangely enough, does not necessarily broach any definite consistency with organisational imperatives over which it is set to command. It is thus not the transitional but rather the full realisation of its modulatory control that seems to provoke engineers of the WBSEDCL to chase after the older legacy system, with its phased integration over segregated silos and servers—a system that has however, been irreversibly replaced by the connected, 'real-time', 'no human touch' world of the WBSEDCL's 'captive' Data Centre and its digitalised logistics.

OF 'LOSS' AND ITS (UN)MANAGEMENT

If even urgent contingencies like actual non-billing of consumers count as anomalies in course of their encounters with the digitised control and feedback system operated through the WBSEDCL Data Centre, it will perhaps not come as much of a surprise that the organisation has not managed to control AT&C losses as much as it would have wanted to. That this system continued to be pushed by upper layers of the electrical bureaucracy is also perhaps not entirely counter-intuitive, given our preceding analysis which showed that within the digitised control established to arrest loss was also born a particular re-centralisation of administrative power within the WBSEDCL.

However, within the scope of this chapter, there is still some cause for exploring what the (un)management of losses amounts to within the WBSEDCL's digitalised operations, if only to continue unpacking the encounters between control and 'feedback'. To commence this exploration, it requires mention that over the first few years of the implementation of a Data Centre-led architecture of management, the WBSEDCL seemed to have been on track to a definite improvement. By 2011, the WBSEDCL had thus registered slim but rare (amongst Indian utilities) profit margins (Pargal and Banerjee 2014: 110). AT&C losses too had dipped between 2008 and 2011 from 33.24 per cent to 27.4 per cent, thus meeting preset annual reduction targets (PFC 2016: 69). But by 2015 there was again a visible rise in loss figures, that by September 2015 had gone up to a worrying 35.35 per cent (PFC 2017: 126). In a report discussing the performance of the WBSEDCL alongside other discoms, the central government funding agency, the Power Finance Corporation (PFC) attributed the rise in losses to the 'massive' rural electrification that took place in the state of West Bengal over the five preceding years. It further noted that this rural electrification was quite prone to technical and commercial losses as it was extended by means of low tension lines and because it suffered from lower billing efficiencies (PFC 2016: 69–70). Officials at WBSEDCL's headquarters in Kolkata broadly repeated this same rationale while explaining the rise in losses in the course of the interviews conducted for this study. But as a senior REM cell official added, these losses kept increasing also because of the relatively delimited scope of action that the organisation could resort to in matters of theft and non-payment of bills in rural areas. The official did not however express any urgent concern about arresting power theft, especially theft conducted by consumers connected with relatively smaller loads (that is, with small consumption demands). According to him, this helped maintain something of a balance between 'profit objectives' and 'socio-economic issues', a balance that was urged by current 'government policy'.

Government policy here referred to the initiative of the party, the Trinamool Congress (TMC), of supplying 'pro-poor' electricity lines at relatively decreased expenses to potential consumers since 2011, when the party came to power in West Bengal after a long era of Left rule in the state. While this erstwhile Left regime had found it difficult to distribute power to areas of low or shallow demand in semi-urban and rural locations (Kale 2014: 170–175), the TMC made it their policy to explicitly target these areas over and above pre-fixed goals of existing central government schemes of rural electrification.[19] This electrical policy of the current West Bengal state government can be understood as following from the characteristically populist politics of the TMC that allows it to claim social legitimacy against an earlier strictly political party-oriented model of clientelism practised by the Left regime (Samaddar 2015). The TMC's populist policies have been accused of foregoing economic logic for a stop-gap politics of delivering 'sops' and 'doles'; yet its remarkable electoral victories till date allow it to push through the possibility of moving beyond market mechanisms in order to allot welfare objects directly, and at times in a relatively unregulated fashion, amongst the large rural and poor population of the state of West Bengal (*The Wire* 2016). In 2012, the party also removed several existing restrictions based on farm-size and geography on the use of electricity-operated groundwater pumps for irrigating agriculture in major parts of West Bengal (Mukherji et al. 2012). Between 2011 and 2016, the number of electricity connections in the state thus nearly doubled from 8.57 million to 16.37 million, with most of these being the rural connections provided by the state-operated WBSEDCL (*Moneylife* 2016).

One particular point that was uniformly confirmed by most interlocutors of this study was that the newer metering arrangements set up by the WBSEDCL had been fairly effective in governing this new expanded landscape of electrification in the state of West Bengal. Especially with the Feeder/DTR metering arrangement devised under the AMR system, locating both the particular regional character of everyday load requirements as well as the streaks of unusually 'excess demand' over particular wire-DTR clusters was both easier and more accurate now. This has apparently made system planning and maintenance a lot more proactive. Within this narrative, the 'feedback' of loss data parsed through the MDAS enterprise and its fault monitoring arrangement was actually creating a push towards greater technological amendment to the network in tandem with expected load values. Of course, the same metering infrastructure of loss calculation also made theft/pilferage more detectable past a particular DTR. The discom, as affirmed by many, is in fact now even more certain about the location and magnitude of such 'leakages', though clearly it has to measure its responses in accordance with existing political mediation. If losses consequently multiplied within the WBSEDCL's electricity distribution network, the network seems to nonetheless be more technologically responsive and robust to handle such demands of 'populism' on its material constitution. Somehow then, losses while not being controlled, were certainly being 'factored in' within the calculative schemas by which the WBSEDCL was conducting its activities.

The critical issue that seems to stem from this evolving situation of the (un)management of losses within the WBSEDCL's digitised operations can be appropriately posed within the framework developed in this chapter, of tracing the dynamic field of encounters between forms of digitalised control, and the terrain of feedback that emerges within the WBSEDCL's scheme of operations. The question that could then be asked is whether the new kinds of data emerging from the digitised operations of the discom were proving ineffective as a kind of 'feedback' when it came to the organisational imperative of controlling losses. Could it also be the case otherwise, that eventually the parametric affordances of WBSEDCL's digitised operations admitted such 'feedback' without quite making this amenable to the objective of loss control, a possibility that we have already encountered in our discussion of the working of ERP software at the organisation? One route to approaching these possibly not-so-contradictory questions could be through highlighting the scope for further technical enhancement within the WBSEDCL's scheme of digitised operations. Here we could refer to proposals being discussed for at least ten odd years in India, for installing 'smart' meters for electricity consumers that can anticipate the probability of power theft from patterns of unusually 'excess' demand, and effect automatic disconnections when detecting this 'excess' (*The Hindu* 2013). This would presumably entail a levelling up from the current metering arrangement of the WBSEDCL to eventually install the parametric command of its data management system as the key agency of exercising sovereignty in matters of power theft and unpaid bills.

The preceding discussions in this chapter do however urge some apprehension about immediately subscribing to such promises of digitalised 'innovation'. We do not yet know if 'smart' meters will learn the vagaries of power consumption in particular localities well enough to offer a considered decision of disconnection, or whether they will offer their own disciplines of power consumption instead of curbing the potential or magnitude of theft. More significantly, such parables of 'smart' innovations seem to harbour a peculiar presupposition that in turn aids the imagination of an effective syncing between processes of digitalised control and the terrain of 'feedback'. This presupposition is that of power being finally treated as a perfectly commodifiable object within the operations of Indian discoms. Will parametric control be able to ensure this on its own? Returning to the actually existing scenario of the WBSEDCL that has been described so far, we can respond to this provocation by finally making certain concluding points that might shed light on both the politics as well as the possible political economy of setting up digitalised control systems to govern power distribution in contemporary Indian settings.

As already discussed, the calculative matrix of 'loss'-control—both on a 'technical' count as well as in terms of the measures of theft—is actually already available within the WBSEDCL's schema of digitised operations. But quite obviously, the actual control of loss yields scope in a way to other operations of power, those that exist in spite of digitalised control through channels of populist claim-making. This is not so much any natural shortcoming of the digital, since its relentless pursuit of calculative schemas has already penetrated deep into the landscape of 'loss'. Rather the seeming gap between data and action can in a way be conceptualised as following from a certain kind of layering between the digital and the non-digital, which will probably be the subject of variable negotiations in the years to come. At present this layering is well described by how the feedback of 'loss' enables particular forms of technological enhancements of the electrical network in question, while awaiting a different political logic to emerge in order to tide over problems of theft, pilferage, and commercial losses. This layering is itself forged by a particular combination of technical capacities and the peculiar pact between the status of electricity as a de-commodified endowment of sorts,[20] and the demands of electoral populism that compels the current TMC government to ratify this status. To ascribe a certain kind of sovereignty to the automatism of parametric control would involve a breaking of this pact. But as of now, it does not seem that this major alteration in the terms on conceiving electricity as a de-commodified resource of citizenship in India[21] can be independently assigned to the affordances of digitalised control. Or to put it in a different way, parametric control would have to stake its claims to sovereignty not so much by replotting existing modes of governing the already commodified object of electricity, but rather by literally bringing into being a novel arena of commodifiable power, unhinged from its existing status as an object of exchange between political power and the citizenry in contemporary India.

CONCLUSION

In conclusion, let us reassemble here the analysis concerning the dynamic interaction of control and feedback that has been the central concern of this chapter. To begin with, we have tried to show with the case of the WBSEDCL that the translation of particular contingencies as organisational imperatives through the mediation of digitalised control is very much subject to the self-referential formats and demarcations that allow digital control to realise itself primarily on its own terms. The model of digitalised control is in this sense, not all-inclusive by way of some meta-operation of code and data but quite delimited in its scope and the constitution of its relevance. This delimitation could be in the form of parametric punctuating of the encounter with feedback (as in the fault-monitoring system). It could be otherwise in the form of an ironic parametric eschewal of feedback (like in the case of ERP implementation and the problem of unbilled consumers) that confirm the self-sufficient logics of software while negating other essential organisational objectives. And finally, this delimitation could occur in spite of a penetration of the digital, as a kind of occupying of a layered existence by the forces of digitalisation (as in the case of the [un]management of 'loss') in relation to currents like those of electrical (electoral) populism.

Yet it has also been a central contention of this chapter that such forms of delimitation need not describe any vacuum of power and efficacy. The Data Centre-led operations of the WBSEDCL will perhaps continue to render 'captive' a wide range of informatic and organisational vectors of power to yield further levels of centralisation. This very likely will yield a different order of informatics and logistical concentration as the WBSEDCL is beginning to open up to third party Data Centre providers. How this will affect the attendant hierarchies of bureaucracy and the tiered encounter between 'feedback', 'loss' management, and control will be for a future study to discuss. But it could be intuited here that as forms of electrical data come to ascend the levels of a virtually stacked up system of logistical governance, they are likely to exert their own kinds of pressure over the domain over which they govern. The extent to which this pressure will create its own domain of sovereignty, however, will depend on both the parametric constitution of digitalised governance, as well as on how this constitution comes to admit contingencies from other worlds of political and economic logics. A final claim in this chapter then is that the work of Data Centres is perhaps best grasped by prising open the forms in which such admittance takes place (or not). The encounter between feedback and control is thus being proposed as a key and dynamic field of investigation that cannot be presupposed as a uniform set of causes and events. It will be essential to delve into this field if any sense is to be made of contemporary Data Centre-led digitised operations and how they are changing the world around us. It is perhaps only through such a vantage point that we can analyse the abstract power of digital governance as it works through the gap between the totalising imperatives of digital control, and the less-than-total layering of such control against a world of other logics and claim-making.

End Notes

Acknowledgements: One part of this research was conducted during the course of working on a project entitled 'Big Data for Development', organised by the Centre for Internet and Society, India, the University of Manchester, and the University of Sheffield. The rest of the study was as part of a project on 'Data Centres', organised by the Western Sydney University in which Calcutta Research Group partnered for the Indian portion of the research. I want to thank Ranabir Samaddar, Sunila Kale, Elizabeth Chatterjee, Richard Heeks, Christopher Foster, Sumandro Chattapadhyay, Priya Sangameswaran, Debarun Sarkar, and Ritajyoti Bandyopadhay for discussions on various aspects of this research.

1. It is the largest discom (electricity distribution company) in the state of West Bengal and distributes electricity to over 95 per cent of the state's geographical territory. Its main functions include buying power from generation and transmission companies and distributing it to 16.5 million customers.

2. This scheme has since been modified to recently launch the Integrated Power Development Scheme (IPDS).

3. See https://www.ipds.gov.in/Forms/Know_More.aspx (accessed May 2022).

4. AT&C losses are calculated as the difference between the power injected into a distribution grid, and the revenue collection realised in equivalent units and as a percentage term. The technical component of the loss consists of dissipation of the energy being transmitted over varying voltages in a distribution network. Some technical loss will always be there in an electricity network but can be minimised by choice of appropriate voltages and wire structures with which to transmit electricity. Commercial losses result from theft, pilferage, and billing inefficiencies mainly.

5. This account of the history of the Indian electricity sector is drawn from Kale (2014), Gupta (2015), and Dubash and Rajan (2001).

6. In this chapter, the approach of thinking of technological forms beyond 'innovation-centrism' is taken from David Edgerton's (2011) historical scholarship.

7. See WBSEDCL's tender notice issued on 21 August 2017: https://www.wbsedcl.in/irj/go/km/docs/internet/new_website/pdf/Tenders/AMR_NIT.pdf (accessed 14 May 2020).

8. See for a discussion of such issues regarding TCS, letter from WBSEBEA to Director (Dist.), WBSEDCL dated 04.07.2014. Reprinted in *Power News*, August 2014, p. 21. Available at http://www.wbsebea.org/media/filer_public/04/60/04600744-fe1c-43bd-92d5-9391317b9902/power-news-apr-sep-2014.pdf (accessed May 2022).

9. The account of the restructuring of the WBSEDCL builds upon interviews conducted, Elizabeth Chatterjee's recent study (2017) and a report by PricewaterhouseCoopers (2009). Chatterjee's study while illuminating otherwise, seems to append the technological changes following the adoption of a Data Centre-led digitised functioning to a general evolution of corporate governance. In contrast, what is emphasised here is to what extent 'technocratic' reforms were also technological reforms, and the multiple potentially conflicting issues arising out of organisational 'restructuring' effected through the adoption of a Data Centre-d architecture of information management.

10. See 'WBSEDCL Case Study 2013–2016: Implementation of Billing Services at Kolkata, West Bengal'. Available at https://drive.google.com/drive/

folders/1yaoQET952D-JC73AsVTZ9Jm4df59edvi?usp=sharing (accessed May 2022).

11. The WBSEDCL currently operates by a organisational hierarchy of the headquarters, five zonal offices, sixty-seven Divisional offices and 490 Customer Care Centres (CCCs). What was abolished in the course of restructuring was a set of sub-Divisional offices under the Divisional units (apart from the CCCs) that coordinated the main tasks of billing and meter reading, and by implication contributed to 'loss' measurement. This change comes into focus as having been rather contentious, as could be gathered from the multiple communications of the WBSEBEA to the WBSEDCL management.

12. The PwC report (understandably) but also Chatterjee's study seem to skip the very conflict-ridden character of technocratic 'restructuring', marked by a series of oppositions articulated by the WBSEBEA as well as national engineers' organisations (as elaborated here).

13. Letter from the AIPEF (All India Power Engineers Federation) to the Chief Minister, West Bengal, dated 11.10.2011 on the subject of 'Restructuring of W. B. State Electricity Distribution Company Limited'. Available at https://drive.google.com/drive/folders/1yaoQET952D-JC73AsVTZ9Jm4df59edvi (accessed May 2022).

14. Letter from the WBSEBEA to the Chairman and Managing Director, WBSEDCL, dated 17.08.2012 on the subject of 'Submission of Restructure Review Committee Report prepared by the WBSEBEA'. Available at https://drive.google.com/drive/folders/1yaoQET952D-JC73AsVTZ9Jm4df59edvi (accessed May 2022). This is also striking since the WBSEBEA has time and again also complained to the WBSEDCL authorities about the shortage of manpower emerging since the days of 'unbundling'.

15. This new ordering of territoriality via the work of variegated centralisation performed by the Data Centres perhaps, resembles what is described by Rossiter (2017: 3) following Deborah Cowen (2014) as 'the production of space beyond territory'.

16. See TCS's document 'Transformers West Bengal Electricity Case Study'. Available at https://drive.google.com/drive/folders/1yaoQET952D-JC73AsVTZ9Jm4df59edvi?usp=sharing (accessed May 2022).

17. See footnote 60 in Rossiter (2016: 50): 'Since logistics software operates as a closed environment that *does not* accommodate feedback as a correctional process through the modification of form, it is not properly a cybernetic system' (emphasis mine). Further, '...the overall level of entropy, or disorder, tends to probabilistically increase in any closed system...It is in this respect that one wonders how logistics does not break down into frequent chaos.'

18. See for instance, 'Minutes of the 3rd CEC Meeting of WBSEBEA for the year 2016–2017 held on 25.06.2016'. Reprinted in *Power News*, July 2016, p. 10.

Available at http://wbsebea.org/media/filer_public/3f/51/3f51156b-6ab4-4513-8a29-b18f9a06902a/power-news-apr-oct-2016.pdf (accessed May 2022).

19. Also see https://powermin.gov.in/sites/default/files/uploads/joint_initiative_of_govt_of_india_and_West_Bengol.pdf (accessed May 2022).

20. On the historically recurring process of de-commodifying electricity in India, see Chatterjee (2020).

21. On the relationship of citizenship and electricity consumption in India, see Gupta (2015) and Cross (2019).

References

Amoore, L. 2016. 'Cloud Geographies: Computing, Data, Sovereignty'. *Progress in Human Geography* 42(1): 4–24.

Bain & Company. 2017. 'Global In-house Centers in India', 20 April. Available at https://www.bain.com/insights/global-in-house-centers-in-india (accessed May 2022).

Bratton, B. 2016. *The Stack: On Software and Sovereignty*. Cambridge, MA: MIT Press.

Chattapadhyay, S. 2013. 'Of identity, platform, and "new" information infrastructure of governance: Situating the Aadhaar project within the history of electronic governance in India'. Paper presented on 14–16 November at 'The Social and Cultural Life of Information' Conference, Sarai-CSDS (Centre for the Study of Developing Societies), New Delhi, India.

Chatterjee, E. 2017. 'Insulated Wires: The Precarious Rise of West Bengal's Power Sector'. Working Paper, Mapping Power Project, Centre for Policy Research, New Delhi and Regulatory Assistance Project.

———. 2018. 'The Politics of Electricity Reform: Evidence from West Bengal, India'. *World Development* 104: 128–139.

———. 2020. 'The Asian Anthropocene: Electricity and Fossil Developmentalism'. *The Journal of Asian Studies*, 79(1): 3–24.

Cowen, D. 2014. *The Deadly Life of Logistics: Mapping Violence in Global Trade*. Minneapolis: University of Minnesota Press.

Cross, J. 2019. 'No Current: Electricity and Disconnection in Rural India'. In *Electrifying Anthropology: Exploring Electrical Practices and Infrastructures*, S. Abram, B. R. Winthereik and T. Yarrow (eds), 65–82. London: Bloomsbury.

Customer 1st Communications. 2017. 'Data Centre Tiers Explained'. Available at https://www.c1c.net/blog/data-center-tiers-explained/ (accessed May 2022).

Deleuze, G. 1992. 'Postscript on the Societies of Control'. *October* 59: 3–7.

Dey, I., R. Samaddar, and S. K. Sen. 2016. *Beyond Kolkata: Rajarhat and the Dystopia of Urban Imagination*. New Delhi: Routledge India.

Dubash, N. K. and S. C. Rajan. 2001. 'Power Politics: Process of Power Sector Reform in India'. *Economic and Political Weekly* 36(35): 3367–3390.

Dutta, K. 2013. 'Issues in Implementation of SAP in WBSEDCL Business Domain'. *Power News*, [West Bengal State Electricity Board Engineers' Association (WBSEBEA)] April–October: 3–7. Available at http://wbsebea.org/media/filer_public/3b/e4/3be43174-d983-4d26-b3f7-a229a719494f/power-news-apr-oct-2013.pdf (accessed May 2022).

Easterling, K. 2014. *Extrastatecraft: The Power of Infrastructure Space*. London and New York: Verso.

Edgerton, D. 2011. *Shock of the Old: Technology and Global History since 1900*. London: Profile Books.

Everest Group. 2012. 'Why We Are Changing to "Global In-house Center" (GIC) over "Captive" | Sherpas in Blue Shirts', 6 September. Available at https://www.everestgrp.com/2012-09-why-we-are-changing-to-global-in-house-center-over-captive-sherpas-in-blue-shirts-10098.html/ (accessed May 2022).

Frost & Sullivan (F&S). 2017. 'Not All Data Centres Are Equal—Understanding the Global Best Practices of Data Centres that Power the Cloud'. A Whitepaper by Frost and Sullivan for Macquarie Telecom. Available at https://silo.tips/download/not-all-data-centres-are-equal-understanding-the-global-best-practices-of-data-c (accessed May 2022).

Gupta, A. 2015. 'An Anthropology of Electricity from the Global South'. *Cultural Anthropology* 30(4): 555–568.

Hogan, M. 2015. 'Data Flows and Water Woes: The Utah Data Center'. *Big Data & Society* 2(2): 1–12.

IAMAI (Internet and Mobile Association of India). 2016. 'Make in India: Conducive Policy & Regulatory Environment to Incentivize Data Center Infrastructure', May. PLR Chambers. Available at https://www.medianama.com/wp-content/uploads/iamai-make-in-india-data-centerreport-india.pdf (accessed May 2022).

Johnson, A. and M. Hogan. 2017. 'Introducing Location and Dislocation: Global Geographies of Digital Data'. *Imaginations: Journal of Cross-Cultural Image Studies* 8(2): 3–6.

Kale, S. S. 2014. *Electrifying India: Regional Political Economies of Development*. Stanford: Stanford University Press.

Larkin, B. 2013. 'The Politics and Poetics of Infrastructure'. *Annual Review of Anthropology* 42: 327–343.

Maguire, J. and B. Ross Winthereik. 2021. 'Digitalizing the State: Data Centres and the Power of Exchange'. *Ethnos* 86(3): 530–551.

Mattern, S. 2016. 'Cloud and Field'. *Places Journal* August. Available at https://placesjournal.org/article/cloud-and-field/ (accessed May 2022).

Ministry of Electronics and Information Technology (MeitY). n.d.-a. 'National e-Governance Plan'. GoI. Available at https://www.meity.gov. in/divisions/national-e-governance-plan (accessed May 2022).

———. n.d.-b. 'State Data Centre'. GoI. Available at https://www.meity.gov. in/content/state-data-centre (accessed May 2022).

Moneylife. 2016. 'West Bengal power sector illustrates the difficulties of power reform', 09 June. Available at https://www.moneylife.in/ article/west-bengal-power-sector-illustrates-the-difficulties-of-power-reform/47171.html (accessed May 2022).

Mukherji, A., T. Shah, and P. Banerjee. 2012. 'Kick-starting a Second Green Revolution in Bengal'. *Economic and Political Weekly* 47(18): 27–30.

Neilson, B. and T. Notley. 2019. 'Data Centres as Logistical Facilities: Singapore and the Emergence of Production Topologies'. *Work Organisation, Labour & Globalisation* 13(1): 15–29.

Neilson B. and N. Rossiter. 2021. 'Automating Labour and the Spatial Politics of Data Centre Technologies'. In *Topologies of Digital Work*, M. Will-Zocholl and C. Roth-Ebner (eds), Dynamics of Virtual Work, 77–101. Cham: Palgrave Macmillan.

Pargal, S. and S. Ghosh Banerjee. 2014. *More Power to India: The Challenge of Electricity Distribution*. Washington DC: World Bank

Power Finance Corporation Ltd. (PFC). 2016. *Report on Operational Study of Ten Selected DISCOMS where AT&C Losses have Reduced in the Last Five Years*, March, New Delhi. Available at https://drive.google. com/drive/folders/1yaoQET952D-JC73AsVTZ9Jm4df59edvi?usp=sha ring (accessed May 2022).

———. 2017. *Report on the Performance of State Power Utilities for the Years 2013–14 to 2015–16*. Available at https://pfcindia.com/Document Repository/ckfinder/files/Operations/Performance_Reports_of_State_ Power_Utilities/1_Report%20on%20the%20Performance%20of%20 State%20Power%20Utilities%202013-14%20to%202015-16.pdf (accessed May 2022).

PricewaterhouseCoopers (PwC). 2009. *West Bengal Power Sector Reforms: Lessons Learnt and Unfinished Agenda*, Report 68330. PricewaterhouseCoopers and WB-AusAID. Available at https:// openknowledge.worldbank.org/handle/10986/12375 (accessed May 2022).

Ramanathan, U. 2011. 'The Myth of Technology Fix'. *India-Seminar* 617.

Rossiter, N. 2016. *Software, Infrastructure, Labor: A Media Theory of Logistical Nightmares*. New York and Oxon: Routledge.

———. 2017. 'Imperial Infrastructure and Asia beyond Asia: Data Centres, State Formation and Territoriality of Logistical Media'. *The Fibreculture Journal* 29: 1–20.

Samaddar, R. 2015. 'Why High Politics in Bengal Speaks the Language of the Lower Depths?' *The Wire*, 8 July. Available at https://thewire.in/politics/why-high-politics-in-bengal-speaks-the-language-of-the-lower-depths (accessed May 2022).

———. 2018. *Karl Marx and the Postcolonial Age*. Cham: Palgrave Macmillan.

Sengupta, U. 2013. 'Inclusive Development? A State-Led Land Development Model in New Town, Kolkata'. *Environment and Planning C: Government and Policy* 31(2): 357–376.

The Hindu. 2013. 'The "smart meter" solution to the problem of power theft', 01 October. Available at https://www.thehindu.com/news/national/karnataka/the-smart-meter-solution-to-the-problem-of-power-theft/article5186952.ece (accessed May 2022).

The Wire. 2016. 'Populist Governments With Strong Leaders Like Mamata Are Here to Stay', 19 May. Available at https://thewire.in/politics/populist-govts-with-strong-leaders-like-mamata-are-here-to-stay-says-political-scientist-ranabir-samaddar (accessed May 2022).

Tongia, R. 2003. 'The Political Economy of Indian Power Sector Reforms'. Working Paper No. 4, Centre for Environmental Science and Policy, Stanford University.

Zehle, S. and N. Rossiter. 2016. 'Mediations of Labor: Algorithmic Architectures, Logistical Media, and the Rise of Black Box Politics'. In *The Routledge Companion to Labor and Media*, R. Maxwell (ed.), 40–50. New York and London: Routledge.

IV

Transforming Urban Form and Emergent Extrastatecraft

Data Centres in Navi Mumbai

MANISH K JHA AND RISHI JHA

Cities provide space and scope for economic development, human reproduction, and social interaction in dynamic and diverse ways. As the site of capitalist production and extension, modern cities exhibit deployment of technologies and management of the network of technologies in their fold. Modern cities are considered as the growth engines of global capitalism, the expansion of which unfolds as the 'global urban strategy' (Smith 2002). The emergence of specialised, privatised, and customised reordering of urban infrastructure depicts the interplay of population, territory, and technology, and its implications for the city and society (Graham and Marvin 2001).

At macro levels, the world is seen in forms of planetary urban agglomeration of cities weaved into a universal fabric towards city-centered growth (Scott and Storper 2014). Most of the non-Western cities in the world adapt to the forces and processes of agglomeration through a vast array of global and local strategies that Roy and Ong (2011) call 'worlding'. However, a postcolonial critique of this eurocentric theorisation emanates multi-fold contradictions—inherent and emergent—that lie within the urbanisation processes, and transformative relations amongst state, capital, land, and labour in the global South. The urban turn in the postcolonial cities has retained their paradoxical physiognomies. The bourgeois imagination of an infrastructure-rich, middle class- and elite-centric, and service sector-based global city is juxtaposed with its immanent other—the burgeoning cartographies of informal and illegal spaces, population flux, informal economy, and the bio-political governance of population (Sanyal 2007). The contemporary postcolonial capitalism and emergent urban form(s) are predominantly grounded in a complex combination of the primitive and the virtual forms of accumulation. The political economy places a focus on land and resources in the expansion of capitalism, a reconfiguration of the spaces of capital through the creation of specialised zones and corridors, emergent salient labour forms and regimes, and the persisting significance of the state as a facilitator of the conditions of accumulation and circulation (Samaddar 2018a: 77–78). In this context, these postcolonial cities, while delving into the future and contesting with the present circumstances, do not entirely merge in the global urban and remain as the 'subjects of transnational or international urban system' (Samaddar 2018b: 21).

This brings us to the moot question—what is this 'urban turn' and the 'urban form' that is being created? Since the 1950s, the satellite township model or peripheral expansion model appeared as the state's blueprint to deal with contradictions inherent in urbanisation, to emanate urban forms, economy, and governance, and to adapt to the global financial networks. On the one hand, it facilitated decongestion of the urban-core, inhibited inner-city sprawl of metropolitan population, and created provisions for infrastructure and amenities. On the other hand, it also facilitated the spatial and institutional expansion of urban production and circulation centres. Following the trends of Japan, Hong Kong, South Korea and China in South Asia, the Indian state also introduced several satellite townships around its major metropolitan centres. It established six town rings around the National Capital Territory—New Delhi, four around its silicon city—Hyderabad, three around its biggest southern city—Chennai, two around the eastern metropolitan—Kolkata and one in conjunction with its financial capital—Mumbai (See, Dick and Rimmer 1998; Shaw 2004).

The chapter locates the genealogical transformations of Navi Mumbai as the case-in-point to explore three basic dimensions of this urban turn. First, how did Navi Mumbai evolve and transmute into the spatial, economic, demographic form of a data processing and data infrastructure hub since its inception as the world's biggest planned 'people-centric' city? Second, and alternatively, in what ways do the policies, politics, and processes of the making of Navi Mumbai reflect a postcolonial pathway of modern city-making? And third, in what ways does the city facilitate the advanced forms of IT infrastructures like Data Centres (DCs) leading to the emergence of a security-economic-administrative complex? In broader contexts, these explorations cumulatively respond to the postcolonial state's ambiguous relationship with the global capital circuits—the differential function of the capital, the emergent urban form, the biopolitics of the emergent subject, and the emergent extrastatecraft (Samaddar 2018a).

The transforming nature of the postcolonial state and its interplay with capital, urban formations, and rapid urban reordering, and evolving forms of government remain central to this exploration. The chapter critically engages with *Extrastatecraft: The Power of Infrastructure Space* (Easterling 2014) in postcolonial urban contexts and draws insights from spatial, state, and institutional ethnographies through fieldwork engagements with Navi Mumbai and Data Centres. In this exploration, we engage with collection and analysis of data from crucial sources like archival records, government documents, published and unpublished reports and board resolutions from various government departments responsible for urban development. Further, an ethnographic exploration of the biggest Data Centre located in Navi Mumbai traces its specific operation, management, and government vis-à-vis the urban form. An intensive exploration of institutional texts, emergent material ramifications of the developmental policies and practices, and ethnographic field research are presented in the chapter. The following section brings out an inherent contradiction within urban planning, and explains the interplay of land, capital, and urban form through the phases of urban transformation. Subsequent sections engage with the present city-zone as a neoliberal 'city-state', and explore the enhanced capacity of the urban form through its digital infrastructures' assemblage. Finally, it explores new labour regime, biopolitics, and subjectivity of the modern subject in the Data Centre; and analyses the emergent 'extrastatecraft' through the triad of data infrastructures, business districts, and the urban form.

EVOLUTION OF NAVI MUMBAI: INHERENT PLANNING CONTRADICTIONS

The postcolonial urban planning inherits a particular logic of development of capital in the form of inputs of 'public interest' by 'public institutions' for 'public processes', and through 'public finance'. Pioneers in this process, Post-World War Development Committee and Modak-Mayer's 'The Master Plan in Outline' (1948) acknowledged mainland development across Mumbai. However, due to insufficient institutional and funding support, significant growth of suburbs could not be materialised. Second to it, the introduction of the Town Planning Act (1954) instrumentalised the development plan and commissioning of the Modak-Mayer report, and brought focus on zoning-based land, which created complications. Following the recommendations, new industrial units were prevented in Mumbai's inner city, and the policy of controlled industrial growth was introduced. Besides, the creation of industrial estates in and around the business district was recommended, and a North–South corridor for infrastructure and transport projects was designed. The spatial limitation of being an archipelago city restricted the city's expansion effects (MCGB 1964).

Conscious of the intense complexities, the Bombay Metropolitan Regional Planning Board proposed four alternatives for Bombay's revival. First, an internal restructuration of the megacity with new commercial and financial centres at Bandra-Kurla Complex; second, multi-town peripheral expansion; third, development of urban corridors emanating from the city centres; and, fourth, development of a twin city of Bombay with similar 'scale' and 'strength' (BMRPD 1970). This futuristic urban form (of Navi Mumbai) also required to reorient Bombay's growth by inducing and relocating the sophisticated tertiary sector away from Bombay's southern tip (ibid.: 104). In doing so, the 'entrepreneurial state' (Mazzucato 2013) machinery shifted its attention from the pressing challenges of the existing financial capital. It attested to the need for its twin city, Navi Mumbai, 'against its earlier piecemeal and internal reconstruction models' (MARG 1965: 30). The spatial limitation and institutional bottlenecks made it difficult to achieve significant transformations from the first three approaches, and an 'extravagant evasion of problems' (Harris 1978: 60) came to being in the form of a new city.

The imagination of Navi Mumbai gave birth to the City and Industrial Development Corporation of Maharashtra (CIDCO), globally renowned for its present tagline—'We Make Cities', as a public limited company under the Indian Companies Act (1956), which later became the New Town Development Authority in the year 1971. The introduced 'New Bombay: Draft Development Plan 1973' (CIDCO 1973) emphasised upon 'common-man centric' and 'amenity-oriented' thrust over a 'high-end city'. Its spatial architecture would generate an inter-connected and self-sustainable 'metropolitan matrix' (Shaw 1999; 2004) of sixteen townships, making it economically comparable to the 'order' and 'character' of Bombay[1](Correa and Patel 1965).

The 'Draft Development Plan' (CIDCO 1973: Foreword) highlighted planners' resistance against the temptation of a city with an architectural grandeur or being elite-centric instead of promoting public good: 'New Bombay, then, will not be another grand city; it will be a city where the common man would like to live'. Paradoxically, the same plan also envisioned New Bombay as a centre of tertiary employment comprising mainly white-collar jobs with limited attention to secondary sector jobs. The first development plan categorised the city as a 'single major urban centre' of 'equal prestige and importance' as of Bombay which would 'provide the equilibrium necessary between the old and the new developments' (MARG 1965: 36) in the region. Following the luxurious spatial expansion, it could also house the expanding sophisticated tertiary sector away from the overcrowded Bombay's southern tip (Correa and Patel 1965). These plans also emphasised on certain 'tacit' inter-institutional agreements amongst the various government departments for the relocation of their offices in the new urban centre as a measure to stabilise Mumbai's business district.

The logic of developmental planning incorporated the futuristic needs of the new urban form as it simultaneously planned for decongestion of the core, dispersal of population, and resettlement of heavy industries. One of the eminent contributors of MARG and CIDCO stressed that

> New Bombay promises sufficient excitement to attract the best talent of India and perhaps some from the rest of the world. Since we start with a clean slate, it promises the opportunity to try the totally new urban system, designed to meet the urban activities of the new century (Patel 1970: 1018).

The systemic contradictions amongst the articulated tertiary sector functions, futuristic urban trajectories, and creation of a people-centric urban form were further deepened. The contradictions made Harris (1978: 57) observe:

> One is left with the impression that the central purpose is solely to create an attractive built environment: that the plan is a program for improved consumption, improved welfare for those fortunate enough to live...The danger is that scarce resource will be used to create a high-income suburb, zoned physically to be a separate area of Bombay, an escape for higher income groups who wish to aspire to higher standards of public amenity.

In the subsequent planning process, meticulous institutional efforts were made to earmark precise spaces and link them to specific identities, functions, and properties. Therefore, the spaces become legible for explicit people and purposes at given places and times. Idealist representation of space was forwarded to pin down inseparable connections amongst prominent places, people, actions, and things to normalise the transforming land use in Mumbai and Navi Mumbai. The new bureaucratic spatial paradigm was envisioned with magnificent imagination:

> Imagine that the Mantralaya were to shift lock, stock and barrel in New Bombay. So also, the Legislative Assembly. Each MLA might than have a bungalow in New Bombay instead of a room in a hostel. Our senior civil servants would live in houses with gardens, like their New Delhi colleagues, rather than stuffy little flats (Dwivedi and Mehrotra 1995: Foreword; also see Patel 1993).

Further, financialisation of the old bureaucratic spaces in Mumbai was imagined as:

> The floor space vacated by the government would happily [be] snapped up by the financial institutions...the floor of assembly might become the trading floor of the National Stock Exchange...there are innumerable government offices in south Bombay which could just as effectively function from New Bombay (Dwivedi and Mehrotra 1995: Foreword).

The planning process of the city reflects the postcolonial state's ambiguities regarding a modern utopian urban that is reflected in the socio-spatial complexities of the region, uncertainties in the planning process, formulation of contradictory institutional narratives, and incomplete implementation. The conception of the self-contained urban form insulated from the 'disorder and chaos' (Datta 2015: 6) of Mumbai and coupled with an imagination of a people-centric city equipped the local government to undertake the project for its socio-economic requirements in the future. These contradictions influenced the city-state to formulate the rhetoric of people-centric and pro-middle class narratives to appease bureaucrats, professionals, and civil society alike. This propelled the state-led urban expansion project, but also made the process less disruptive and inevitable socio-spatial transformations acceptable across its stakeholders (Bapat 1990; Sheth 1992).

Policy documents unfold ambiguous planning intentions and imperatives; however, an intensive engagement and a detailed analysis establish how the postcolonial state has promoted the city as an 'extrastate urban-space' (Easterling 2014: 11, 65–81). These spaces remained largely insulated from the inefficient state bureaucracy, instrumentalised as an isomorphic exurban enclave within the upgraded urban setting through exceptional legal, administrative, and governance interventions. The next three sections of this chapter explain a classic case of establishment and sequential transformations within this extrastate urban space, like 'zone urbanism' (Ong 2006), through the unfolding phases of fragmentary policy implementation, development of the present-form city-zone, and amplified capacity of the city-zone through data infrastructures. The state's planning dispositifs anchored rapid 'mutation' in its urban form through policy priorities and interventional mechanisms. The phased transformations establish Navi Mumbai as the 'double' of Mumbai which subsequently 'hijacked the place and power of its counterpart' (Easterling 2014: 125) and strengthened Mumbai's territory, significance, and power in the world in general and in the global South in particular.

Fragmentary Implementation: Interplay of Land and Capital in the Urban Form

Navi Mumbai's contemporary form that facilitates advanced IT infrastructures is a succession from its secondary sector growth (1970–1980), logistical development (1990s), and service sector boom (2000s) (Also see Shaw 1999, 2004; Vedula 2007). The principal economic drivers in the first phase of development in Navi Mumbai were three-fold: the establishment of an industrial corridor in the Trans Thane Creek (TTC), which stretches for 16 kms along the east of the Thane-Belapur Road; the initiation of development of central business districts (CBDs) in Vashi and Belapur; and proliferation of heavy industries in the TTC Industrial Area. Large petrochemical and pharmaceutical industries along with associated industries (especially Naphtha-based), which were connected with the refineries located in the north eastern part of Mumbai through pipelines burgeoned in the region. The impetus for investment in these industries came from the overgrown character of Bombay region (Bhattacharya 1971). The designated economic zone in the city provided vast land, water reservoirs, safe environment, and spatial proximity to Bombay. Availability of unconstrained and cost-effective resources expanded the manufacturing sector in the TTC, and as a multiplier effect, small and medium industries also flourished in mutual dependences and generated skilled and unskilled employment (CIDCO 1984).

The TTC demonstrates a concentration of capital- and resource-intensive industries, intensive capital, infrastructure inputs, and high capital gains but comparatively lower employment outcomes (Shaw 2004). The investment-employment mismatch existed in the developing zone since its establishment as it contributed over 5 per cent of the total output of the state but offered only less than 2 per cent of its employment (Bhattacharya 1971: 7). The scales of 'inter-industry transactions', measured in terms of demand for inputs from other industries within the region, and 'forward and backward linkages', estimated in terms of utilisation of raw materials and products, reflected aspects of unsustainability and intra-regional imbalance. While the manufacturing sector industries located in Navi Mumbai depended on petrochemicals, the forward-backward linkages within other sectors did not appear to be strong, giving way to poor intra-regional feeding, and fewer opportunities for expansion of down-stream (dependent) industries.

Resultantly, during the 1970s, despite the expansion of the downstream industries, the total consumption of petrochemical industries within the TTC was hardly a third of their total output. However, overlooking the emerging industrial unsustainability, the report, 'A Study of Industries in Trans-Thane Belt' (Bhattacharya 1971), emphasised the need for sizeable industrial investment on one hand, and essential public and social infrastructures for approximately half of its workforce that stayed in the region, on the other hand. Beyond financial investment, logistical development in forms of better connectivity with Mumbai, Mumbai Metropolitan Region (MMR), and other parts of India was emphasised, loosening the previously imagined self-contained nature of the new urban form.

The phase of 'vibrant development' (1980–1990) unveiled CIDCO's expansion plan and intensive industrial and infrastructure development in seven of its fourteen nodes.[2] Commercial complexes over the prominent railway stations, Vashi and Belapur, located on the trans-harbour railway, opened up new revenue generation schemes for CIDCO. An analysis of 'A report on the survey of industries in New Bombay' (CIDCO 1990, 1984) spells out its mutating characteristics in two ways. Firstly, industrial units proliferated multi-fold, from 44 in 1970–1971 to 533 in 1984 and over 1374 in 1990, and capital and resource investment per capita employment produced also increased over twice, from Rs 1.10 lakhs in the 1970s to Rs 2.42 lakhs in the 1980s. This locates the growth industries with high capital investment for employment generation. And second, the industrial zone located poor inter-industry feeding as over 98 per cent of its inputs materials were procured from outside Mumbai. In fact, CIDCO could not promote tertiary sector establishments in this phase (CIDCO 2010: 32).

As a compensatory logic and with an intensive logistical focus, wholesale and retail trade were relocated in the region, especially in Vashi. Strengthening the territorial robustness of Mumbai, areas like Kalamboli, strategic for their location and connectivity across the Mumbai–Pune Highway and the Mumbai Metropolitan Region (MMR) were converted into wholesale market for iron and steel. The commissioning of Jawaharlal Nehru Port Trust (JNPT) in 1989 along with port-based industrial zones strengthened the logistics infrastructure and the emergent economy in the region. Following the economic transformations, the workforce, work-related commutation, and housing provisioning requirements witnessed significant changes. Commutation for work from Mumbai, Thane, and urban villages increased from over 40 per cent in 1971 to over 60 per cent in 1984. To deal with the pressing housing needs of over 200,000 inhabitants in the city, CIDCO, which controlled the housing market, constructed over 77 per cent of the total housing stocks (CIDCO 1984, 1988, 2010). However, amongst the total developed housing stocks, housing developed for the high-income group and the medium-income group became predominant with 54 per cent and 35 per cent, respectively, which left minuscule space for low-income groups.

Moreover, the post-liberalisation decade (1990–2000) exhibits the most significant transformation towards the contemporary urban form. The capital- and resource- intensive and labour non-intensive heavy chemical and engineering industrial units that had dominated the industrial corridors (until 1990) registered an unprecedented decline. Being increasingly capital-intensive, the gross value per employment had increased over twice, from Rs 170,000 in 1984 to Rs 370,000 in 1990. However, employment generation did not register any significant change, as it increased from Rs 34,000 in 1984 to Rs 40,648 in 1990 (CIDCO 1990). Also, over 700 industrial units were closed and the average employment per industry dropped approximately by half from 108 workers in 1984 to 58.5 workers during this phase. Meanwhile, JNPT expanded and emerged as India's largest port, handling more than 60 per cent of the total cargo of Indian ports. With CIDCO's focus on modernisation of facilities and infrastructure, the service sector expanded, and trading, transportation, communication, and business services supplemented the growing service industries. During this phase, service and maintenance contributed a massive 54.7 per cent of the total industrial and commercial set-ups that accounted for 22.8 per cent of the total employment. It managed to produce an additional employment of 74,731 workers in a total of 245,000 in Navi Bombay (CIDCO 2006). Increasing service sector employment, higher wages, and the dominance of the private sector in real estate and housing sector impacted the socio-spatial dimensions of the city. Daily commuters from adjoining areas reduced and the city's population stabilised as over half of the industrial employees stayed in CIDCO-developed colonies. By 2000, the city's overall population reached 1.10 million, however, CIDCO's share in housing construction dipped from the last decades. CIDCO could only contribute 44 per cent of the total construction now (ibid.), and for the first time, the private construction sector surpassed the state facilitated housing. These phased transformations situate the momentum for the city's contemporary urban form.

Today's Navi Mumbai as a City-Zone

Geographically, the city-zone is spread over 344 sq. km. land area with lavish 45 per cent green zones and accommodates fourteen well-planned commercial and residential nodes. Navi Mumbai has comparative advantage upon Mumbai on environmental and security parameters. Unlike Mumbai which remains prone to perennial waterlogging and flooding, Navi Mumbai has storm-water management and flood risk control mechanisms through catchment areas, alternative traditional solutions like Ughadi, detention ponds, holding ponds, and modern drainage systems like two-tier drains and central overflowing channel. Even though the site is located in the vicinity of Mumbai, it is seismologically safer and also fortified through military and naval bases.

Navi Mumbai is proximate to the most modern seaport of India—JNPT, and one of the most prominent upcoming international airports of India—Navi Mumbai International Airport. A transport infrastructure that constitutes of 650 kms of the highway network, and rapid-networked road, rail, and water transport corridors assure the logistical robustness of the city. Its redundant water resource infrastructure ensures uninterrupted supply to the city's industrial and residential requirements. It has the capacity for amplified future needs.[3] Advanced electricity infrastructure and continuous supply, a product of the institutional collaboration between CIDCO and Maharashtra State Electricity Distribution Company is on one side, whereas robust infrastructure and supply from dual power sources, such as hydropower and fossil power, and technical innovations like Supervisory Control and Data Acquisition, are on the other.

The city-zone, predominated by digital infrastructures, is a result of shifts in its industrial zones and spatial transformations: large-scale chemical and pharmaceutical industries, established in its early phase, gradually became irrelevant and closed down (CIDCO 1998, 2010). Several institutional attempts to relocate the government departments into the CBD also failed as the tacit agreement between the government departments and CIDCO could not be materialised.[4] The CIDCO had relied on these institutional measures to stabilise its emerging urban form, the failure of which also ceased the coupling effect of private capital investment that is expected with synergistic growth of government institutions, mainly in the housing sector and infrastructure development. Nevertheless, CIDCO followed the new economic regime to liberalise its taxation and governance further, and banked on the upcoming tertiary sector industries to put to use its unoccupied space and unutilised infrastructure (CIDCO 1998).

To incentivise the tertiary sector, neoliberal measures of revamped land use, subsidised taxes, sector-specific concession, and liberalised governance were introduced. Restrictive land use through zoning techniques was reworked, and IT and ITES (Information Technology Enabled Services) were allowed to open in any zone. Permissible floor surface index—a measure of maximum development on land—that too without any premium or extra tax was introduced for IT and ITES industries. Additional incentives like liberated land use in terms of up to more than half of the land use for Integrated IT Townships (IITT), including DCs, concessional property tax regime comparable to residential units and mixed land use were allowed. Moreover, exemptions from VAT, stamp duty, e-duty, tariff subsidy, escort tax, local body tax, Octroi tax, entry tax and other cess and taxes were provided, and up to 100 per cent incentives on fixed capital investment were provided to the growing IT-based industries and mega and ultra-mega IT projects.[5]

By way of further impetus, sector-specific concession including dedicated infrastructures like approach roads of 15 m. to the industrial units, premium locations free from any encumbrances, and any form of contagious elements were ensured. Enrolment of several policies like Telecom policy, Software and Technology Park policy, and related institutional incentives by the central government and their adoption by the state government propelled high-skill service sector industries in the region. The state government also established a single window clearance policy to combat technical and administrative hassles in licensing, approvals, consents, and establishments. The upcoming sophisticated IT, ITES, and IITT industries were allowed to operate round the clock with relaxed or decentralised labour and governance regulations.

The IT-based spatial transformations are the *raison d'être* of the new urban form. The subsequent establishment of IT parks at Vashi,

Reliance Knowledge City in Kopar Khairane, IT zone, and Bio-Tech Park in Mahape boosted the new economic regime. Simultaneously, five million sq. m. of TTC, which was earlier designated for the manufacturing industries, has been released for IT-ITES industries. Public-private partnership unfurled as a new model of investment in its making. As an innovative model, CIDCO partnered with one of the biggest international players in IT industries—the Reliance group to establish an industrial city with an expansion in 22 sq. km. To venture into new routes of capital investments and to unleash the underlying potential of the zone, the city-state has opened an exclusive duty-free enclave of 16 sq. km. in the hitherto unexplored nodes of Dronagiri, Ulwe, and Kalamboli—which is called the Navi Mumbai Special Economic Zone (SEZ). These nodes are proximally located and strongly networked with the CBD, the upcoming international airport, transport corridors, and the expanding port. This special economic zone is planned to be developed with substantive state spending towards infrastructure development with planned interventions from the corporates. These strategic developmental paradigms supplement the robustness of the futuristic urban form.

Beyond the concentration of IT industries, Navi Mumbai's CBD, which expands to 5.75 million sq. m., is twenty times larger than Mumbai's CBD-Nariman Point. Its commercial infrastructure is spread over 55,000 sq. m. at the International Infotech Park in Vashi, 92,000 sq. m. of International Technology Centre in CBD Belapur, and 1.4 million sq. m. of SEZs in Ulwe (CIDCO 2014). Cumulatively, these aim to offer over 825,000 high-skilled service sector jobs in the near future. Following the trends, jobs created in the service sector during 2000–2010 have outnumbered the other sectors. Also, while the city exhibited a slow-down in job creation in the last three decades (CIDCO 2009), IT-based industries are now celebrated as the most prominent driver for creating incremental jobs for its highly skilled demographic dividend (CIDCO 2014; MEDC 2013). These developments speak for the city-zone, which is well equipped for the futuristic needs of the dominant IT-based service sector.

The CIDCO had invested Rs 109.8 billion in infrastructure development until 2008–2009, and as a signifier of the state-led development, it had also successfully 'crowd[ed] in' substantial private sector investment over the last four decades (CIDCO 2012, 2009; MEDC 2013: 40). Since the beginning of the 1990s, the multiplier effect of private capital investment in the service sector transformed it into a zone with high Net Domestic Product. The CIDCO, as a para-state administrative agency, with corporate model governance through designated departments offers a bureaucracy-free territory, and caters to decentralised planning and management functions and administers Navi Mumbai as a 'city-state' (Easterling 2014). Following the new economic policy of 1991, the Government of India pushed for a decentralised governance model for its cities through the 74th constitutional amendment. Leaping forward, Navi Mumbai Municipal Corporation (NMMC) was established in 1992 which now administers the civic management, while CIDCO continues to administer urban planning, financial management, infrastructure development, tax collection, and overall governance. In this way, institutional engineering, and devolutions of operational and administrative functions in Navi Mumbai demarcate an 'extreme case of key economic operation' (Sassen 2014: 9) of the city-state.

These economic transformations steered rapid spatial, economic, and social transformation in the city. A recent socio-economic study highlights 'high visibility of existing and proposed projects; its new class of urban elites; young professional population; prominent educational institutions and commercial establishments...' (MEDC 2013: 41). While the city's population almost doubled during 2005–2010, CIDCO's skewed attention and deregulation towards the creation of housing stocks gradually transformed the use value of the privatised space. CIDCO, which earlier claimed its authority over the housing sector, systematically withdrew and as a result, the private real-estate builders hegemonised the sector (CIDCO 2009, 2012). However, as a revenue generation model, CIDCO introduced procurement, development, and sale of developed land to the private builders, which further distorted the housing market. A withdrawal by the CIDCO led to shrinkage of affordable housing stocks for the low-income group but an extensive development of premium flats for the growing middle class and the elites.

The socio-economic profile of households in planned nodes in Navi Mumbai (CIDCO 2010) establishes an unspoken relationship between its economic landscape and the socio-economic profile of its inhabitants. Based on a robust sample size of over 15,000 households from across the developed nodes, it mentions that the inhabitants owned more than 80 per cent of the sample flats. Further, middle-income group housing has swelled to a whopping 70.7 per cent, high-income group housing has also dramatically increased to 14 per cent. However, low-income group housing shrunk to the record low of 16.5 per cent of the total housing stocks. These figures indicate that not only the average built-up area of houses, but also the affordability of expensive housing has increased. But in the city also inhabits an abysmally low proportion of low-income groups. Cumulatively, it is explicit that Navi Mumbai has moved towards a relatively stabilised high-earning population with an amplified requirement, affordability, and utility of the privatised urban space.

The state's role in influencing urban form shifted from state-controlled monopoly to a public-private partnership to private sector-led development. The state's work is now shared and even outsourced in private interests or pursued through the pervasive logics of public-private partnership (Neilson and Mezzadra 2014). The institutional outsourcing lately transformed the 'public' dimensions of public 'interests', 'institutions,' and 'processes' that had emerged in its primordial stages. The stronger regulatory state from the decades of manufacturing-sector dominance has mutated into an enabler 'economic actor' of service sector phase through its particular relations with the specific fractions of capital (ibid.). Central to this is the emergent dimensions of the new spatial and state form. These developments guided, as the section described, an exceptional proliferation of the urban form in terms of specialised zones through decentralised governance, liberalised economy, ambiguities towards self-sustainability, and internal rearrangements to allure the global capital that gradually attested to the postcolonial developmental urges. Exploring further, the following section will establish an emergent turn of data infrastructure based-agency and enhanced capacity of the urban form.

DATA CENTRES AND CAPACITY OF NAVI MUMBAI

Data Centres, as advanced IT industries, are material exigencies of digital capitalism and governance in the postcolonial landscape. These material exigencies locate the emergent 'variegated' or 'graduated sovereignty' (Krasner 1999; Ong 2006: 7), or rescaling of the postcolonial state's power in two distinct ways: first, through its materiality, as the assemblage of DCs in the urban form, and second, through its operation, as the rising power of the postcolonial state. Unlike the old developmental feature of the postcolonial state that aimed at nationwide uniform models, this post-developmental assemblage utilises an astute logic to create and operate variegated zones of political and economic exception. It enables regulatory but differential effect on the rights and privileges of different segments of the population. For example, on the one hand, distinctive re-territorialisation focuses on the development and management of spaces and populations within this zone to achieve developmental targets and calibrate for futuristic needs. On the other hand, such interventions enforce economic networks and foster political integration at nationwide scales.

Returning to the aspect of materiality, this section locates how the DCs' physical existence, spatial location, redundant infrastructure, standardised operation, and (de)centralised management demonstrate variegated sovereignty of the spatially fragmented city-zone that allow positive exceptions and opportunities. It presents a spatial cum institutional ethnography of Asia's most significant DC, CtrlS, alongside the city's economic landscape. It strikes a chord amongst the establishment, operation, and management of the DCs vis-à-vis the unfolding security-finance-governance complex of Navi Mumbai. In doing so, it demonstrates how these institutional processes and their implementation enhances the 'agency' of the city (Thrift 2014: 7).

Developed bottom-up on barren land in the electronic zone and surrounded by software industries, CtrlS reflects its autonomy concerning its establishment, operation, and management.[6] Taking advantage of a long-term lease of land for ninety-nine years, the facility has been constructed with an elevation of 3.5 m. from the ground that eliminates chances of flooding. Secluded location within the electronic zone maintains a safe distance from the other institutions and industries like suburban railways, roadways, and offices of public interests. It restricts human or material flows which supplement its security and anonymity requirements. Special permissions from Maharashtra Industrial Development Corporation (MIDC) allows the facility to maintain high walls defending its perimeter. Sharing boundaries with a modern warehouse, Writer Information Management Firm, and research and development institution, Mahanagar Telephone Nigam Limited, on its lateral sides ensures restricted human influence, reinforces anonymity, and allows additional spatial security at local levels. Alongside, exceptionally wide approach roads at both the anterior and the posterior sides supplement supply and logistical redundancy.

Being resource-hungry, these sophisticated data infrastructures hinge on the urban form through resource dependencies. CtrlS needs more than 50 Mega Watts of electricity, and is exceptionally allowed to have dual power supply from Mahape and Airoli, and is connected to fossil fuel and hydropower power stations. The connection is established through dedicated electrical supply ducts between the transmission station and the facility and special express feeder equipment that ensures a stable supply. Located in the industrial zone, electricity is supplied at commercial rates without extra charges, which reduces operation costs. Power redundancy is also supplemented through the facility's additional arrangements—high power dual generators, dedicated biogas plant, back-up fuel for ninety-six hours, and a contract with fuel station regarding supply within four hours of the demand even in case of a calamity, disaster, or an emergency.

CtrlS also needs 840,000 gallons of water per day for its cooling requirements, which is provided by the MIDC at industrial rates. It also has a world-class water-cooling tower and a 2N infrastructure for failproof cooling.[7] Geographical isolation and a safe distance from hazardous industries and green coverage provides contamination-free air supply without additional filters, reduces pollution-related operational investments, and ensures against damages or any additional operational costs.[8]Additionally, the city supports DCs through the internet, business, and logistical infrastructures. While the National Internet Centre in Vashi provides multiple as well as maximum possible internet bandwidths for DC's telecommunication and data processes, the CBD at Belapur offers luxurious but subsidised spaces for government and corporate institutions.

Beyond its resource dependence on the city, the DCs operate through the principle of total ownership, differential, hierarchical yet synchronised governance, operations, and management of multiple components and processes within the unified infrastructure facility. Enhanced security for the smooth operation of digital infrastructures is a postcolonial predicament. Location in a no-fly zone, a safe distance of 30 kms from the sea, warehouse-model external structure, earthquake-resistant infrastructure, and outer concrete shields protect the facility from any unforeseen environmental or structural dangers. Beyond locational and structural robustness, CtrlS establishes a militarised zone of security through a combination of anthropocentric, mechanical, electronic, and software mechanisms.

Access inside the DC is governed through eight-layered inner security zoning: zone 1 of crash-proof entrance and perimeter security, zone 2 of armed guards around the establishment and on watchtowers, zone 3 of electronic IDs-based entrance inside the facility, zone 4 of physical and digital security checks, zone 5 of man-trap,[9] zone 6 of electronic IDs-based access to elevators connecting server floors, zone 7 of biometric security for main DC area, and zone 8 of biometric security for data racks.

The 'soft laws of global exchanges' (Easterling 2014: 12) administered by the global institutions validate DC's specific parameters on globally rationalised and accepted standards, and allows soft governance in foreign—but shared, networked, and dependent—infrastructural spaces. These soft laws even bypass the local complex socio-political situations, conflicts, and adversities, and produce a hyper-sovereignty to facilitate the operation of DCs as infrastructure-based extrastatecraft in the global networks of capital. Telecommunication Industry Association (TIA) and Uptime Institute Certification (UIC), being the pioneers in assessing DCs, categorise and certify them into Tiers 1, 2, 3, and 4 based on over 1,800 parameters covering geographical location, physical infrastructure, security arrangements, operation management, redundancy and fault tolerance, power efficiency, and overall management.[10]

Compliance to International Organization for Standardization (ISO) protects the DC's clients at the international scale. ISO certification is based on certain standards of network, quality, service and governance parameters that are set irrespective of the DC's spatial, juridical, or administrative boundaries and these standards are recognised globally.[11] Moreover, secret, hierarchical, multi-dimensional security strategies and international certifications deliver end-to-end assurance, from physical perimeter to server rooms, from data racks to data clouds. Multiple undisclosed firewalls and software securities, including 448 Bit military-level encryption protection that requires a supercomputer-level algorithm and more than 1 billion attempts per second, makes it almost impossible to hack. For additional security redundancy, the facility does not allow any electronic device within its secured zones.

The DC hosts multiple tenants within its unified facility. Each floor is customised for the facility's specific infrastructural, technical, and management needs: ground floor comprises of shared working areas that offer business continuity services (conference rooms, meeting rooms), space for client-service provider interface and additional work places; first floor anchors telecom, internet, and other components and upper floors host data servers. The operational architecture allows the 'meet-me room' to converge internet from leading internet providers; 'staging room' controls storage and network operation, 'telecom room' has six internet providers, 'control room' has CCTV camera-monitored 'work areas' and conference rooms, and most importantly, there are 'server rooms' with data racks.

CtrlS's robust physical infrastructure attributes to a huge load-bearing capability of the server rooms, 1500–2100 kg/sq. m., that are equipped with the latest technologies ensuring fire and thermal insulation, moisture and heat sensitive sensors, and automated cooling mechanisms. More than 31,000 sq. m. of server space with an operational capacity of over 20,000 racks, the functional architecture is future-ready. Resource, operation, and management are optimised, and convergent multi-scaler governance is materialised through an assemblage of building infrastructure and IT applications into one space. Four teams of administrators work round the clock to keep a manual and electronic check on thousands of the DC's components and processes. Staff who are critical for DC's specialised operation reside in the housing zones developed in the close vicinity of the facility (within 5 kms), thus supplementing workforce redundancy, and maintaining uninterrupted workforce availability in case of any emergency.

Besides, DCs constitute an ultramodern techno-space of the city's physiognomy. This assemblage spatialises DC's material and immaterial components, technology-driven and automatic operations, shared and oblivious anatomies, and anthropocentric, machine-controlled, and man-machine interfaces. The advanced capitalist economies in Europe and the US still rely on Tier 3 DCs owing to dependable infrastructure and resource supply.[12] Navi Mumbai competes with the Western standards by incorporating additional redundancies in the form of Tier 4 DCs, which is like a double infrastructure complex. Having mentioned so, Tier 4 DCs also consume two–three times more resources; however, factoring in an uninterrupted and low-cost supply of resources from the city-state, and the multiplier effect leading to competition and growth amongst the DC's resource-providing firms (based on increased demands from the DCs), make the operation of DCs cost-efficient and profitable. It is through these variegated sovereignties, local configuration and arrangements amongst the institutions and regimes that these zones in the postcolonial economy network and compete with the global capitalist and financial circuits.

CtrlS is the most prominent amongst over thirty recorded and dozens of unrecorded DCs in Navi Mumbai.[13] It hosts data of over a hundred clients including government departments, manufacturing companies, financial and banking organisations, insurance companies, public sector undertakings, e-commerce businesses, investment banking companies, Infotech companies, business solution consultants, power sector companies, multi-company brands, medical research organisations, infotainment industries, machinery and automobile giants, logistics companies, among many others.[14] A composite hosting in the DC networks the operations and management of the government, public-private partnerships, and private, international, and regional institutions within its spatial, technological, and infrastructural capabilities.

Most of the clients depend on DCs for 'Infrastructure as a Service' (IaaS) and 'Software as a Service' (SaaS) models.[15] This dependence frees the clients from infrastructure, software, management, and operations components of data management—such as servers and data hosting, storage and maintenance components—through a hassle-free, cost-efficient, and secured outsourcing. Its complete infrastructure solution—infrastructure, migration, virtualisation, automation, software solutions—enables the clients to pick services as per their specific requirements. Product bundles like storage as service, network as service, dynamic scaling of the services, resource subscription models like pay-per-use and pay-per-resource deliver optimised services based on usage-linked billing and ensures uninterrupted uptime, business continuity, and product management while significantly reducing operational costs.

Complete outsourcing of data storage at ubiquitous locations supplements the organisation's measures of the government of risk. This outsourcing eliminates the client's capital investment in hardware, software, and associated infrastructure and human resource. Alternatively, the client's human resources are freed for software solutions and innovation, which supplements their business growth and market value. As a result of this symbiotic relationship amongst the DCs, service providers, and clients, a large number of DCs mushroom over the city's landscape, leading to an Indianisation of DCs in Navi Mumbai's landscape.[16] Such a proliferation supplements the city's security-finance-governance complex and enhances the city's agency. An investigation into this economic landscape, its operation and management unfold an emergent labour territory and specific labour subjectivities.

Emerging Labour Territory: Regime, Subject, and Subjectivity

Data Centres are similar to an advanced IT industry. Based on the engagements with the DCs in Navi Mumbai, it is possible to locate a two-fold typology of the labour workforce that corresponds to its infrastructure, software, digital, and computing operations: administrative and technical. The administrative workforce is involved in sales, security, management, and administration departments and their processes. Further, technical workforce includes hardware engineers, software engineers, and data scientists. In this way, while the administrative workforce involves dependent processes, the technical workforce involves core processes of the DCs. The most significant DCs that host critical data from various organisations mostly hire skilled and experienced taskforce from advanced IT firms or IT sector, for both administrative and technical categories. Administrative workforce shares their spatial allocation in the offices at the CBDs as well as the DCs. However, as a principle, a critical administrative workforce is maintained for its operation, and all other uncritical business activity is alienated from the DCs, and is operated from their corporate offices in the CBDs in other state-capitals or international offices. On the other hand, the technical workforce is distributed in different work areas within and amongst the DCs, the host and the networked institutions.

The variegated sovereignty of the zone requires a new labour regime for its operation. It creates exceptional opportunities for the minority of new experts, professionals, consultants, and gurus—the 'new prophets of capital' (Aschoff 2015). They enjoy accommodations and conditions not granted to the rest of the workforce. In the profoundly altered landscapes of neoliberalism, labour standards and work conditions are administered and managed through international and inter-institutional guidelines that ensure flexible work conditions and comparatively higher pay packages. However, an exploration of the work conditions and emergent subjectivities also inform about spoken and unspoken demands of the workplaces, psycho-social conditions of work and involved precarity that juxtaposes the pronounced advantages of the new labour regimes.[17] An exploration into this labour territory, through the labour subjects, who form the material or immaterial labour, and perform administrative or technical tasks, explicates the unique spatiality of the DCs and its specific requirements.

We recognise that the spatial, existential, and operational camouflage evolve to deal with postcolonial predicaments of material and financial insecurities prevalent at local levels. During one of the visits to the DCs, a technical team-head mentioned, 'We have to ensure safety from "outside" as well as "inside" of the DC; the threat could be from anywhere.' To minimise risks associated with its spatiality, DCs become an exclusive space for data storage, and as mentioned earlier, other non-critical business processes are located away from it but, in the CBDs. Further, a sales manager informed:

> The facility appears analogous to its surrounding, so we keep it low-profile. Vehicular and human movement is controlled and restricted: only supply and maintenance vehicles are allowed. It is maintained like a warehouse. Otherwise, being a high-profile industry, it might be targeted by local politicians or goons for donations (*chanda*) or hackers that could compromise its safety, anonymity and reputation.

The technical organisation, hierarchical operation, and centralised control of the security infrastructure minimises any risk emanating from within and/or outside the facility. A security supervisor mentioned:

> No one is exceptional to the layered security system. Different security firms [individually] control the eight layers and report to the central security monitoring system. Only after clearance from the central monitoring system, one has access to zones six, seven and eight of the facility.

Focusing on the specific security infrastructure, he explained:

> The employment of different agencies ensures that no one agency has the full authority to all the layers of security and even if there is a breach by one of the security firms at the penultimate level, it will be caught by another firm at the next stage.

The security apparatus hence creates a segmentation within the layers, induces the principle of mutual unreliability, and operates in hierarchical and complementary fashion to govern any unforeseen risk. The security apparatus also compartmentalises 'critical' from 'less critical' infrastructure, and complements DC's disguised morphologies and anatomies. A sales manager explained:

> Corporate visits are necessary for business processes and to address the client's apprehensions. We showcase physical infrastructure, certifications, audit reports and less critical infrastructural settings. If required, we display a few data servers of low-profile clients, like manufacturing firms. However, we can't even disclose servers or cloud storage of several international clients with 'no disclosure contracts' with us.

The security needs and the governance of risk associated with the industry in general and the facility in particular direct its employees towards an intense encounter with the security complex. A system engineer explained, 'Like any profession, e.g., 1st grade or 4th grade government job, we also develop a kind of mentality. This mentality is guided by the specific work environment, work culture, and terms of requirements, terms of contact, superintendence, and locale of the work environment'. Security and governance of this new labour territory get ingrained into the employees' everydayness and engender subjectivities, as the employees initially struggle and finally adapt to the specific requirements of the labour territory. As a software professional explained:

> Working here does not mean that I will have access or authority to every business process. It is significantly hierarchical and demands specific clearances: reaching the workstation, access to the server racks and access to data, processes of maintenance or

trouble-shooting require specific clearances. This is an integral part of the work conditions.

Supplementing the relevance of security labyrinth, a junior engineer mentioned:

> We work under highest possible surveillance: Every movement, every log-in and activity is recorded and scrutinised; and employees from a different team, like technical or HR, keep track of the employee's activities. At times, clients also covertly monitor the various critical data processes. The safety of data is ensured through the composite security arrangements.

A system engineer emphasised on the emergent contention within the man-machine interface:

> Data is more important than any employee. An employee could be replaced, but a breach could compromise our credibility and business. So, even if hyper-surveillance and clearance-needs are annoying, and technical assignments and reporting are shared across multiple departments, we understand that these are steps towards the facility's overall governance. Moreover, we adapt to the specific provisions, which eventually stop bothering us.

On its operational fronts, DCs requires advanced capabilities and continuous performances, especially from its technical workforce. 'Your work-shift is primarily your team's responsibility and risk', another system engineer mentioned. A minor issue detected in an application could be ascertained and addressed from the desk located in the DC, sister DC, backup DC, and even client's work stations. However, issues become critical if hard disk or servers exhibit symptoms of predictive or network failure, or if it requires an upgrade. For them, 'Such an emergency could happen anytime, and the system engineers and data administrators have to work tirelessly even beyond their time-shifts; we need utmost endurance'.

Situations that have the potential to affect the uninterrupted business processes is categorised as an emergency. An exploration into the dimension of the labour regime and labour processes during such an emergency highlights its precarity. Servers have a placement sequence in the numbered racks that are compact, to optimise space utility, energy efficiency, and operational costs, and do not allow service desk space. A system engineer, from a Tier 3 DC, shared the practice of fixing the servers and his attempts towards maintaining an uninterrupted uptime,

> You work in standing, squatting or sitting position based on the server's locations. In one such case, it was upside down and took 4–5 hours to identify the faulty hard disks. The supplier took 3–4 hours to deliver the required disks, and it took another 4–5 hours for the assembly. Replacement, data replication, and synchronisation of 12 Tera Bytes took 15–17 hours; so, a total of 27–30 hours.

Explaining the needs of the emergency, he explained, 'During such an emergency, time slot or work hours are not counted. Change in shift could complicate the issue or linger the maintenance process. Based on the requirements, big DCs could mobilise human resource across projects and divisions'.

On similar lines, backup storage of data—incremental, differential, or full—is either partially or fully automated. In any case, every fraction of a second's data is crucial for the client's business processes, and a lag, discontinuity, or loss in the backup at the front-end or/and in the backup servers hosted at various DCs might cause disruption and hence, needs uninterrupted human attention, supervision, and engagement. Moreover, server upgrade during occasional increased traffic, additional software or server deployment, an upgrade, online or offline maintenance, and issues of backup and recovery also require extended and complicated interfaces of the employees, the human beings, and DC's infrastructure, the machines.

The stringent work regime induces certain rationalities amongst the employees who seek opportunities in an advancing industry. 'An IT professional with advanced skill-sets, like Java, Dot Net, Angular or Python, and 4–5 years of work experience will not succumb to a strenuous condition or an emergency', a data administrator explained. Elucidated further, 'He would not exhibit anger or frustration on the servers, wouldn't cut the network cables loose or resist storage or backup; instead, he will exhibit his work experience, maturity, confidence, endurance and expertise in dealing with exigencies and behave as a dependable employee'. Another data administrator supplemented:

> Working tirelessly and taking extra precautions to avoid escalation of the problem will be an achievement for one's professional record. The industry pays well and provides growth opportunities, but it also runs on the principle of hire and fire, with no scope for human error. So, understanding this, we also internalise what this industry demands, what it offers, and what is at stake.

Employees with extensive work experience observe this as a 'paradigm', while new entrants encounter this as an 'exception'. A recently joined software professional mentioned, 'One could get fired for a single mistake. The [DC] firm should treat employees with dignity and honour, not like cheap labour. Terminating them without any warning should not be a code of conduct'.

The new labour territory of DCs emanates an intersection of labour and technocratic workspace that is highly hierarchical, segmented, and extremely surveilled. The governance of the produced labour subjects and the labour territory is dramatically stringent. With the infrastructural turn of capitalism, the labour becomes conditionally visible and invisible; they are individually compromised through the new workspace, its regime, and overlapping man-machine interfaces. Conjointly, their novel scale of operation intensifies and multiplies the extractive capacities of digital infrastructures. Such regimes acquire a geopolitical significance as they ensemble new relations of capital and labour that unfold over a vast expanse of the dense congregation of digital technologies, automated operations on the one side and dependent human processes on the other. Here, alienated labour, invisible labour, and machine-human interlinked processes lead to the production, function, storage, and maintenance of a new kind of immaterial commodity in the form of data (also see Introduction, this volume). Although nascent and still-developing, the profoundly altered techno-spaces in DCs spatialise the transition of labour, labour processes, and labour values from individualised bodies of factory floors to an immaterial commodity of the DCs, which is imperative to postcolonial extrastatecraft.

EMERGENT EXTRASTATECRAFT: THE TRIAD OF DATA CENTRES,
CBD, AND THE URBAN FORM

The triad of the new urban form, digital infrastructures, and the central business district forward a logical argument about the evolving governance in the postcolonial economic and political milieu. A gradual movement from 'public-exclusive' to 'public-private' collaborative to 'private-exclusive', however state-dependent—in parallel with the partnership and the rivalry of the state—has been phenomenal and led to the creation of the urban form, as in the case of Navi Mumbai. The created urban form with state-of-the-art infrastructure, synergistic state governance and boundless economic freedom expands the postcolonial state's linkages with the global circuits of neoliberal capitalism. Within this, the 'premium networked spaces' (Graham 2000) of IT infrastructures, DCs, service sector industries, and the CBD in the city-zone's assemblage caters spatiality to integrated cyber-physical spaces of institutions and extraordinary circulation of technology, operations, logistics, and services that cater to governments, businesses, and citizens (Yovanof and Hazapis 2009).

An emergent rhizomic infrastructural power in the form of a web of connections that traverse stakeholders in opaque and codified structures describes the materialisation of data as a critical component of neoliberal capitalism (Hansen and Verkaik 2009: 20; Larkin 2013). This allows the global financial institutions, nation-states, corporation and other institutions to operate beyond multiple jurisdictions with potentially conflicting allegiances, laws, and geographical sovereignties. The security-administrative-governance complex, hence created, acts as a site of multiple, overlapping, or nested forms of sovereignty, whereby the domestic and transnational infrastructure spaces and their rhizomic network function and create 'extrastatecraft'—a portmanteau describing the often undisclosed activities outside of, in addition to, in juxtaposition to, in collaboration, and in partnership with statecraft (Easterling 2014).

This emergent extrastatecraft is imperative for the management of postcolonial societies hitherto considered unmanageable and anarchic. Data governance draws from experiences of the Indian state in dealing with society, population groups, security, and welfare needs and territorial management (Samaddar 2018a: 134), of which the triad of DCs–CBD–city is an evolving form. DCs constitute the material significance of the 'big data revolution' (Mayer-Schönberger and Cukier 2013), as over three-fourth of the total data of an organisation stays in DCs at any time. Based on the operation of the triad, a new form of 'algorithmic governance and governmentality' (Introna 2016; Leszczynski 2016: 1692) is unleashed in which the government, market, and civic institutions, and the new human subjects engage with the processes of data production, synthesis, collection, storage, assimilation, and analysis. This gives rise to a new wave of understanding about the role of data within capitalism—data which is materialised, operated, and governed through the technocratic 'platform', and propels towards 'platform capitalism' (Srnicek 2017).

> Capitalism has turned to data as one way to maintain economic growth...based on changes in digital technologies, data have become increasingly central to firms and their relations with workers, customers, and other capitalists. The platform has emerged as a new business model, capable of extracting and controlling immense amounts of data (Srnicek 2017: 6).

Such trends are already visible in banking and finance, e-commerce, and governance in India.

From ledger-based banking (1980s), computerised operations (1990s), internet banking (2000s) to the current core-banking solutions, India's banking sector's service and its customer interface have transformed drastically. Foreign direct investments, mergers and acquisitions, banking reforms, and the advent of international financial institutions have created competitive pressure in the banking sector. On the one hand, the banks have to respond to the new consumer needs, increased competition within the sector, and stringent regulations from the governing authorities, and on the other hand, they also have to upgrade their infrastructure and introduce innovative business models that forge sustenance, efficacy, and growth. The 'new-age banking' aims at 'collaboration among service providers with financial institutions partnering with telecom, technology, and consumer product providers to create an enabling environment' (Chakraborty 2013). This would make India the third largest banking industry in the world in 2025 from being the fifth largest in 2020.

While expected financial growth is a measure of Big Data phenomenon, India simultaneously also suffers from a 'sparse data syndrome'[18] (Demirgüc-Kunt et al. 2018). The contradictory dualism of amassing wealth, growing service sector, bourgeoning and aspiring middle-class and elite on one side, and poverty amongst a large section of Indian population outside a formal banking network on the other, is redefining the roles of the banking sector. Amidst the shrinking welfare state and hysterical market ambitions, remodelling welfare through financial inclusion of the subjects, projecting welfare onto 'missions' and 'models', and financialisation of the welfare provisions is the latest rule.[19] In this new turn, while capital investments in banking infrastructure development are drastically reducing, alternate infrastructures like banking kiosks, micro-credit institutions, and mobile branches are mushrooming. These new infrastructures not only promise to bring a large population into the formal financial network and make them bankable, but also pave a way towards harnessing their untapped economic potential. Evolving and expanding banking services rely on the DC–CBD–city triad and the emerging extrastatecraft for their operations and management. The advanced, technologically capable, secured, and institutionally compliant physiognomy of DCs provides IaaS, SaaS, co-location, and server hosting as well as automated scale-up and scale-down. It allows pay-as-you-go services, among many others, to the banking and financial services partners.[20] A symbiotic association enables the banking partners to have a benevolent approach towards the unreached; however, it also frees the sector from having and maintaining physical infrastructures of their own. Infrastructural and operational dependencies between the data infrastructures and the banks benefit the banking sector with lower per capita bank branches nationwide as opposed to a trend of branch-based banking penetration in the last several decades.[21] Further, headquarters of the banking and financial firms have a dual advantage in this urban form by first, co-axially locating corporate office operations in the secured and subsidised premium spaces of the CBD, and hosting their critical servers in its premier IT zones, and second, having access to a stable, qualified, and comparatively cheaper workforce.

Banking and financial sector firms have burgeoned in the CBD. A proximal location vis-à-vis the DCs also allows test and pilot run of new products and services, better bureaucratic control, and circulation of their IT staff between their core teams and their DCs to their advantage. International firms also have an added benefit of accessing the infrastructure of global standard as well as a competitive workforce at cheaper rates.[22] Cumulative operation of the 'public', the 'public-private', and the 'private' organisations at transnational, inter-institutional and inter-departmental levels situate a rhizome of infra-power that acts as the apparatus of this extrastatecraft.

Expansion of safe digital banking services has also influenced the e-commerce sector in India. E-commerce in India has grown by 34 per cent (CAGR) since 2009 and has a huge potential for e-commerce with a high demographic dividend.[23] On similar lines, the Asia-Pacific region is emerging as the strongest Business-to-Consumer (B2C) e-commerce region in the world. It is not a matter of surprise that expansion of e-commerce, and mergers and acquisitions among the e-commerce giants like Flipkart, Amazon, Alibaba, and subsidiary units like Myntra have grabbed the attention of several blue-chip private equity firms' investments. Coaxially, ancillary services, e-commerce firms, online payments companies, and logistics partners are collaborating with each other.

The material implications of these business processes could be observed in the postcolonial megacities in terms of business interface and consumer behaviour. For example, over eleven malls have been closed in Mumbai—a city that grew from mills to malls between 2010–2015, citing poor business and imbalance of trade amidst inflated real estate market (*The Times of India* 2017). Alternatively, e-commerce is mutating from its physical landscape to a digital interface, of which data hosting, computation, and management through the DCs is crucial. The new interface is administered through data-influenced choice-making and pricing, e-payments through banks' services and e-wallets, internet-based instant billing, instant convergence with logistical and warehouse partners and doorstep delivery provisions.

The logistical warfare—a demand and supply rivalry of e-commerce—is mediated through digital infrastructures: its operation depends on continuous data flows between the users, sellers, and the intermediate agencies like the logistical, warehouse, sales, and other divisions across agencies like the seller, payment banks, courier partners, and users that are spread in unrelated, but digitally connected geographies. Extensive computation enables a harmonic operation of the logistics of the consumer goods across diverse geographical and national boundaries, and optimises their production, storage, circulation, transit, and distribution. On the operational levels, the robustness of digital infrastructures and real-time coordination between the banks, service providers, clients and the users; measures of transparency; and efficient information management attributing to the sector's viability correspond to its estimated growth. On an advanced algorithmic level, the bulk of customers' data—including individual profile, demographic and geographic details, banking information, creditworthiness, credit and debit details, buyer's behaviour, product or service search, and overall browsing history influence buying practice and product performance. An algorithmic computation of the generated, stored, and shared data from across the stakeholders, routed through the data infrastructures supplements the business redundancy of the sector by providing insights about current paradigms, future potential, or unforeseen risks.

Likewise, data, its 'bigness' and applicability of data infrastructures are becoming central in the operation, management, documentation, service delivery, and inter-department coordination for government organisations. New governmental techniques aim to inculcate higher transparency, better coordination and co-operation amongst the government departments, ministries, and associated civic institutions, and private firms for faster roll-out of statutory laws, government policies, welfare administration, and ensure accountability across the levels of government. Quick and effective delivery of services at reduced service delivery costs thrusts the implementation of technology-driven welfare and overall data-based governance. The trinity of direct subsidy—Aadhaar, mobile, and direct transfer—is a new way of welfare administration. In this new arrangement, Aadhaar helps in personal identification and mobile serves as digital validation to allow the direct cash transfer to happen digitally. This arrangement supersedes the age-old contentious mechanisms of identification of beneficiaries or subjects worthy of welfare, inclusion and exclusion errors, leakage and mismanagement of project funds.[24] The new data-based apparatus enables centralised governance, lesser bureaucracy, and reduced state spending.

On macro-economic and political fronts, an effort towards efficient governance makes the postcolonial state depend on the emerging extrastatecraft to remove the bottlenecks of age-old licence raj and corruption, and to allow market, institutions, policies, and processes to be transparent, trackable, manageable, and governable by the international financial organisations, and multinational and international companies. Technically, it also hints at hybrid governance models amongst its multiple tiers and stakeholders through devolution and sharing of bio-data and data-based algorithmic governance.

Following this logic, the apex body of planning in India, Niti Aayog 'has already begun exploring ways in which advanced encryption technologies can be used so that data can be used for training Artificial Intelligence algorithms' (*The Indian Express* 2018). Working in its advanced phase to develop a National Data and Analytics Portal, and the accomplishment of the world-famous Aadhaar project, big data theory is set to facilitate a policy support system through accurate sourcing, storing, analysing, and presentation of data in a usable and visually appealing manner. The infusion of technology into the frameworks of governance aims to reach the hitherto unreached, instrumentalise minimum government and maximum governance, escalate market reforms, and roll out welfare and economic policies. It also infuses a hope of 'smart' governance against the endemic and incorrigible plague of embedded corruption, red-tapism, and unaccountable political society. It is irrefutable to acknowledge the worth of such futuristic social, economic, and political turns.

Succinctly, through this chapter, we aimed to comprehend how the Data Centre, its geographical location and physiological operation, provoke and influence our understanding of the city, its activities, transformations, social fabric, infrastructure, and overall governance mechanism. With the push to recognise data as a 'public good' within the nation-state, and the politics around the flow of data across borders, the relationship amongst data, society, and institutions is going to dominate political economy discourses locally and globally. While the upcoming digital postcolonial future is contested, an exploration through this chapter elucidates the role of transforming relations of capital, land, and labour in the contemporary and emerging postcolonial landscape.

End Notes

1. Airoli, Ghansoli, Koper Khairane, Jui Nagar, Vashi, Sanpada, Juhu Nagar, Nerul, CBD Belapur, Kharghar, Kamothe, New Panvel, Kalamboli, Ulwe, Pushpak, and Drongiri.

2. Vashi, New Panvel, Nerul, Airoli, Sanpada, Koperkhairane, and Kalamboli.

3. From Morbe dam, Balganga dam, and Hetawane water supply project.

4. Out of the planned 12,000 government jobs only 1,200 were shifted to Navi Mumbai and emerged as corporate relocation scheme in a failed CBD. See Vedula 2007.

5. Octroi tax is a state tax, and the applicable rate was between 3–6 per cent. It is now subsumed within the centralised Goods and Services Tax system (GST).

6. CtrlS's details are based on institutional visits and observations, accessed documents and reports, and interviews and discussion with employees facilitating the study.

7. 2N refers to a fully redundant, mirror system of infrastructure with two independent distribution systems that ensures uninterrupted supply and accommodates increased load. This redundancy eliminates potential downtime.

8. For more information on gaseous contamination in Malad, Mumbai and its impacts on DC's operation, see https://www.bryair.com/case-studies/gas-phase-filtration/gaseous-contaminants-threatening-servers-of-malad-area (accessed on 21 May 2019).

9. A man-trap is an access control system with a small space and interlocked doors. One set of the doors must close before the other one can be opened so that a person with unauthorised access is 'trapped' in between.

10. Tier 1: basic requirements, 99.671 per cent uptime; Tier 2: redundancy components, 99.749 per cent uptime; Tier 3: concurrently maintainable components, 99.982 per cent uptime; Tier 4: autonomous fault tolerance, 99.995 per cent uptime. Tier 1 has a maximum of 28.8 hours, and Tier 4 has a minimum of 26.28 minutes of downtime per year. See Uptime Institute at https://uptimeinstitute.com/ (accessed on 21 May 2019).

11. ISO 27000 series, ISO 2000 series, ISO 22301: 2012, ISO: 9000, ISO 9001: 2015, ISO 27001: 2013 among many others. See Easterling (2014: 28) and ISO's homepage https://www.iso.org/home.html (accessed on 21 May 2019).

12. See 'Tiers is the global language of Data Centre performance' and distribution of Tier based DCs across the world on https://uptimeinstitute.com/uptime_assets/Tier-Example-Sites-2018.pdf (accessed on 21 May 2019).

13. Accurate listing of all the DCs in Navi Mumbai is not available; See https://cloudscene.com/search/data-centers?searchTerm=navi%20mumbai (accessed on 21 May 2019). At least a few of the government and private DCs maintain absolute locational anonymity and do not even appear on the available listing or Google maps. For example, the Reserve Bank of India's DC is located in its residential complex in Navi Mumbai. They also camouflage themselves as IT industries.

14. State Bank of India, National Bank of Singapore, Axis Bank and HDFC Bank, Paytm, Alibaba, L&T Infotech, Tata Services, Cognizant Business Consulting, National Thermal Power Corporation, Mahindra & Mahindra, Mercedes-Benz, Nagarjuna Fertilizers, Deepak Fertilizers and Chemicals, Gati Corporation, HDFC Life Insurance, Reliance Power, Siro Group of Companies, Parallels, Research in Motion (India), Ask Investments, Municipal Corporation of Greater Mumbai (MCGM), Rajiv Gandhi Cancer Institute and Research Centre, Muse Art Gallery among many others. Many of these organisations share operations with sister DC establishments located in Hyderabad, Delhi, and Bangalore in India.

15. See the specific details of IaaS and SaaS services on https://www.ibm.com/cloud/learn/iaas-paas-saas (accessed on 21 May 2019).

16. India is the second-largest market for DCs in the world and a prominent player in the global South. According to the National Association of Software and Service Companies (NASSCOM), the DC market aims to register aggressive growth from US$ 3.4 billion per annum to up to US$ 6–8 billion per annum by 2025.

17. The DCs and their employees follow a strict non-disclosure policy. Keeping this in mind, the respondent's identities and institutional affiliation have been anonymised. However, they represent the three most-prominent DCs in Navi Mumbai.

18. For example, India has emphasised on core banking solutions, and there is an unprecedented growth in Banking, Financial Services and Insurance sector; financial inclusion within the city has remained abysmally low at around 40 per cent till 2018.

19. Forty-four Mission Mode Projects with multiple components and service delivery verticals have been introduced through the new National e-Governance Plan (NeGP), see https://www.meity.gov.in/divisions/national-e-governance-plan. Remodelled poverty-alleviation schemes include nationwide Rural Livelihoods Mission, Urban Livelihoods Mission, and others like Conditional Cash Transfer initiatives.

20. The Reserve Bank of India; the Insurance Regulatory and Development Authority (IRDAI); the Securities and Exchange Board of India's guidelines; the Information Technology Act 2000; and the Gopal Krishnan Committee recommendations are among the most prominent in setting up frameworks for online payments.

21. India globally ranks 74th with 14.06 branches per 100,000 people, see https://www.theglobaleconomy.com/rankings/bank_branches/ (accessed on 21 May 2019).

22. US$ 20–25 per hour in India as compared to US$ 60–75 per hour in other markets, see https://www.datacenterdynamics.com/news/india-a-future-proofed-market/ (accessed on 21 May 2019).

23. E-commerce in India: Accelerating growth—a study by PWC; see https://www.pwc.in/assets/pdfs/publications/2015/ecommerce-in-india-accelerating-growth.pdf (accessed on 21 May 2019).

24. Aadhaar is a 12-digit biometric signifier for Indians; it is also the world's largest biometric ID system. See http://uidai.gov.in (accessed on 21 May 2019).

REFERENCES

Aschoff, N. 2015. *The New Prophets of Capital*. London: Verso.

Bapat, M. 1990. 'Allocation of Urban Space: Rhetoric and Reality'. *Economic and Political Weekly* 25(28): 1502–1507.

Bhattacharya, A. 1971. *A Study of Industries in Trans-Thane Belt*. Bombay: CIDCO.

BMRPD (Bombay Municipal Regional Planning Board). 1970. *Report on the draft regional plan of Bombay Metropolitan Region 1970–1991*, 2 vols. Mumbai: BMRPD.

Chakraborty, S. 2013. 'Indian Banking Set to Become Fifth Largest by 2020: KPMG-CII Report'. *Business Standard*, 13 September. Available at http://www.business-standard.com/article/finance/indian-banking-set-to-become-fifth-largest-by-2020-kpmg-cii-report-113091300822_1.html (accessed May 2022).

CIDCO (City and Industrial Development Corporation of Maharashtra). 1973. *New Bombay: Draft Development Plan*. Mumbai: CIDCO. Available at https://dspace.gipe.ac.in/xmlui/bitstream/handle/10973/38163/GIPE-150789-Contents.pdf?sequence=2&isAllowed=y (accessed May 2022).

———. 2005. *Revised Budget Estimates 2003–04*. Navi Mumbai: CIDCO.

———. 2009. *39th Annual Report 2008–09*. Navi Mumbai: CIDCO.

———. 2012. *42nd Annual Report 2011–12*. Navi Mumbai: CIDCO.

CIDCO Economics Department. 2006. *Executive Summary—Socio-economic Survey of Households in Navi Mumbai's Planned Nodes*. Navi Mumbai: CIDCO.

CIDCO Economics and Statistics Departments. 2014. *Project Report of Navi Mumbai*. Navi Mumbai: CIDCO.

CIDCO Economics Section. 1984. *A Report on Survey of Industries in Thane-Belapur Area in New Bombay*. New Bombay: CIDCO.

———. 1988. *Socio-economic Survey of Households in Various Nodes in New Bombay*. New Bombay: CIDCO.

———. 1990. *A Report on the Survey of Industries in New Bombay*. New Bombay: CIDCO.

CIDCO Public Relations Office. 1998. *Navi Mumbai: The Corporate World's New Address in 21st century*. Navi Mumbai: CIDCO.

CIDCO Statistics Department. 2010. *Socio-Economic Profile of Households in Planned Nodes in Navi Mumbai*. Navi Mumbai: CIDCO.

Correa, C., P. Mehta, and S. B. Patel. 1965. 'Planning for Bombay'. *MARG* 18(3): 30–56.

Datta, A. 2015. 'New Urban Utopias of Postcolonial India: "Entrepreneurial Urbanization" in Dholera Smart City, Gujarat'. *Dialogues in Human Geography* 5(1): 3–22.

Demirgüç-Kunt, A., L. Klapper, D. Singer, and S. Ansar. 2018. *The Global Findex Database 2017: Measuring Financial Inclusion and the Fintech Revolution*. World Bank Publications.

Dick, H. W., and P. J. Rimmer. 1998. 'Beyond the Third World City: The New Urban Geography of South-east Asia'. *Urban Studies* 35(12): 2303–2321.

Dwivedi, S. and R. Mehrotra, R. 1995. *Bombay: The Cities Within*. Bombay: India Book House.

Easterling, K. 2014. *Extrastatecraft: The Power of Infrastructure Space*. New York: Verso.

Graham, S. 2000. 'Constructing Premium Network Spaces: Reflections on Infrastructure Networks and Contemporary Urban Development'. *International Journal of Urban and Regional Research* 24(1): 183–200.

Graham, S. and S. Marvin. 2001. *Splintering Urbanism: Networked Infrastructures, Technological Mobilities and the Urban Condition*. London: Routledge.

Hansen, T. B. and O. Verkaik. 2009. 'Introduction: Urban Charisma—On Everyday Mythologies in the City'. *Critique of Anthropology* 29(1): 5–26.

Harris, N. 1978. *Economic Development, Cities and Planning: The Case of Bombay*. Mumbai: Oxford University Press.

Introna, L. D. 2016. 'Algorithms, Governance, and Governmentality: On Governing Academic Writing'. *Science, Technology, & Human Values* 41(1): 17–49.

Krasner, S. D. 1999. *Sovereignty: Organized hypocrisy*. Princeton, New Jersey: Princeton University Press.

Larkin, B. 2013. 'The Politics and Poetics of Infrastructure'. *Annual Review of Anthropology* 42: 327–343.

Leszczynski, A. 2016. 'Speculative Futures: Cities, Data, and Governance Beyond Smart Urbanism'. *Environment and Planning A: Economy and Space* 48(9): 1691–1708.

MARG (Modern Architects Research Group). 1965. 'Bombay: Planning and Dreaming'. *MARG* 18(3).

Mayer-Schönberger, V. and K. Cukier. 2013. *Big Data: A Revolution That Will Transform How We Live, Work, and Think*. Boston, New York: Houghton Mifflin Harcourt.

Mazzucato, M. 2013. *The Entrepreneurial State: Debunking Public Vs. Private Sector Myths*. New York: Anthem Press.

MCGB (Municipal Corporation of Greater Bombay). 1964. *Report on the Development Plan for Greater Bombay*. Mumbai: Government Central Press.

MEDC (Maharashtra Economic Development Council). 2013. *Repositioning Navi Mumbai as a Growth Engine*. Navi Mumbai: Statistics Department, CIDCO.

Modak, N. V. and A. Mayer. 1948. *The Master Plan in Outline*. Bombay: The Bombay Municipality and the Government of Bombay. Available at https://dspace.gipe.ac.in/xmlui/bitstream/handle/10973/45577/GIPE-022418-Contents.pdf?sequence=2&isAllowed=y (accessed May 2022).

Neilson, B. and S. Mezzadra. 2014. 'The State of Capitalist Globalization'. *Viewpoint Magazine*, 4 September. Available at https://www.viewpointmag.com/2014/09/04/the-state-of-capitalist-globalization/ (accessed May 2022).

Ong, A. 2006. *Neoliberalism as Exception: Mutations in Citizenship and Sovereignty*. Durham, NC: Duke University Press.

Patel, S. B. 1970. 'Regional planning for Bombay'. *Economic and Political Weekly* 5(26): 1011–1018.

———. 1993. 'A Second Financial Centre for Bombay: Where Should It Be?' *Economic and Political Weekly* 28(32/33): 1631–1635.

Prakash, Gyan. 2002. 'The Urban Turn'. In *Sarai Reader 02: The Cities of Everyday Life*, Ravi Vasudevan et al. (eds), 2–7. Delhi: Centre for the Study of Developing Societies.

Roy, A. and A. Ong. (eds). 2011. *Worlding Cities: Asian Experiments and the Art of Being Global*. Malden, Oxford: Wiley-Blackwell.

Samaddar, R. 2018a. *Karl Marx and The Postcolonial Age*. Switzerland: Palgrave Macmillan.

———. 2018b. 'The Urban Turn'. *Policies and Practices* 96. Mahanirban Calcutta Research Group, Kolkata, India. Available at http://www.mcrg.ac.in/pp96.PDF (accessed June 2022).

Sanyal, K. 2007. *Rethinking Capitalist Development: Primitive Accumulation, Governmentality and Post-Colonial Capitalism*. New Delhi: Routledge.

Sassen, S. 2014. *Expulsions: Brutality and Complexity in the Global Economy*. Cambridge, MA: Harvard University Press.

Scott, A. J. and M. Storper. 2014. 'The Nature of Cities: The Scope and Limits of Urban Theory'. *International Journal of Urban and Regional Research* 39(1): 1–15.

Shaw, A. 1999. 'The Planning and Development of New Bombay'. *Modern Asian Studies* 33(4): 951–988.

———. 2004. *The Making of Navi Mumbai*. Hyderabad: Orient Longman.

Sheth, D. L. 1992. 'Movements, Intellectuals and the State: Social Policy in Nation Building'. *Economic and Political Weekly* 27(8): 425–429.

Smith, N. 2002. 'New Globalism, New Urbanism: Gentrification as Global Urban Strategy'. *Antipode* 34(3): 427–450.

Srnicek, N. 2017. *Platform Capitalism*. Cambridge and Malden: Polity Press.

The Indian Express. 2018. 'Three Years of Formation: Niti Aayog working to Adopt AI, Blockchain in Governance', 4 January. Available at http://indianexpress.com/article/business/business-others/three-years-of-formation-niti-aayog-working-to-adopt-ai-blockchain-in-governance-5010639/ (accessed June 2022).

The Times of India. 2017. 'Mumbai Mega Mall Fails, Turned into Offices', 07 April. Available at https://timesofindia.indiatimes.com/city/mumbai/mumbai-mega-mall-fails-turned-into-offices/articleshow/58057231.cms (accessed June 2022).

Thrift, N. 2014. 'The "Sentient" City and What it May Portend'. *Big Data and Society* 1(1): 1–21.

Vedula, A. 2007. 'Blueprint and Reality: Navi Mumbai, a City of the 21st Century'. *Habitat International* 31(1): 12–23.

Yovanof, G. S. and G. N. Hazapis. 2009. 'An Architectural Framework and Enabling Wireless Technologies for Digital Cities & Intelligent Urban Environments'. *Wireless Personal Communications* 49(3): 445–463.

Make in India: Conducive Policy & Regulatory Environment to Incentivize Data Center Infrastructure. Internet and Mobile Association of India (IAMAI), May 2016

Excerpts:

Chapter One
Global Data Centre Market and India's Share

1.1 GLOBAL DATA CENTRE IT INFRASTRUCTURE MARKET BY GEOGRAPHY 2015

Data Centre IT infrastructure investments globally, including total spending on servers, storage, networking, security and virtualisation, reached $170 billion in 2015,[1] a 23% increase over the 2012 levels[2] and is estimated to reach $175 billion by 2016 at 2% on an average p.a., much of which will be accounted from Asia-Pacific.

Large data centres will lead this expansion with an average annual increase of 8% over the period till 2016–17. Much of this infrastructure

Figure 1.1: Investments ($Bn)

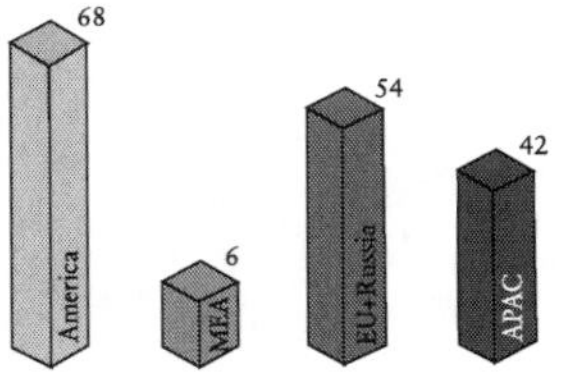

Figure 1.2: Market share in spending ($Bn)

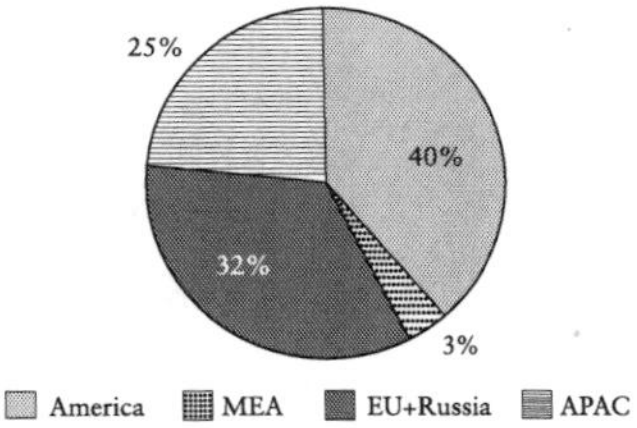

Source: Data Centre Dynamics Intelligence 2015

will be used to form the backbone of cloud services for both consumer and commercial customers. Cloud computing and Analytics will be the biggest driver of large Data Centre investment globally.

Global Data Centre market is dominated by the Americas with 40% of market share at $68 billion followed by Europe and Russia together at 32% or $54 billion. The APAC market is growing rapidly with a 25% market share at $42 billion[3] and lastly, the Middle East and Africa region hold a 3% share with nearly $6 billion in investments.

Global investments in large Data Centre segments are estimated to grow at 8% in 2016 whereas Asia Pacific will be the fastest growing region over the next five years. Today, APAC accounts for a quarter of worldwide Data Centre infrastructure spend at $42 billion. Regions such as Asia Pacific and Latin America are the ones really fuelling global Data Centre investment levels. China and India stand to exploit the market the most and fuel the growth in APAC[4]. Growth rates in the mature Data Centre markets have slowed down and will remain sluggish,[5] North America (US 3.8%, a point down from 2012), Western Europe (3%, a point up from 2012) and Japan (-0.1%, from flat to negative). [6]

1.2 India's Data Centre Market 2015

Data Centre facilities are of two types: captive (firms setting up centres for their own use) and third-party (hosting/co-location/outsourced). Data Centre market in India is seeing a good growth since the past few years due to the explosion of data through smartphones, social networking sites, e-commerce companies and Government's initiated projects. In India, the market is dominated by third-party Data Centre providers like Netmagic (NTT Com), CtrlS and telecom firms like Reliance, Tata Communications, etc.[7]

The Data Centre IT infrastructure investments, including total spending on servers, storage, networking, security and virtualisation stood at $2.2 billion (2015) and is expected to reach $2.29 billion by the year 2018.[8] Within the Indian IT infrastructure market, server growth reached $658 million in 2015, a marginal increase over 2014 levels. Enterprise networking and storage are the biggest segments with revenue reaching $944 million and $426 million in 2015, a 5.5% and 10% growth over 2014 respectively. Data Centre consolidation and virtualisation, cloud and mobility, are the key trends influencing network purchases.

Date Centre IT Infrastructure Growth by Technology

In Million USD	2014	2015
Servers	656	658
Storage	382	426
Enterprise Networking	892	944
Total	1929	2228

Source: Gartner 2015

India's Data Centre Market Share

As per the above figures, India shared around 1.2% of the world Data Centre IT infrastructure and 5.23% in APAC in 2015. As per

Figure 1.3: India has 1.2% share in the global market

Figure 1.4: India has 5.23% share in APAC

India Size
1.2%

India Size
5.23%

Source: Data Centre Dynamics Intelligence 2015

Gartner, India is the 2nd largest market for Data Centre infrastructure and 2nd fastest growing market in Asia/Pacific after China in 2015.[9]

India's Data Centre Hosting and Co-location Market

Co-location denotes the provisioning of a third party space to maintain an end-user's servers and the associated equipment. Growth of Data Centre market in terms of hosting and co-location market is going to experience a consistent growth through 2018.

India's Data Centre hosting and co-location market size stood at $638 million[10] in 2014 and is predicted to reach $1.3 billion in 2016 and 1.8 billion by 2018 at a CAGR of 21% as per Gartner.[11] There will be an increased outsourcing of Data Centre requirements in the forecast period due to demands from BFSI, social media, entertainment, e-commerce and telecom industries. This 3rd party segment contributed 30% in 2012 to the total Data Centre market and contributes nearly 40–45% at present.

Figure 1.5: Captive Data Centre and hosting & co-location market outlook

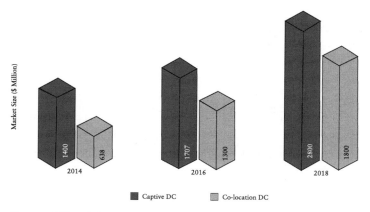

Source: CII and Gartner

1.3 INDIA DATA CENTRE MARKET OUTLOOK 2014–2020

India will be a $4.5 billion Data Centre market by 2018 as per Cyber Media Research[12] and will reach $7 billion by 2020 at a growth rate of 23% and with the current investment in Data Centre infra business by the various companies this would further enhance India's market share in the global and APAC markets, thus making India an attractive destination for the Data Centre business in the region. As per the current growth rate estimation, India's share in the global market and APAC could go up to 4.5% and 12% respectively.[13]

Figure 1.6: Investments ($Bn)

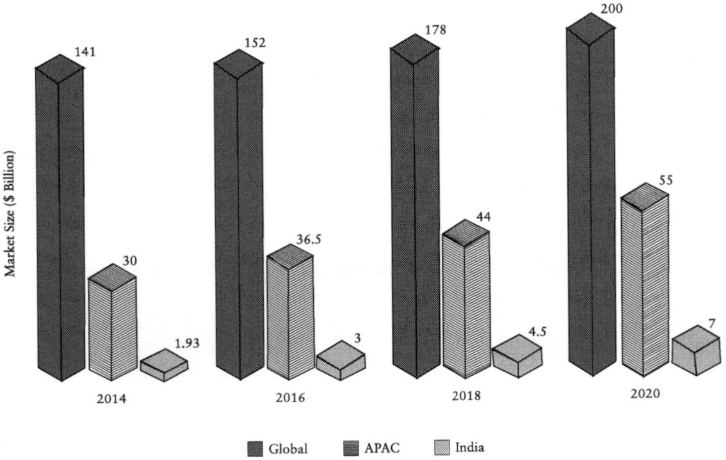

Source: Gartner, IDC and Cyber Media Research

Cloud Computing and Virtualisation will lead the technology evolution and continue to trigger growth in the Data Centre services market provided there is a seamless movement of data across national borders benefiting both businesses and consumers, enabling them to access the best available technology and services wherever those resources may be located.

Chapter Two
Trans Border Data Flows and Data Centres: Key to Future Growth

2.1 TRANS BORDER DATA FLOWS: STEADY CONTRIBUTION TO INDIAN ECONOMY

With the liberalisation of the Indian economy, the Information Technology and Business Process Management (IT-BPM)[14] sector has seen exponential growth in the country—from a mere 1.2% of the GDP in 1998 to 9.5% in 2015.[15] There is also evidence to show that India's leading role in IT-BPM services exports, i.e. trade from data flows, has had a spillover effect. With strong IT-capable human resources, the country's data processing needs are only going to expand with the growth in digital business and the thrust towards e-governance. India's technology and BPM sector (including hardware) has generated US$ 146 billion[16] in revenue during FY15, growing by 13% over the previous year[17] where the sector earned $118 billion in revenues. This growth has been largely backed by the export of IT-BPM services with industry driving non-linear growth through platforms, products and automation, leading to 1.2 times increase in revenues and employees since 2009.[18]

Worldwide IT-BPM spend was US$ 2.3 trillion, growing at 4.6% over 2013–2015, and India holds a massive 55% market share. The industry today is India's largest and most diverse private sector employer, with a direct workforce nearing million, and effecting over 10 million indirect jobs.

The IT industry growth is backed by 76% of exports of services and there are several economic effects of Transborder Data Flows (TBDF). As witnessed in India, TBDF provides economic benefits to industries, businesses and organisations that are able to adapt and change their internal practices to take advantage of developments in ICT and emerging technologies. Some of the economic benefits[21] that have been identified are[19]:

- **Economies of Scope:** The ability to centralise functions such as data storage, processing and management to reduce costs and take advantage of specialisation within the firm.
- **Increased Trade in Information and Communication Technologies and Services Fuelling Market Growth:** AAs trade in ICT takes place, prices are reduced and the market expands. This increased globalisation and economic expansion creates new activities and new companies that are engaged in cross-border trade and investment. As per Mckinsey Global Report[20], India has average to high participation across all flows (much of this growth has been in IT service exports including IT consulting, systems integration, call centers, and outsourcing of back-office functions) and ranks as the 30th most connected country overall, up 16 places from 1995.

- **Leveraging Global Supply Chains by Outsourcing Support Functions Allows for Renewed Focus on Core Business:** Outsourcing tasks that would otherwise need to be done in-house at either lower levels of efficiency or at higher costs enables firms to focus on their core functions. This leads to more effective use of internal resources and accelerated growth.

- **Access to Knowledge:** The growth of knowledge-based industries within the North American economy has elevated the importance of a firm's ability to effectively manage, create and disseminate knowledge within their organisation. A firm's ability to successfully control their information holdings is crucial to their success within their market.

- **Medical Data Transfers[21]:** In several cases ease in data flows can literally save lives of the patients, as some of the data that is transported are used for the purposes well beyond commercial including public health and safety.

- **International Growth Opportunities:** Through the use of TBDF, companies are able to enter foreign markets without necessarily having a physical presence there. This can result in significant cost savings and the ability to enter certain markets that may not have been economically viable if a physical presence was required.

- **Increased Productivity:** TBDF allows for multifaceted use of technology. This enables firms to improve their ability to maintain and share knowledge among their employees, which can help increase individual productivity. Improvement in productivity by enabling workers to use their skills effectively contributes to the company's bottom line.

- **Foster Innovation:** The ability to share data across borders, both between and within companies, fuels research and development and brings about additional ways of doing business, while providing new opportunities for emerging business models. Access to customer data allows businesses to analyse the success of past ventures and develop innovative approaches to better address customer needs or internal processes. In terms of a quantitative analysis of the economic impact of TBDF, it has been estimated that globally 75% of the value added by the Internet and data flow is in traditional industries, in part through increase in productivity.[22] Therefore, TBDF and domestic data flows are key to encouraging public/private enterprise as well as providing economies of scale and penetration to the NeGP for citizen-centric services in India.

The onus is on both governments and businesses to facilitate the flow of information data and communication around the world. Both will need to negotiate a range of challenges and risks to data privacy and security that are part and parcel of an increasingly data driven world to avoid misguided policies that could stifle job growth and lead to economic stagnation.

2.2 GOVERNMENT FOCUS ON DATA, DATA FLOWS AND DATA CENTRES[23]

Focus on data and, consequently, dataflow is not restricted to the private sector. Governments are increasingly reliant on IT-intensive services to improve their performance and organise the Government to Citizen (G2C) delivery platforms—including e-forms, public service grievance redressal, etc. For example, the National eGovernance Plan (NeGP) has more than 31 Mission Mode Projects[24] in its initial years[25]; the NeGP itself requires several data centres and needs yet more to support the various Business to Citizen (B2C) services.

The Government has a vision of making all services accessible to common man to achieve the citizen centric service delivery goal with three core infrastructural NeGP pillars:

- State Wide Area Network (SWAN)
- State Data Centres (SDCs) and
- Common Service Centres (CSCs)

The State Data Centre scheme has been approved for all States by Government of India with an outlay of Rs 1623.20 crores ($266 million) over a period of 5 years.[26]

In the United States, between 1998 and 2010, the number of federal data centres jumped from 432 to 2,094. In order to enhance efficacy of e-Governance and reduce costs, countries such as the US and the UK have defined the Cloud as an integral part of the government's IT strategy,[27] and are gradually moving towards a paperless government. These countries have realised the value to the economy from potential data flows and the consequent importance of data centres: Cloud First Policy (US), Integrated Strategy (EU), G-Cloud Strategy (UK), Strategic Direction Paper (Australia) and Smart Cloud Strategy (Japan) are all hallmarks of their respective governments' focus on strengthening data flows and building a robust Data Centre friendly environment. Common features of these government initiatives include driving *cloud adoption, friendly legal framework, and devising a technology and international collaboration strategy.*

Quantitatively, the impact of cloud computing on Data Centre traffic is clear. It is important to recognise that most of the Internet traffic since 2008 has originated or terminated in a Data Centre. According to one of the top-line projections, 69% of Data Centre traffic in the world will be cloud traffic by 2017.[28]

The Government of India's Cloud initiative—MeghRaj (GI Cloud)—was started with this vision: '*To accelerate delivery of e-services provided by the government and to optimize ICT spending of the government hence to support overall vision of NeGP (improved government services to common man)*'.

The Government of India has already begun rolling out of the GI Cloud with the launch of Phase-I of the National Cloud[29], which introduced the National AppStore and allowed the State Data Centres to be Cloud-enabled.

Under the NeGP, the NIC has established three major data centres, besides the one at its headquarters in New Delhi. These are the National Data Centre (NDC), New Delhi, NDC Pune and NDC Hyderabad. Under the same plan, state governments were expected to establish SDCs to enable e-governance, database management and digitisation of governmental information. Several states have created data centres, some with the help of the private sector. So, the data centres have private 'State Consultants' and 'Data Centre Operators'— primary players include Tata Consultancy Services, Wipro and Sify, with HCL, Reliance and Spanco also playing an important role.

The SDC, Maharashtra, has already moved from first generation data management to having a fully operational cloud earning the distinction of being the first state to do so. The private sector has also kept pace with the government and established data centres across the country, with Mumbai, Hyderabad and Bangalore being the most important locations.

With the rise in e-governance projects and governments relying on a strong digital infrastructure to support its operations, the demand for more secure and sophisticated technologies is definitely going to be explored. According to Government of India's GI Cloud Strategic Direction Paper, the key drivers and potential benefits for GI Cloud will be the following: Optimum utilisation of existing infrastructure; rapid deployment and reusability; manageability and maintainability;

scalability; efficient service delivery and agility; security; ease of first-time IT solution deployment; reduced effort in managing technology; and increased user mobility.

It is important to note that the GI Cloud[30] will not be a standalone private cloud but will consist of several categories such as government-owned and-operated cloud as well as government-shared cloud, owned and operated by the private sector. With managed services provider models[31] increasingly being used for service delivery to citizens by the Government (G2C), the GI Cloud categories evince the critical role of private sector participation in data management, data flows and data centres in India.

2.3 EFFECTS ON INDIAN INNOVATIONS

It should also be kept in mind that the freedom of data flow has been a boon to the innovation landscape in India. Zoho Corp., founded in 1996 in Chennai, Tamil Nadu, operates data centres in California and New Jersey.[32] Myntra, an e-commerce platform, and redBus, an online bus ticketing company, have also hosted their servers with cloud service providers such as Amazon Web Services.[33] Flipkart, one of the largest e-commerce platforms, relied on data centres in Canada for its initial operations.[34] Fortis Healthcare has migrated from its own corporate Data Centre to the cloud service provided by Windows Azure, leading to significant cost savings, and it intends to use the cloud for remote healthcare monitoring and remote healthcare delivery (Telemedicine).[35]

Restricting data flow via data localisation requirements would, therefore, hamper the next generation of disruptive start-ups from incubating in India. It would have a damaging effect on the investment climate, leading to trade deficit and impacting national GDP. These opportunities cannot be realised by attempting to achieve them through government mandates, but require market driven opportunities and incentives. A mandate-based approach —in the form of forced data localisation—will restrain the free flow of information in a way that will constrain the opportunity for growth.

'Make in India' would remain a dream for many entrepreneurs rather than a reality and it is critical to make India a preferred destination for data flows/centres rather than impose chilling data localisation requirements.

End Notes

1. http://www.gartner.com/newsroom/id/3186517.

2. http://www.canalys.com/newsroom/data-center-infrastructure-market-will-be-worth-152-billion-2016.

3. http://www.cio.in/content/asia-pacific-account-25-global-data-centre-infrastructure-spending-2016.

4. http://www.canalys.com/newsroom/data-center-infrastructure-market-will- be-worth-152-billion-2016.

5. IDC Predictions 2014: Battles for Dominance—and Survival—on the 3rd Platform (Page 5).

6. In the year 2014.

7. http://www.datacentermap.com/india/new-delhi/.

8. http://articles.economictimes.indiatimes.com/2015-05-11/news/62039831_1_infrastructure-market-infrastructure-spending-storage-market.

9. http://www.gartner.com/newsroom/id/2857217.

10. http://articles.economictimes.indiatimes.com/2014-12-26/news/57420683_1_india-enterprise-business-cloud-storage-data-centers.

11. http://datacenters.lbl.gov/sites/all/files/CII%20Energy%20Efficieny%20in%20Indian%20Data%20Centers-%20Present%20Trends%20and%20Future%20Opportunities.pdf.

12. http://cmrindia.com/cybermedia-research-india-data-center-services-market-review-2011-india-data-center-services-market-to-grow-at-a-23-cagr-over-the-three-years-to-2012-to-touch-rs-11800-crore/.

13. This estimate is under the business as usual scenario, keeping the economic conditions constant; the estimation could be bigger if the market situation gets conducive.

14. Includes IT enabled services for the purposes of this paper.

15. The IT-BPM Sector in India Strategic Review, NASSCOM.

16. http://www.ibef.org/industry/information-technology-india.aspx.

17. NASSCOM Report 2015.

18. NASSCOM—India IT-BPM Overview (Available at: http://www.nasscom.in/indian-itbpo-industry).

19. Report on the Trilateral Committee on Transborder Data Flows—North American Leaders Summit, Digital Policy Branch (Available at: https://www.ic.gc.ca/eic/ site/ecic-ceac.nsf/eng/gv00548.html).

20. Global flows in a digital age: How trade, finance, people, and data connect the world economy—McKinsey Global Institute 2014.

21. Business Without Borders: The Importance of Cross-Border Data Transfers to Global Prosperity (Page 7)—Whitepaper at Hunton & Williams LLP.

22. McKinsey Center for Business and Technology, Perspectives on Digital Business (Jan 2012).

23. https://negp.gov.in/images/guidelines.pdf.

24. eGovernance initiatives covering various streams identified and funded by the Central Government for implementation by the various State Governments in India.

25. Rolled out/approved in May 2006.

26. http://www.doitc.rajasthan.gov.in/_layouts/15/Doitc/User/ContentPage.aspx?Id=264&LangID=English.

27. The World Bank, Next Generation eGovernment: The Cloud and Beyond, eGovernment Summit; CII-KPMG Cloud Report 2012.

28. Cisco Global Cloud Index: Forecast and Methodology, 2012–2017 (Available at: http://www.cisco.com/c/en/us/solutions/collateral/service-provider/global- cloud-index-gci/Cloud_Index_White_Paper.html).

29. February 2014, as per DeiTY reports.

30. As per Department of Electronics & Information Technology, Ministry of Communications & IT, Government of India.

31. BSP for Aadhaar, Driving License projects across several states.

32. Bernard Lunn, Zoho: The Little Engine That Could (Take on Both Microsoft and Google) (8 September 2008) available at http://readwrite.com/2008/09/18/zoho_ the_little_engine_that_could.

33. Amazon Web Services Launches 'The Lean Cloud' Program for Start-Ups in Asia Pacific (3 April 2012), available at http://yourstory.com/2012/04/amazon-web-services-launches-the-lean-cloud-program-for-start-ups-in-asia-pacific/.

34. Rebuilding Flipkart's Data Centres (12 June 2014), available at http://www.cioandleader.com/cioleaders/cio-transforms/40294/rebuilding-flipkarts- centres.

35. Microsoft is Powering the Cloud Transition in India (20 March 2014), available at http://www.microsoft.com/en-in/news/Press/2014/Mar14/MicrosoftisPoweringt.aspx.

BIBLIOGRAPHY

Abraham, I. 2017. 'From the Commission to the Mission Model: Technology Czars and the Indian Middle Class'. *The Journal of Asian Studies* 76(3): 675–696.

Amoore, L. 2016. 'Cloud Geographies: Computing, Data, Sovereignty'. *Progress in Human Geography* 42(1): 4–24.

Appel, H., N. Anand, and A. Gupta. 2018. 'Introduction: Temporality, Politics, and the Promise of Infrastructure'. In *The Promise of Infrastructure*, H. Appel, N. Anand, and A. Gupta (eds), 1–38. Durham: Duke University Press.

Aronova, E. 2017. 'Geophysical Datascapes of the Cold War: Politics and Practices of the World Data Centers in the 1950s and 1960s'. *Osiris* 32(1): 307–327.

Aronova, E., C. V. Oertzen, and D. Sepkoski. 2017. 'Introduction: Historicizing Big Data'. *Osiris* 32(1): 1–17.

Aschoff, N. 2015. *The New Prophets of Capital*. London: Verso.

Banerjee, P. S. 1983. 'Induction of Computers in India'. Occasional paper no. 56, Centre for Studies in Social Sciences (CSSSC). Calcutta: CSSSC.

Bapat, M. 1990. 'Allocation of Urban Space: Rhetoric and Reality'. *Economic and Political Weekly* 25(28): 1502–1507.

Basu, A. and K. Nachiappan. 2020. 'India and the Global Battle for Data Governance'. *Seminar* 731, July. Available at https://www.india-seminar. com/2020/731/731_arindrajit_and_karthik.htm (accessed April 2022).

Bates, J., Yu-Wei Lin, and P. Goodale. 2016. 'Data Journeys: Capturing the Socio-Material Constitution of Data Objects and Flows'. *Big Data & Society* 3(2): 1–12.

Bhattacharya, A. 1971. *A Study of Industries in Trans-Thane Belt*. Bombay: CIDCO (City and Industrial Development Corporation of Maharashtra).

Bigo, D., E. Isin, and E. Ruppert (eds). 2019. *Data Politics: Worlds, Subjects, Rights*. New York: Routledge.

Blum, A. 2012. *Tubes: A Journey to the Center of the Internet*. New York: Harper Collins.

BMRPD (Bombay Metropolitan Regional Planning Board). 1970. *Report on the Draft Regional Plan of Bombay Metropolitan Region 1970–1991*, 2 vols. Mumbai.

Bouk, D. 2017. 'The History and Political Economy of Personal Data over the Last Two Centuries in Three Acts'. *Osiris* 32(1): 85–106.

Brandt Commission. 1980. *North-South: A Program for Survival, Report of the Independent Commission on International Development Issues*. Cambridge, MA: MIT Press.

Bratton, B. 2016. *The Stack: On Software and Sovereignty*. Cambridge: MIT Press.

Breman, J. 2013. *At Work in the Informal Economy of India: A Perspective from the Bottom Up.* Oxford: Oxford University Press.

Broad Group. 2019. *Data Centres India.* Available at https://www.broad-group.com/reports/data-centres-india (accessed May 2022).

Burrington, I. 2015a. 'The Strange Geopolitics of the International Cloud'. *The Atlantic*, 17 November. Available at https://www.theatlantic.com/technology/archive/2015/11/the-strange-geopolitics-of-the-international-cloud/416370/ (accessed May 2022).

———. 2015b. 'A Visit to the NSA's Data Center in Utah'. *The Atlantic*, 19 November. Available at https://www.theatlantic.com/technology/archive/2015/11/a-visit-to-the-nsas-data-center-in-utah/416691/ (accessed May 2022).

Carruth, A. 2014. 'The Digital Cloud and the Micropolitics of Energy'. *Public Culture* 26(2): 339–364.

Carse, A. 2016. 'Keyword: Infrastructure'. In *Infrastructures and Social Complexity: A Companion*, P. Harvey, C. Bruun Jensen, and A. Morita (eds), 27–39. New York: Routledge.

Chakraborty, S. 2013. 'Indian Banking Set to Become Fifth Largest by 2020: KPMG-CII Report'. *Business Standard*, 13 September. Available at http://www.business-standard.com/article/finance/indian-banking-set-to-become-fifth-largest-by-2020-kpmg-cii-report-113091300822_1.html (accessed April 2022).

Chander, A. and U. P. Lê. 2015. 'Data Nationalism'. *Emory Law Journal* 64(3): 677–739.

Charlie, A. 2014. 'India Losing out Data Centre Business to Small Nations'. *The Hindu*, 2 June. Available at https://www.thehindubusinessline.com/info-tech/india-losing-out-data-centre-business-to-small-nations/article23152064.ece (accessed April 2022).

Chattapadhyay, S. 2013. 'Of identity, platform, and "new" information infrastructure of governance: Situating the Aadhaar project within the history of electronic governance in India'. Paper presented on 14–16 November at 'The Social and Cultural Life of Information' Conference, Sarai-CSDS (Centre for the Study of Developing Societies), New Delhi, India.

Chatterjee, E. 2017. 'Insulated Wires: The Precarious Rise of West Bengal's Power Sector'. Working Paper, Mapping Power Project, Centre for Policy Research and Regulatory Assistance Project. Available at http://www.raponline.org/wp-content/uploads/2017/05/rap-india-mappingpower-west-bengal-2017-may.pdf (accessed April 2022).

———. 2020. 'The Asian Anthropocene: Electricity and Fossil Developmentalism'. *The Journal of Asian Studies* 79(1): 3–24.

Chatterjee, P. 2004. *The Politics of the Governed: Reflections on Popular Politics in Most of the World.* New York: Columbia University Press.

CIDCO (City and Industrial Development Corporation of Maharashtra). 1973. *New Bombay: Draft Development Plan*. Mumbai: CIDCO.

———. 2005. *Revised Budget Estimates 2003–04*. Navi Mumbai: CIDCO.

———. 2009. *39th Annual Report 2008–09*. Navi Mumbai: CIDCO.

———. 2012. *42nd Annual Report 2011–12*. Navi Mumbai: CIDCO.

CIDCO Economics Department. 2006. *Executive Summary—Socio-Economic Survey of Households in NM's Planned Nodes*. Navi Mumbai: CIDCO.

CIDCO Economics and Statistics Departments. 2014. *Project Report of Navi Mumbai*. New Bombay: CIDCO.

CIDCO Economics Section. 1984. *A Report on Survey of Industries in Thane-Belapur Area in New Bombay*. New Bombay: CIDCO.

———. 1988. *Socio-Economic Survey of Households in Various Nodes in New Bombay*. New Bombay: CIDCO.

———. 1990. *A Report on the Survey of Industries in New Bombay*. New Bombay: CIDCO.

CIDCO Public Relations Office. 1998. *Navi Mumbai: The Corporate World's New Address in 21st Century*. Navi Mumbai: CIDCO.

CIDCO Statistics Department. 2010. *Socio-Economic Profile of Households in Planned Nodes in Navi Mumbai*. Navi Mumbai: CIDCO.

Correa, C., P. Mehta, and S. B. Patel. 1965. 'Planning for Bombay'. *MARG* 18(3): 30–56.

Couldry, N. and U. A. Mejias. 2018. 'Data Colonialism: Rethinking Big Data's Relation to the Contemporary Subject'. *Television & New Media* 20(4): 336–349. Available at https://journals.sagepub.com/doi/abs/10.1177/15 27476418796632?journalCode=tvna (accessed April 2022).

Cowen, D. 2014. *The Deadly Life of Logistics: Mapping Violence in Global Trade*. Minneapolis: University of Minnesota Press.

Cross, J. 2019. 'No Current: Electricity and Disconnection in Rural India'. In *Electrifying Anthropology: Exploring Electrical Practices and Infrastructures*, S. Abram, B. R. Winthereik, and T. Yarrow (eds), 65–82. London: Bloomsbury.

Datta, A. 2015. 'New Urban Utopias of Postcolonial India: "Entrepreneurial Urbanization" in Dholera Smart City, Gujarat'. *Dialogues in Human Geography* 5(1): 3–22.

———. 2018. 'The digital turn in postcolonial urbanism: Smart citizenship in the making of India's 100 smart cities'. *Transactions of the Institute of British Geographers* 43(3): 405–419.

Dattani, K. 2020. '"Governtrepreneurism" for Good Governance: The Case of Aadhaar and the India Stack'. *Area* 52(2): 411–419.

Deleuze, G. 1992. 'Postscript on the Societies of Control'. *October* 59: 3–7.

Derrida, J. 1996. *Archive Fever: A Freudian Impression*. Chicago: University of Chicago Press.

Deshpande, S. 1993. 'Imagined Economies: Styles of Nation-Building in Twentieth Century India'. *Journal of Arts and Ideas* 25–26: 5–35.

Dey, I., R. Samaddar, and S. K. Sen. 2016. *Beyond Kolkata: Rajarhat and the Dystopia of Urban Imagination*. Kolkata: Routledge India.

Dharia, N. and N. Trisal. 2017. 'Demonetization: Critical Responses to India's Cash(/less) Experiment'. Hot Spots series, *Fieldsights*, 27 September. Available at https://culanth.org/fieldsights/series/demonetization-critical-responses-to-indias-cash-less-experiment (accessed April 2022).

Doctorow, C. 2008. 'Welcome to the Petacentre'. *Nature* 455(4): 16–21.

Dubash, N. K. and S. C. Rajan. 2001. 'Power Politics: Process of Power Sector Reform in India'. *Economic and Political Weekly* 36(35): 3367–3390.

Dutta, K. 2013. 'Issues in Implementation of SAP in WBSEDCL Business Domain'. *Power News*, [West Bengal State Electricity Board Engineers' Association (WBSEBEA)] April–October: 3–7.

Dwivedi, S. and R. Mehrotra. 1995. *Bombay: The Cities Within*. Bombay: India Book House.

Easterling, K. 2014. *Extrastatecraft: The Power of Infrastructure Space*. London and New York: Verso.

Edgerton, D. 2011. *The Shock of the Old: Technology and Global History since 1900*. London: Profile Books.

Edwards, P. 1996. *The Closed World: Computers and the Politics of Discourse in Cold War America*. Cambridge: MIT Press.

Friendly, M. 2008. 'The Golden Age of Statistical Graphics'. *Statistical Science* 23(4): 502–535.

Frost and Sullivan (F&S). 2017. 'Not All Data Centres Are Equal—Understanding the Global Best Practices of Data Centres that Power the Cloud'. A Whitepaper by F&S for Macquarie Telecom.

Fuster, G. G. 2014. *The Emergence of Personal Data Protection as a Fundamental Right of the EU*, Law, Governance and Technology series, Vol. 16. London: Springer Science & Business.

Gabrys, J. 2011. *Digital Rubbish: A Natural History of Electronics*. Ann Arbor: University of Michigan Press.

Galloway, A. R. 2013. 'The Poverty of Philosophy: Realism and Post-Fordism'. *Critical Inquiry* 39(2): 347–366.

Ghosh, A. 2013. *Branding the Migrant: Arguments of Rights, Welfare and Security*. Kolkata: Frontpage.

———. 2016. 'Accepting Difference, Seeking Common Ground: Sino-Indian Statistical Exchanges 1951–1959'. *BJHS Themes* 1: 61–82. Available at https://doi.org/10.1017/bjt.2016.1 (accessed April 2022).

Ghosh, J., C. P. Chandrasekhar, and P. Patnaik. 2017. *Demonetisation Decoded: A Critique of India's Currency Experiment*. London and New York: Routledge.

Graham, M. and T. Shelton. 2013. 'Geography and the Future of Big Data, Big Data and the Future of Geography'. *Dialogues in Human Geography* 3(3): 255–261.

Graham, S. 2000. 'Constructing Premium Network Spaces: Reflections on Infrastructure Networks and Contemporary Urban Development'. *International Journal of Urban and Regional Research* 24(1): 183–200.

Graham, S., and S. Marvin. 2001. *Splintering Urbanism: Networked Infrastructures, Technological Mobilities and the Urban Condition*. London: Routledge.

Gupta, A. 2015. 'An Anthropology of Electricity from the Global South'. *Cultural Anthropology* 30(4): 555–568.

Hacking, I. 1990. *The Taming of Chance*. Cambridge: Cambridge University Press.

Hansen, T. B. and O. Verkaik. 2009. 'Introduction: Urban Charisma—On Everyday Mythologies in the City'. *Critique of Anthropology* 29(1): 5–26.

Hardt, M. 1999. 'Affective Labour'. *Boundary 2* 26(2): 89–100.

Harris, N. 1978. *Economic Development, Cities and Planning: The Case of Bombay*. Mumbai: Oxford University Press.

Hogan, M. 2015a. 'Data Flows and Water Woes: The Utah Data Center'. *Big Data & Society* 2(2): 1–12.

———. 2015b. 'Facebook Data Storage Centers as the Archive's Underbelly'. *Television & New Media* 16(1): 3–18.

Hogan, M. and A. Vonderau. 2019. 'The Nature of Data Centers'. *Culture Machine* 18. Available at https://culturemachine.net/vol-18-the-nature-of-data-centers/ (accessed April 2022).

Hu, T-H. 2015. *A Prehistory of the Cloud*. Cambridge: MIT Press.

IAMAI (Internet and Mobile Association of India). 2016. 'Make in India: Conducive Policy & Regulatory Environment to Incentivize Data Center Infrastructure', May. PLR Chambers. Available at https://www.medianama.com/wp-content/uploads/iamai-make-in-india-data-center-report-india.pdf (accessed May 2022).

Introna, L. D. 2016. 'Algorithms, Governance, and Governmentality: On Governing Academic Writing'. *Science, Technology and Human Values* 41(1): 17–49.

Jacobson, K. and M. Hogan. 2019. 'Retrofitted Data Centres: A New World in the Shell of the Old'. *Work Organisation, Labour & Globalisation* 13(2): 78–94.

Jakobsson, P. and F. Stiernstedt. 2012. 'Time, Space and Clouds of Information: Data Center Discourse and the Meaning of Durability'. In *Cultural Technologies: The Shaping of Culture in Media and Society*, Göran Bolin (ed.), 103–118. New York: Routledge.

Johnson, A. 2019. 'Emplacing Data within Imperial Histories: Imagining Iceland as Data Centres' "Natural" Home'. *Culture Machine* 18.

Available at https://culturemachine.net/vol-18-the-nature-of-data-centers/emplacing-data/ (accessed April 2022).

Johnson, A. and M. Hogan. 2017. 'Introducing Location and Dislocation: Global Geographies of Digital Data'. *Imaginations: Journal of Cross-Cultural Image Studies* 8(2): 3–6. Available at http://imaginations. glendon.yorku.ca/?p=9950 (accessed April 2022).

Joshi, D. 2020. 'Interrogating India's Quest for Data Sovereignty'. *Seminar* 731, July. Available at https://www.india-seminar.com/2020/731/731_ divij_joshi.htm (accessed April 2022).

Kale, S. S. 2014. *Electrifying India: Regional Political Economies of Development*. Stanford: Stanford University Press.

Kharbanda, V. 2019. 'An Analysis of the RBI's Draft Framework on Regulatory Sandbox for Fintech'. *The Centre for Internet and Society Blog*, 8 May. Available at https://cis-india.org/internet-governance/files/ analysis-of-the-rbi2019s-draft-framework-on-regulatory-sandbox-for-fintech (accessed April 2022).

Khera, R. 2019. 'Aadhaar Failures: A Tragedy of Errors'. *Economic and Political Weekly* 54(14). Available at https://www.epw.in/engage/article/ aadhaar-failures-food-services-welfare (accessed April 2022).

——— (ed.). 2019. *Dissent on Aadhaar: Big Data Meets Big Brother*. Hyderabad: Orient BlackSwan.

Kitchin, R. 2014. *The Data Revolution: Big Data, Open Data, Data Infrastructures and their Consequences*. London: Sage.

Klose, A. 2009. *The Container Principle: How a Box Changes the Way We Think*. Cambridge: MIT Press.

Kohli, A. 1987. *The State and Poverty in India: The Politics of Reform*. New York: Cambridge University Press.

Koops, B. J. and R. Leenes. 2014. 'Privacy regulation cannot be hardcoded. A critical comment on the "privacy by design" provision in data-protection law'. *International Review of Law, Computers & Technology* 28(2): 159–171.

Korsmo, F. L. 2010. 'The Origins and Principles of the World Data Center System'. *Data Science Journal* 8: 55–65.

Krasner, S. D. 1999. *Sovereignty: Organized Hypocrisy*. Princeton: Princeton University Press.

Kumar, A. 2017. *Demonetization and Black Economy*. New Delhi: Penguin Random House India.

Larkin, B. 2013. 'The Politics and Poetics of Infrastructure'. *Annual Review of Anthropology* 42: 327–343.

Latour, B. 1993. *We Have Never Been Modern*, C. Porter (trans.). Cambridge: Harvard University Press.

LeCavalier, J. 2016. *The Rule of Logistics: Walmart and the Architecture of Fulfillment*. Minneapolis: University of Minnesota Press.

Leszczynski, A. 2016. 'Speculative Futures: Cities, Data, and Governance Beyond Smart Urbanism'. *Environment and Planning A: Economy and Space* 48 (9): 1691–1708.

Lewis, M. W. and K. E. Wigen (eds). 1997. *The Myth of Continents: A Critique of Metageography*. Berkeley: University of California Press.

Lippert, R. K. and K. Walby. 2016. 'Governing through Privacy: Authoritarian Liberalism, Law, and Privacy Knowledge'. *Law, Culture and the Humanities* 12(2): 329–352.

Liu, X., N. Iftikar, and X. Xie. 2014. 'Survey of Real-Time Processing Systems for Big Data'. In *IDEAS '14: Proceedings of the 18th International Database Engineering & Applications Symposium*, Ana Maria Almeida, Jorge Bernardino, and Elsa Ferreira Gomes (eds), 356–361. New York and USA: ACM. Available at https://dl.acm.org/doi/10.1145/2628194.2628251 (accessed April 2022).

Liu, Y., J. K. Muppala, M. Veeraraghavan, D. Lin, and M. Hamdi. 2013. *Data Center Networks: Topologies, Architectures and Fault–Tolerance Characteristics*. Cham: Springer.

Liu, Z., Z. Wang, X. Cheng, C. Jia, and K. Yuan. 2013. 'Multi-User Searchable Encryption with Coarser-Grained Access Control in Hybrid Cloud'. In *2013 Fourth International Conference on Emerging Intelligent Data and Web Technologies*, IEEE, 249–255. Available at https://ieeexplore. ieee.org/abstract/document/6631626 (April 2022).

Luque-Ayala, A. and S. Marvin. 2015. 'Developing a Critical Understanding of Smart Urbanism'. *Urban studies* 52(12): 2105–2116.

Lynskey, O. 2015. *The Foundations of EU Data Protection Law*. Oxford: Oxford University Press.

Lyon, D. 1994. *The Electronic Eye: The Rise of Surveillance Society*. Minneapolis: University of Minnesota Press.

Maguire, J. and B. Ross Winthereik. 2021. 'Digitalizing the State: Data Centres and the Power of Exchange'. *Ethnos* 86(3): 530–551.

Malecki, E. J. and H. Wei. 2009. 'A Wired World: The Evolving Geography of Submarine Cables and the Shift to Asia'. *Annals of the Association of American Geographers* 99(2): 360–382.

MARG (Modern Architects' Research Group). 1965. 'Bombay: Planning and Dreaming'. *MARG* 18(3).

Marx, K. 1867. *Capital: A Critique of Political Economy, Volume I: The Process of Capitalist Production*. Charles H. Kerr and Company. Available at https://oll.libertyfund.org/title/marx-capital-a-critique-of-political-economy-volume-i-the-process-of-capitalist-production (accessed May 2022).

———. 1885. *Capital: A Critique of Political Economy, Volume II: The Process of Circulation of Capital*. Charles H. Kerr and Company.

Available at https://oll.libertyfund.org/title/marx-capital-a-critique-of-political-economy-volume-ii-the-process-of-circulation-of-capital (accessed May 2022).

Marx, K. 1894. *Capital: A Critique of Political Economy, Volume III: The Process of Capitalist Production as a Whole*. Charles H. Kerr and Company. Available at https://oll.libertyfund.org/title/marx-capital-a-critique-of-political-economy-volume-iii-the-process-of-capitalist-production-as-a-whole (accessed May 2022).

———. 1993 [1939–1941]. *Grundrisse: Foundations of the Critique of Political Economy*. Penguin Classics. Also available at https://www.marxists.org/archive/marx/works/1857/grundrisse/ (accessed March 2022).

Mattern, S. 2016. 'Cloud and Field'. *Places*, August. Available at https://placesjournal.org/article/cloud-and-field/ (accessed April 2022).

Mazzucato, M. 2013. *The Entrepreneurial State: Debunking Public vs. Private Sector Myths*. New York: Anthem Press.

MCGB (Municipal Corporation of Greater Bombay). 1964. *Report on the Development Plan for Greater Bombay*. Mumbai: Government Central Press.

MEDC (Maharashtra Economic Development Council). 2013. *Repositioning Navi Mumbai as a Growth Engine*. Navi Mumbai: Statistics Department, CIDCO.

Mehmood, T. 2008. 'Notes from a Contested History of National Identity Card in India: 1999–2007'. *South Asia Citizens Web*, 9 December. Available at http://www.sacw.net/article391.html (accessed April 2022).

Menon, N. 2018. '"Fancy Calculating Machine": Computers and Planning in Independent India'. *Modern Asian Studies* 52(2): 421–457.

Mitchell, T. 2014. 'Economentality: How the Future Entered Government'. *Critical Inquiry* 40(4): 479–507.

Mitra, I. K., R. Samaddar, and S. Sen (eds). 2017. *Accumulation in Post-Colonial Capitalism*. Singapore: Springer.

Modak, N. V. and A. Mayer. 1948. *The Master Plan in Outline*. Bombay: The Bombay Municipality and the Government of Bombay. Available at https://dspace.gipe.ac.in/xmlui/bitstream/handle/10973/45577/GIPE-022418-Contents.pdf?sequence=2&isAllowed=y (accessed May 2022).

Mosco, V. 2014. *To The Cloud: Big Data in a Turbulent World*. New York: Routledge.

Mukherji, A. 2006. 'Political Ecology of Groundwater: The Contrasting Case of Water-Abundant West Bengal and Water-Scarce Gujarat, India'. *Hydrogeology Journal* 14(3): 392–406.

Mukherji, A., T. Shah, and P. Banerjee. 2012. 'Kick-Starting a Second Green Revolution in Bengal'. *Economic and Political Weekly* 47(18): 27–30.

Neilson, B. 2014. 'Beyond Kulturkritik: Along the Supply Chain of Contemporary Capitalism'. *Culture Unbound: Journal of Current Cultural Research* 6(1): 77–93.

Neilson, B. and S. Mezzadra. 2014. 'The State of Capitalist Globalization'. *Viewpoint Magazine*, 4 September. Available at https://www.viewpointmag.com/2014/09/04/the-state-of-capitalist-globalization/ (accessed May 2022).

Neilson, B. and T. Notley. 2019. 'Data Centres as Logistical Facilities: Singapore and the Emergence of Production Topologies'. *Work Organisation, Labour & Globalisation* 13(1): 15–29.

Nemani, R. 2011. 'The Journey from Computer Time-Sharing to Cloud Computing: A Literature Review'. *International Journal of Computer Sciences and Engineering* 1(6): 267–273.

Newbigin, E. 2020. 'Accounting for the Nation, Marginalizing the Empire: Taxable Capacity and Colonial Rule in the Early Twentieth Century'. *History of Political Economy* 52(3): 455–472.

Nilekani, N. 2009. *Imagining India: The Idea of a Renewed Nation*. New Delhi: Penguin.

———. 2017. 'Why India needs to be a data democracy'. *Livemint*, 27 July. Available at http:// www.livemint.com/Opinion/gm1MNTytiT3zRqxt1d XbhK/Why-India-needs-to-be-a-data-democracy.html (accessed April 2022).

Oertzen, C. V. 2017. 'Machineries of Data Power: Manual versus Mechanical Census Compilation in Nineteenth-Century Europe'. *Osiris* 32(1): 129–150.

Ong, A. 2006. *Neoliberalism as Exception: Mutations in Citizenship and Sovereignty*. Durham: Duke University Press.

Paidipaty, P. 2020. 'Testing Measures: Decolonisation and Economic Power in 1960s India'. *History of Political Economy* 52(3): 473–497.

Pargal, S. and S. Ghosh Banerjee. 2014. *More Power to India: The Challenge of Electricity Distribution*. Washington: World Bank.

Park, H. W. and Z. Xu. 2010. 'Turnover Time and its Relation to the Rate of Profit', 17 October, Conference at University of Massachusetts. Available at http://www.peri.umass.edu/fileadmin/pdf/conference_papers/newschool/NS-UMASS_conference_2010.docx (accessed April 2022).

Patel, S. B. 1970. 'Regional Planning for Bombay'. *Economic and Political Weekly* 5(26): 1011–1018.

———. 1993. 'A Second Financial Centre for Bombay: Where Should It Be?' *Economic and Political Weekly* 28(32/33): 1631–1635.

Postone, M. 1978. 'Necessity, Labor, and Time: A Reinterpretation of the Marxian Critique of Capitalism'. *Social Research* 45(4): 739–788.

Rajaraman, V. 2012. 'History of Computing in India, 1955–2010'. Supercomputer Education and Research Centre, IISc Bangalore. Available at https://history.computer.org/pubs/2012-12-rajaraman-india-computing-history.pdf (accessed May 2022).

Ramanathan, U. 2011. 'The Myth of the Technology Fix'. *India-Seminar* 617. Available at https://www.india-seminar.com/2011/617/617_usha_ramanathan.htm (accessed April 2022).

Rao, U. 2018. 'Biometric bodies, or how to make electronic fingerprinting work in India'. *Body & Society* 24(3): 68–94.

Rao, U. and V. Nair. 2019. 'Aadhaar: Governing with Biometrics'. *South Asia: Journal of South Asian Studies* 42(3): 469–481.

Reading, A. and T. Notley. 2015. 'The Materiality of Globital Memory: Bringing the Cloud to Earth'. *Continuum* 29(4): 511–521.

Rigi, J. 2014. 'Foundations of a Marxist Theory of the Political Economy of Information: Trade Secrets and Intellectual Property, and the Production of Relative Surplus Value and the Extraction of Rent-Tribute'. *tripleC* 12(2): 909–936.

Rigi, J. and R. Prey. 2015. 'Value, Rent, and the Political Economy of Social Media'. *The Information Society* 31(5): 392–406.

Rose, N. 1996. 'The Death of the Social? Re-Figuring the Territory of Government'. *Economy and Society* 25(3): 327–356.

Rossiter, N. 2016. *Software, Infrastructure, Labor: A Media Theory of Logistical Nightmares*. New York and London: Routledge.

———. 2017. 'Imperial Infrastructure and Asia Beyond Asia: Data Centres, State Formation and Territoriality of Logistical Media'. *The Fibreculture Journal* 29: 1–20.

Roy, A. and A. Ong (eds). 2011. *Worlding Cities: Asian Experiments and the Art of Being Global*. Malden and Oxford: Wiley-Blackwell.

Rudra, A. 1996. 'The Indian Statistical System'. In *Prasanta Chandra Mahalanobis: A Biography*, Ashok Rudra (ed.), 204–213. New Delhi: Oxford University Press.

Ruppert, E. and E. Isin. 2019. 'Data's Empire: Postcolonial Data Politics'. In *Data Politics: Worlds, Subjects, Rights*, D. Bigo, E. Isin, and E. Ruppert (eds), 207–227. New York: Routledge.

Sadowski, J. 2019. 'When Data is Capital: Datafication, Accumulation, and Extraction'. *Big Data & Society*, January: 1–12.

Samaddar, R. 2015. 'Why High Politics in Bengal Speaks the Language of the Lower Depths?' *The Wire*, 8 July. Available at https://thewire.in/politics/why-high-politics-in-bengal-speaks-the-language-of-the-lower-depths (accessed April 2022).

———. 2018a. *Karl Marx and the Postcolonial Age*. Switzerland: Palgrave Macmillan.

Samaddar, R. 2018b. 'The Urban Turn'. *Policies and Practices* 96: 16–23. Available at http://www.mcrg.ac.in/pp96.PDF (accessed April 2022).

Sanyal, K. 2007. *Rethinking Capitalist Development: Primitive Accumulation, Governmentality and Post-Colonial Capitalism*. New Delhi: Routledge.

Sartori, A. 2013. 'Global Intellectual History and the History of Political Economy'. In *Global Intellectual History*, Samuel Moyn and Andrew Sartori (eds), 110–133. New York: Columbia University Press.

Sassen, S. 2014. *Expulsions: Brutality and Complexity in the Global Economy*. Cambridge: Harvard University Press.

Scott, A. J. and M. Storper. 2014. 'The Nature of Cities: The Scope and Limits of Urban Theory'. *International Journal of Urban and Regional Research* 39(1): 1–15.

Sengupta, U. 2013. 'Inclusive Development? A State-Led Land Development Model in New Town, Kolkata'. *Environment and Planning C: Government and Policy* 31(2): 357–376.

Shaw, A. 1999. 'The Planning and Development of New Bombay'. *Modern Asian Studies* 33(4): 951–988.

———. 2004. *The Making of Navi Mumbai*. Hyderabad: Orient BlackSwan.

Sheth, D. L. 1992. 'Movements, Intellectuals and the State: Social Policy in Nation-Building'. *Economic and Political Weekly* 27(8): 425–429.

Sinha, A. and A. Sethia. 2017. 'Aadhaar Case: Beyond Privacy, An Issue of Bodily Integrity'. *The Quint*, 1 May. Available at https://www.thequint.com/voices/opinion/aadhaar-case-privacy-and-bodily-integrity (accessed April 2022).

Sinha, A. and A. Basu. 2019. 'The Politics of India's Data Protection Ecosystem'. *Economic and Political Weekly* 54(49). Available at https://www.epw.in/engage/article/politics-indias-data-protection-ecosystem (accessed April 2022).

Smith, N. 2002. 'New Globalism, New Urbanism: Gentrification as Global Urban Strategy'. *Antipode* 34(3): 427–450.

Solanki, A. 2019. 'Management of Performance and Performance of Management: Getting to Work on Time in the Indian Bureaucracy'. *South Asia: Journal of South Asian Studies* 42(3): 588–605.

Srinivasan, T. N. 1996. 'Professor Mahalanobis and Economics'. In *Prasanta Chandra Mahalanobis: A Biography*, Ashok Rudra (ed.), 225–252. New Delhi: Oxford University Press.

Srnicek, N. 2017. *Platform Capitalism*. Cambridge and Malden: Polity Press.

Star, S. L. and G. C. Bowker. 2002. 'How to Infrastructure'. In *Handbook of New Media*, L. A. Lievrouw and S. Livingstone (eds), 151–162. London: SAGE.

Starosielski. N. 2015. *The Undersea Network*. Durham: Duke University Press.

Subramanian, C. R. 1992. *India and the Computer: A Study of Planned Development*. New Delhi: Oxford University Press.

The Economist. 2017. 'Data is Giving Rise to a New Economy', 6 May. Available at https://www.economist.com/briefing/2017/05/06/data-is-giving-rise-to-a-new-economy (accessed April 2022).

The Indian Express. 2018. 'Three Years of Formation: Niti Aayog Working to Adopt AI, Blockchain in Governance', 4 January. Available at https://indianexpress.com/article/business/business-others/three-years-of-formation-niti-aayog-working-to-adopt-ai-blockchain-in-governance-5010639/ (accessed April 2022).

The Times of India. 2017. 'Mumbai Mega Mall Fails, Turned into Offices', 7 April. Available at https://timesofindia.indiatimes.com/city/mumbai/mumbai-mega-mall-fails-turned-into-offices/articleshow/58057231.cms (accessed April 2022).

Thompson, E. P. 1963. *The Making of the English Working Class.* London: Pantheon Press.

Thrift, N. 2014. 'The "Sentient" City and What it May Portend'. *Big Data and Society* April–June: 1–21.

Tongia, R. 2004. 'The Political Economy of Indian Power Sector Reforms'. Working paper no. 4, Centre for Environmental Science and Policy, Stanford University.

Tsing, A. 2009. 'Supply Chains and the Human Condition'. *Rethinking Marxism* 21(2): 148–176.

UNCTAD (United Nations Conference on Trade and Development). 2016. *Data protection regulations and international data flows: Implications for trade and development.* New York and Geneva: United Nations. Available at https://unctad.org/en/PublicationsLibrary/dtlstict2016d1_en.pdf (accessed April 2022).

Vedula, A. 2007. 'Blueprint and Reality: Navi Mumbai, the City of the 21st Century'. *Habitat International* 31(1): 12–23.

Vigne, B. 2020. 'Omeya: Water, Work and Infrastructure in Ovamboland from 1915 to 1968'. Master's Thesis, Department of Historical Studies, University of Cape Town. Available at https://open.uct.ac.za/handle/11427/32366 (accessed April 2022).

Ward, M. 2004. *Quantifying the World: UN Ideas and Statistics.* Bloomington: Indiana University Press.

Warf, B. 1989. 'Telecommunications and the Globalization of Financial Services'. *The Professional Geographer* 41(3): 257–271.

———. 2007. 'Geopolitics of the Satellite Industry'. *Tijdschrift voor Economische en Sociale Geografie* 98(3): 385–397.

World Bank. 2009. *West Bengal Power Sector Reforms: Lessons Learnt and Unfinished Agenda.* Washington D. C.: World Bank. Available at https://openknowledge.worldbank.org/handle/10986/12375(accessed April 2022).

WSU (Western Sydney University). 2016. 'Data Centres and the Governance of Labour and Territory'. Unpublished project proposal, WSU, Sydney.

Xiang, S., F. Nie, and C. Zhang. 2008. 'Learning a Mahalanobis Distance Metric for Data Clustering and Classification'. *Pattern Recognition* 41(12): 3600–3612.

Yovanof, G. S. and G. N. Hazapis. 2009. 'An Architectural Framework and Enabling Wireless Technologies for Digital Cities & Intelligent Urban Environments'. *Wireless Personal Communications* 49(3): 445–463.

Zehle, S. and N. Rossiter. 2016. 'Mediations of Labor: Algorithmic Architectures, Logistical Media, and the Rise of Black Box Politics'. In *The Routledge Companion to Labor and Media*, Richard Maxwell (ed.), 40–50. London: Routledge.

NOTES ON THE CONTRIBUTORS

Ritajyoti Bandyopadhyay is Assistant Professor in History in the Department of Humanities and Social Sciences at Indian Institute of Science Education and Research (IISER) Mohali. His research areas are urban history, informal economy, and infrastructure studies.

Manish K Jha is Professor of Community Organisation and Development Practice in the School of Social Work at Tata Institute of Social Sciences (TISS), Mumbai. His research interests include migration, disaster response, middle classes, digital governance, social policy, and social justice.

Rishi Jha is Doctoral Researcher in the Faculty of Social Sciences, School of Social Work at Lund University, Sweden. His research interests include postcolonial capitalism, state, urban transformation, governance,inequality, housing, and community change.

Brett Neilson is Professor in the Institute for Culture and Society at Western Sydney University (WSU), Australia. His research and writing aim to provide alternative ways of conceiving globalisation with particular emphasis upon its social and cultural dimensions.

Ritam Sengupta is Post-Doctoral Research Fellow at Leibniz-Zentrum Moderner Orient (ZMO) in Berlin, Germany. His research engagements include energy regimes and the political and economic transformations, small town urbanity, data centres and infrastructure, etc.

Index